W   PLE

WHAT THE MARKET DOES TO PEOPLE

Privatization, Globalization and Poverty

David Macarov

Clarity Press, Inc.
Atlanta

Zed Books
London

What the Market Does to People: Privatization, Globalization and Poverty was first published in the United States by Clarity Press, Inc.

Published outside North America by Zed Books Ltd.

Library of Congress Cataloging-in-Publication Data

Macarov, David.
  What the market does to people : privatization, globalization, and poverty / by David Macarov.
      p. cm.
Includes bibliographical references and index.
  ISBN 0-932863-38-8
  1. Poor. 2. Poverty. 3. Privatization. 4. Free enterprise. 5. Globalization. I. Title.
  HC79.P6M33 2003
  339.4'6—dc21
                                    2002153019

A catalogue record for this book is available from the British Library

Zed ISBN 1 84277 430 1 hb ISBN 1 84277 431 X pb

Cover design by Tricolour Graphics
Typeset by Tricolour Graphics
Printed by Patterson Printing, Michigan

CLARITY PRESS, INC.   ZED BOOKS
Ste. 469, 3277 Roswell Rd. NE   7 Cynthia Street
Atlanta, GA. 30305   London N1 9JF

http://www.claritypress.com   http://www.zedbooks.demon.co.uk

This book is dedicated to my sister Ruby,
with much love

Table of Contents

Introduction

"The belly has no ears, nor is it to be filled with fair words."
Rabelais (1548)

How is it possible that, during a period of unparalleled prosperity, the richest countries in the world are content to allow ten to fifteen percent of their populations to live in abject poverty? How is it possible that after *fifty years* of foreign aid and development assistance, the Third World remains not only basically poor, but also subject to ever-increasing inequality? And why is there no public outcry from the people—including the poor themselves—against this immoral situation? After the Twin Towers destruction, there was a massive public outpouring of grief, including marches and meetings. Relief efforts were so great and so numerous that they literally got in each other's way.[1] No such manifestations against mass poverty have ever been exhibited.

Similarly, the question of abortion raises so many emotional reactions that it has actually led to murders, and demonstrations of the "Right to Life" movement have invariably been met with "Right to Choose" counter-demonstrations. No such conflict between demonstrations against poverty have been recorded, because no such demonstrations have been held. Even the markedly fewer demonstrations conducted by organized labor over recent decades have had specific employer or industry targets and work-related objectives, and cannot be viewed as protests against poverty itself. In such struggles, strikebreakers are often viewed with opprobrium, rather than recognized as yet another sector of the poor who are also in need of a livelihood.

The fight against racial discrimination was rife with marches and meetings, in which both whites and blacks participated. Where were or are the marches against poverty in which both the poor and the non-poor join hands? The Gay Rights Movement demonstrates in many cities, and protest meetings against the closing of naval bases, location of a drug rehabilitation center, and other relatively minor issues have become standard. Only the question of poverty is sidelined, side-stepped, and made into a non-issue. Not since the 1960s – almost half a century ago—when President Johnson declared "war on poverty" (a war that America lost), and Martin Luther King, Jr. initiated a march against it, has any serious attention been paid to the phenomenon. Poverty is simply not on any government's national, regional or local agenda as a serious phenomenon to be addressed.

There is no question that during the last several decades there has been economic improvement for great swathes of populations. For example, in the year 2000, 90 percent of American households owned a vehicle, and 18 percent owned three or more vehicles. This is the highest share of vehicle-ownership ever. In 1990 only 75 percent of the population twenty-five and older had graduated high school, but in the year 2000, 82 percent had. In 1990 only 20 percent had at least a bachelor's degree, and by 2000 this had grown to 25 percent.[2] Towards the end of the millennium the Gross Domestic Product was growing by more than 3 percent a year and unemployment reached its lowest level since World War II.

So why is it that literally millions of people nevertheless live in what has been called "belly-gripping, face-grinding poverty,"[3] and have been doing so for generations? In Europe, too, during the creation of the world's largest market, unemployment and social inequality increased. Is this because governments do not know how to eradicate poverty, or are unable to do so, or don't care about overcoming poverty, or—perhaps—need poverty? And can anything be done to drastically alleviate, if not to eradicate, poverty? These are the questions that this book will examine.

As a foretaste of its findings, it is clear that in addition to the many factors that have created and perpetuated poverty for centuries, the fair-haired twins of modern-day economics—privatization and globalization—are rapidly widening the gap between the rich and the poor, while destroying the environment as a side-effect. The "market-driven society" is despoiling those already poor, and rapidly adding to their numbers. Hence the title of this book.

But many other factors are at work increasing inequality, increasing poverty, and increasing all of the individual and societal ills that flow from being poor. They will be examined within the context of a total look at the configuration of poverty.

However, it should be noted that this book was begun before the Twin Towers tragedy, and the results of that event will inevitably resonate throughout the economy and society of the world. It will be years, and perhaps decades, before new configurations emerge, and we can now only estimate how many people will be plunged into poverty; how social welfare funds and programs will be affected; and where the attention of people and officials will be focused. Nonetheless, while September 11th may mark a significant juncture in world history, we must also recognize that negative economic processes had already set in prior to this event; the crash of the tech sector, the onslaught on social programs, the attack on the working class, and the slide of the economy toward recession and depression were already in play.

Nevertheless, to judge by history, one can be sure that in the end the poor will suffer most. They will pay the highest price for societal change, as they always do. Even immediately after the blasts, several headlines in the *New York Times* foresaw the future: "A Disaster for the Working Poor," "Attacks Hit Low-Pay Jobs the Hardest,"[4] and "Hungry and Jobless." The latter article noted, "In the days and weeks and years to come the impact on the working classes and the poor is likely to be horrific."[5] From a longer-term point-of-view, it is clear that poverty does not arise from any shortage of agricultural or industrial products, and nobody even claims that it does. The reasons are ideological, structural, and —most of all—selfish.

Even though in some regards, in some places, and for some people, poverty has diminished, Sen, the Nobel laureate in economics, cautions us against focusing on this aspect. Regardless of our interpretation of the trend—the magnitude of poverty remaining is unacceptable.[6]

This is admittedly a tendentious book—or what French scholars might term, with more positive connotations, an engaged book. Any arguments that in the long-run privatization and globalization—as well as the other factors that now make for inequality—will make for a better, more just, more compassionate world through efficiency and free-markets are not examined. These are all pie-in-the-sky rationalizations and justifications for the injustices being perpetrated now. There is no point in quoting and arguing about these approaches one by one, since the overwhelming evidence so far, and as far as can now be foreseen, is that they do not and will not help the poor. On the contrary, they almost always worsen the position of poor people, and – in many cases – are designed to do so. This book is focused on the evidence that this is so.

ENDNOTES

[1] Barstow, D., and D. B. Henriques, "Red Tape at Red Cross: Groups Now in a Tangle." *New York Times*, October 28, 2001, internet edition, p. 1.

[2] Schmitt, E., "Census Data Show a Large Increase in Living Standard," *New York Times*, August 6, 2001, p. 1, internet edition.

[3] Gans, H. H., "Income Grants and 'Dirty Work'." *The Public Interest*, 6, *110*, 1967.

[4] Eaton, L., and E. Wyatt, "Attacks Hit Low-Pay Jobs the Hardest." *New York Times*, November 6, 2001, internet edition, p. 1.

[5] Herbert. B., "Hungry and Jobless," *New York Times,* October 31, 2001, internet edition, p. 1.

[6] Wade, R. H., "The Rising Inequality of World Income Distribution," *Finance and Development*, December, 2001, p. 1 (quoting Sen, A., "If It's Fair, It's Good: Ten Truths about Globalization," *International Herald Tribune*, July 14-15, 2001).

CHAPTER I

An Overview of Poverty

WHAT IS POVERTY?

"The greatest of evils and the worst of crimes is poverty."
Major Barbara, G. B. Shaw

For people who are hungry, without drinkable water, living in shanties or on the street and watching their children die from lack of medical care, technical definitions of poverty are sheer mockery. However, all attempts to deal with poverty—its presence, its causes, its effects or its amelioration—necessarily start with at least an assumption as to who is to be considered poor. To understand how poverty is dealt with—or not dealt with—one must be aware of how such definitions are used and how they can be misused.

DRAWING POVERTY LINES

"There are lies, damn lies, and statistics."
Mark Twain

Every government has a method of defining poverty, but it should be understood at the outset that defining poverty—or, in other words, drawing a poverty line—does not necessarily mean that action will follow. Poverty lines simply serve statistical and comparative purposes. When governments establish such a line it does not mean that they are committing themselves to create conditions in which no one is under the line, nor are they undertaking to provide enough social assistance to raise people out of poverty as they themselves define it. This has not always been the case. When Winston Churchill said, in 1906, "We want to draw a line below which we will not allow persons to live and labor,"[1] the intention to act was stated. By now, however, the poverty line is simply a talking point.

For example, although the official poverty line in the United States in 1996 was about $13,000, Alaska and Hawaii, the most generous states, paid in social welfare benefits, respectively, only 92 percent and 95 percent of the poverty line; Alabama paid only 44 percent, and Mississippi paid 40 percent.[2] From 1940 to 1970 welfare payments in the United States rose slowly, but since then they have continuously declined,[3] and in 1997 aid to mothers covered only 60 percent.[4] In Britain, there is a measure known as the Low Cost but Acceptable Incomes for Older People (LCA), which takes into account older people's psychological, social and physical needs, including "the need for a healthy palatable diet, the need to go out and meet friends and family and the need for a healthy environment."[5] This is a lovely formula, but it has no relationship to the old age pensions paid by the British government. In fact, older people in Britain who rely on state pensions, even when supplemented by social welfare payments, face a high risk of poverty.[6] Similarly, in Britain there is a "half of average household incomes measure," (HBAI) but, as has been pointed out, "The HBAI target is a statistical measure of inequality; it is not an adequacy standard because it says nothing about how much money one needs not to be poor, or how well (or badly) one can live on it."[7] In short, poverty lines are simply drawn, and whether anything happens afterwards is another question.

Keeping the Count Down

There is no international consensus as to what constitutes poverty, and consequently the way poverty is defined in one country may differ greatly from that in another. In addition, even various agencies of the same government often use different criteria. For example, the United States Census Bureau lists nine experimental poverty measures.[8] Some countries even refuse to admit that they use a definition of poverty, as though by denying it they eliminate the problem. Before Hong Kong became part of China the Secretary for Health and Welfare there said: "There seems to be a general consensus amongst experts that 'Poverty' as such defies definition—whether in absolute or relative terms or by any other more subjective method."[9] Nevertheless, Hong Kong uses the cost of a "basic foods" basket, which becomes a *de facto* poverty line,[10] and the Hong Kong population does not seem to have benefited by this semantic juggling.

There are also definitions that distinguish between the "near-poor," the "poor," and the "abject poor." It is easy to dismiss the situation of the near-poor as not needing help, but they may be only "one sick child away from destitution."[11] Further, the insertion of the category "abject poor" serves to distract attention from, and thus concern about, those who are "merely" poor, or almost poor. Further, many countries that do not officially proclaim a poverty line nevertheless use the formulae of various research organizations, think tanks, and even individuals in their measurement of poverty.

One thing is certain—each government and agency uses the formula that it thinks will tend to minimize the number of the poor, and for this reason some even change definitions from time to time. Official poverty figures will almost always overstate benefits and understate costs.[12] Consequently, it has been suggested that to Mark Twain's three kinds of lies, mentioned above, a fourth and worse lie should be added, *i. e.*, government statistics.[13]

As one example, the poverty line in Israel is based on 50 percent of the *median* income, which means that the same number of people have incomes above that figure as do those below it. In 1999 the *median* was 2543 shekels, resulting in a poverty line of 1276 shekels. Had it been based on the *average* (or *mean*) income of 3090 shekels, the poverty line would have been 1545 shekels, thus raising the statistical number of the poor in Israel by about 20 percent. There is thus no question as to why the median is the standard of choice.[14] Conversely, long-term social welfare benefits in Israel are based on the *average wage*, the average wage being obviously less than both the median and the average income.

Since the statistical definitions of means (or averages), medians and modes are unfamiliar to most of the public (and to many politicians), the interchangeable use of these terms can be used to obscure the real picture. An Israeli newspaper writer discusses the *mean* disposable income and explains it as the income point at which half the population is above and half below the point—a clear description of the *median*.[15] Even reputable researchers have been known to fall into these confusing semantic traps, *viz:* "...Most researchers use...poverty lines set at 40 percent and 60 percent of *average* equivalent income. Forty percent of the *median* is chosen because... ."[16] Similarly, in Britain, a government report has been criticized for "the frequent lack of clarity as to which definition of poverty it is using at a given point in the text."[17]

Further, when the question arose in Israel as to whether welfare benefits should be in cash or in kind—e. g., home-care, subsidized housing, educational subsidies, counseling, etc.—representatives of the Israeli Ministry of Finance argued for the latter, since cash payments would create a great number of applicants, but there would be a natural reluctance to apply for in-kind help. In particular, fewer elderly people would apply for in-kind benefits, thus reducing the cost of the program. This reasoning prevailed and only in-kind benefits were offered.[18]

The level at which the poverty line is drawn—although not a prescription for action—is of some importance, at least for public relations purposes. "Small changes in the poverty line can produce relatively large changes in the estimates of people living below the poverty line," and further, "it is important to distinguish between overall poverty, and the depth and severity of poverty."[19]

The various methods used to define poverty—either by governments or others—are usually categorized as absolute measures, relative measures, subjective methods, or normative perspectives,[20] although there is inevitably some overlap among these. Before discussing these, it should be pointed out again that no matter what method is used to determine the poverty line, it involves no commitment concerning relief for the poor.

Absolute Measures

"Our bellies are empty. That's where it all begins."
Mack the Knife

An absolute poverty line is based upon a single, universal, arbitrary figure or situation. Everyone under that figure in terms of income and/or assets is *ipso facto* considered poor. The United States government, for example, uses an absolute income amount for measuring poverty. In 1963 Mollie Orshansky[21] took the Department of Agriculture's economy food plan, converted the items in this budget into the money cost of the food, and then multiplied this by three, assuming that food costs were one-third of the total cost of living. With adjustments for inflation, and changes due to differences in family size, this formula has remained the basis of the American poverty line ever since.

The poverty line in the United States in 2001 was $18,104 for a family of four.[22] To understand the real meaning of this figure, one must divide by four to get the figure for one person ($4526), then divide by three to get the cost of food alone for that person ($1509), then divide by 365 for the number of days in the year for the daily figure ($4.13), and finally, divide by three to get the per-meal figure which flows from the poverty line ($1.38). It follows that anyone in a family of four who can afford $1.39 per meal is officially not poor in the United States. In 1999, this figure was $1.29—hardly a heart-warming increase.[23] For individuals, the 1999 figure was $8240,[24] allowing them to spend only $2.50 on every meal, day after day, month after month. The median income for women over 65 in the United States is $10,943,[25] which allows for $3.33 per meal. Since half the women are below the median, the results are predictable. For comparative purposes, it should be noted that even a Big Mac alone costs $2.99. And that's the good news.

Worse news includes the fact that 4.4 percent of the poor in the United States (over 12 million people) had incomes less than 50 percent of the poverty line.[26] Using the Orshansky formula, this allows them only $1.28 per meal. Could it be any worse? It could be and it is.

The real news, and the bad news, is that this figure was based upon food costs constituting one-third of total costs of living. When the original poverty-line formula was devised this was true—but only for affluent families. Low-income families spent at least half their income on food.[27] In Chile today, for example, no less than 80 percent of household income is spent on food, leaving only 20 percent for all other expenses.[28] In the United States, the Department of Labor indicates that food costs, as a percentage of total pre-tax income, range from 13.4 percent to 13.9 percent—or roughly one-seventh—of total expenditures, the differences being between age groups.[29] Using the same calculations as above, but with food figured as one seventh of the total, fifty-nine cents becomes the maximum one may expend per meal while under the poverty line. In other words, anyone who can afford sixty cents per meal would not be counted among the poor if a more realistic formula were used. For those living below 50 percent of the poverty line, the figure becomes negligible.

Connecticut, for example, evidently takes advantage of this change in formula and is more generous. Since welfare there pays $540 per month to a family of three,[30] the per-meal per-person allowance is the magnificent sum of sixty-six cents a meal. It is obviously impossible for someone to eat day in and day out on sixty cents, or even sixty-six cents, per meal, and continue functioning.

In Britain, too, the poverty line originally proposed was based upon the cost of food and other indispensable household items, below which it would be difficult to maintain health and physical efficiency.[31] It has since been changed to a relative measure as discussed below. Nevertheless, the poverty line in Britain in 1998 for a couple with three children was 231 pounds sterling, leaving out housing costs.[32] Using the same formula as before, this can be divided by five to get forty-six pounds, twenty pence per person; then divided by thirty days of the month, arriving at one pound, fifty-four pence per day. If one third of costs is for food, that equals fifty-one pence and dividing that by three for per meal costs allows for seventeen pence per meal. Anyone living in Britain knows what a ridiculous figure on which to try to live this is. An acceptable living standard (without alcohol) in Britain has been postulated as 55.07 sterling a week for a family of four, which works out to sixty-six pence per person per meal.[33] As one British observer puts it: "Women have to be financial wizards…they have to make a meal for five on two pounds every day."[34]

Subjecting the poverty line in Israel at the above-quoted 1276 shekels per individual to the same set of calculations results in about five shekels per meal. On the exchange rate this is about a dollar, but in real terms, one cannot buy even a half-portion of *falafel* in *pita* (Israel's cheapest fast food) for that. And if food costs are less than a third of total income in Britain and in Israel?

But there is even worse news. The United Nations and the World Bank use the figure of *less than* one dollar a day (for total expenditures—not just food) as a worldwide comparative poverty line.[35] True, dollars have different values in various countries, but still—living on less than a dollar a day, or $365 per year, in any economic situation, is horrendous.[36] The 130 million people in Bangladesh—"packed into a territory slightly smaller than Wisconsin"—have an average per capita income of $370.[37]

Could the news get worse? It could and does. In forty of the OAU member states the average person lives on less than $100 per year.[38] Can that really be called living?

But after all, for Westerners, these are strange people and far away. It couldn't happen in the developed world. Or could it? In the United States, state health officials say one of every four families from low- and middle-income neighborhoods in Providence, Rhode Island, is going hungry.[39] In New York at the end of 2001:

> Americans were lining up for emergency food assistance. Those seeking help included the jobless, a majority of whom do not qualify for unemployment benefits; working poor families that do not earn enough money to cover the cost of food as well as their other necessities, like rent and utilities; the elderly, including many men and women faced with the heartbreaking choice of paying for food or paying for medicine; immigrants ineligible for welfare or food stamps; and a wide range of individuals struggling with substance abuse, physical disabilities and mental illness.[40]

As a teaching exercise, to help students understand more personally the meaning of poverty, I have challenged social work students in the United States, Israel and Australia to volunteer to live on the United States poverty-line budget (with food as one-third of costs) for ten days. They were asked to keep a record of the cost of everything they ate and drank (including raw materials when they cooked for themselves), and a diary as to their activities and feelings. The results were very instructive.

Some students gained considerable weight, finding that cheap food was fattening, rather than nutritious. Others lost weight, as they cut down the amount that they normally ate. Students reported their embarrassment at being seen closely examining choices in the supermarket to find the cheapest items—they felt that everyone was watching them, and categorizing them as paupers. Others found themselves resentful of people who were not confined to the same diet, becoming bitter as they watched them choose or eat expensive items. Several became a-social, not wanting to be with people who were not experiencing the same problems, or not wanting to have to explain themselves. Not drinking a beer or eating an ice-cream cone while in a convivial crowd required a good deal of equivocation unless one admitted to being part of an experiment, which was forbidden. One student reported that he found himself driving dangerously because of his jealousy of other (well-fed) drivers. Other—married—students said that they could tolerate the diet for themselves, but there was no way they would put their children on such a diet. One student reported that her husband volunteered to join her in the diet, but dropped out on the third day. In total, students reported themselves as tense, irritable, and in some cases, listless—as well as hungry. No student who completed the experiment reported normal behavior during the period, and especially toward its end. Many said that if they had been forced to continue that life-style, they would have become criminals or even committed suicide. It became clear to the students as a result of this exercise that many of the characteristics often imputed to the poor—that they are lazy, or not ambitious, or incapable of sustained effort, or not motivated—are the results of poverty, not its causes.[41]

This teaching exercise used the poverty line explicated above that allowed for $4.15 per day for food. Consider what the results would have been if the poverty line had been based, as it is by the World Bank, on one dollar per day for *all* costs.[42] As a contrast, consider the CEO of Applied Micro Circuits, who was termed "a paragon of virtue" by the *San Diego Union-Tribune* for taking a salary and bonus of only $600,000. But not to worry—he made $170,000,000 selling his own stock.[43]

Nothing Is More Permanent Than Temporary

Two further aspects of the American poverty line should be, but rarely are, noted. The first is that the Department of Labor's original food budget was intended only for an emergency period of three or four days.[44] That is, if there were an earthquake, or a flood, or some other disaster that cut people off from their normal sources of food, this was presumed to be the minimum that they would need to be able to maintain themselves through such a period. The budget was never intended to be the basis for normal, on-going dietary needs and habits. However, this is how it began to be used when the Department of Health, Education and Welfare adopted it as the official American poverty line in 1976. And then only if "the housewife [*sic*] is a careful shopper, a skillful cook and a good manager, who will prepare all the family's meals at home."[45] With this proviso, and no limitations as to time spent using this budget, this is how poverty in America has been defined ever since.

Calories Don't Count

Second, the nutritional value of that emergency short-period diet was only 1300 calories per day.[46] It has been estimated that a male laborer requires at least 3500 calories a day.[47] Again, there have since been some adjustments, but even now the nutritional value of the food costs at the poverty line is completely insufficient for a healthy maintenance diet. In the Philippines the poverty line diet is based on only 2000 calories a day.[48] In India today—a country not known for overnourished people—only children up to three years of age are said to require 1200 calories per day. From the age of four, this requirement increases until an adult male performing heavy activity needs 3,900 calories a day.[49] In 1997 the daily caloric intake in Somalia—(the lowest figure listed) was 1573—in the United States, it was more than twice that much.[50] In their studies of poverty, malnutrition, etc., the World Health Organization, the Food and Agriculture Organization and other UN organs use cut-off points for needed nutrition that allow for only "minimal physical" and "light" activity;[51] which hardly describe the employment roles prescribed for many of the poor.

In other words, if one can afford to eat more than 1300 calories a day in the United States, or 2000 in the Philippines, one is not considered poor, which means that one is not eligible for governmental help. It is small wonder that people living under such poverty lines become physically and/or mentally ill, and die early.

There are other countries that use an absolute approach in determining poverty, although some of them equivocate concerning use of the term. Hong Kong, as mentioned above, refuses to adopt an official poverty line, but nevertheless defines poverty on an income basis;[52] Zimbabwe also uses a "basket of food" criterion; and the Philippines, as mentioned above, uses an absolute measure as one method among others.[53]

The World Bank also uses a measure of consumption rather than income as a poverty line. This is sometimes termed the Private Consumption Poverty level (PCP).[54] Another measure of poverty has been proposed, based upon net earnings capacity (NEC).[55] Each of these are absolute, although changeable, poverty lines.

Not all absolute measures of poverty are based on income alone. Assets are also sometimes taken into consideration,[56] although usually on a more informal basis. In the very early days of social welfare, the forerunners of social workers—"social investigators"—would make judgments as to a family's eligibility for relief based on their observed living conditions. At one time a rug on the floor obviously meant that the family was not destitute—if they had enough money to buy a rug, rather than using it all for food, they were not entitled to relief. As a rug changed from being a luxury to being an accepted and necessary piece of household furnishings, the electric refrigerator, in place of an icebox, took its place as an evidence of prosperity. There followed radios, and—of course—cars. Indeed, automobiles were considered so clearly an evidence of wealth at one time that there grew up a whole indignant folklore about cheating welfare clients who drove to the welfare office in Cadillacs to pick up their checks. One indefatigable investigator followed up such rumors, and came to the conclusion that they were "horse-feathers swathed in mink,"[57] in other words: nonsense. Today, anyone without some sort of car would probably not be able to get to work, or even to the welfare office. The possession of a television set, and later color television, was at one time enough to cast doubt on one's claim to be poor, while today even in the most abject slums of many large cities, television antennas are an ubiquitous sight, and videos are common.[58] Computers are already moving from the luxury to the necessity category, and cellular phones will soon catch up. Thus, yesterday's luxuries have become today's necessities, and poverty is increasingly now determined by how much income a person or family has, and not how it is spent.

Even the possession of real estate is no longer an evidence of prosperity. Many cases of persons owning their homes but without the income to maintain them, or even to eat properly, abound. This is a modern version of what was once called being "land poor." Selling the property is still often a prerequisite for receiving social assistance in some places, although the assistance that results rarely covers the cost of substitute housing. It has been found that, as far as living on assets is concerned, those who own their homes could probably sell their property and invest the money. However, in very few cases would the proceeds be enough to pay for long-term residential care for any length of time.[59] Assets are still used to determine eligibility for help in some cases. For example, anyone with more than $2000 of disposable assets is not entitled to Food Stamps in the United States,[60] and to be eligible for Medicaid many families have to "spend down" to reduce their assets to the allowable sum.

It should be clear from the above that an absolute measure of poverty requires judgments as to what are needs and what are wants. Indeed, all societies hold that social welfare deals with needs, rather than wants.[61] The distinction between them is not easily drawn, however. One formula distinguishes between *common* human needs, *special* human needs, and *societally induced* needs.[62]

Common human needs are often glibly referred to as food, clothing and housing, but even these needs are relative. I have asked a young man in Western Samoa whether he would be considered poor. He thought for a moment and answered: "There are enough wild coconut and banana trees around so I will never be hungry. I can sleep in any *fala* (a thatched-roof open-sided hut) that I want to. As you can see, I wear only a *lava-lava*. Even without income I will never be poor."

However, even the very existence of these so-called basic needs can be argued. Homeless people, as their name implies, exist in many places without houses, living on the sidewalks, in parks, and other open places. Some desert nomads and Romas (once called Gypsies and still called "Travelers" in some places) live completely without shelter. Australian aborigines, African pigmies and some Papua-New Guineans, until influenced by missionaries, wore no clothing at all. Finally, it is doubtful whether most people would consider the blood sucked from a living cow that, together with milk from the same cow, is the total diet of some Kenyan tribes, to be food in the conventional sense.

On the other hand, even the mere presence of adequate food, clothing and shelter does not satisfy all basic human needs. There are biological, emotional and social needs that may be even more important than those mentioned. Maslow outlines a hierarchy of human needs, with one becoming potent as the previous one is satisfied.[63] These range from the physiological through the need for security, love, and self-esteem, ending with the need for self-actualization. Others speak of the need to belong (or not to be excluded); to be free of humiliation;[64] and to be empowered, among others. For example, the mother who deprives herself of food to take care of her children is exhibiting a need more powerful than the mere biological, as is the girl who starves herself to have a fashionable figure and the homeless person who prefers the park bench to the indignities of the shelter. Religion, too, has long been a priority in the concerns of large masses of people, even when it is used to promote notions or ideologies counter to their economic well being.

Jencks says that all of us have seen poor people buy things that we would not allow ourselves, like the woman on Food Stamps who buys a product that others see as very expensive. The reason: most people find that spending all their money on necessities is unbearably depressing. "Neither morality nor common sense requires human beings to value their health and physical comfort more than their honor, pleasure, or self-respect."[65]

Special human needs include those of the incapable, the unprepared, disaster victims and the nonconforming. Societally-caused needs include those attributable to discrimination, economic structures, and unequal resource distribution, among others.[66]

Absolute measures of poverty, however, do not take any needs other than income into consideration. Poverty lines based on income alone assume that sufficient money can purchase everything lacking among poor people. However, there are places without safe drinking water, without educational opportunities, and without adequate medical care, and these lacks are not caused by insufficient buying power. Persons lacking access to these items are really poor, regardless of their incomes. As one researcher puts it: "The poverty of inadequate household cash incomes may only be one cause, among others, of peoples' deprivations and social exclusion. Deficiencies in the labor market and in the collective supply of goods and services, whether public or private, as well as environmental diswelfares, are also significant causes of these social evils."[67]

Despite the seemingly definitive nature of absolute measures of poverty, they nevertheless contain some relative elements. The thirteen hundred daily calories below which an American is considered poor might seem like a banquet to people in some parts of the world, while to others (CEOs of multinational corporations, for instance) such a diet is simply unimaginable. Even housing, as such, is not a definitive term. As a member of the Israeli Knesset recently declared: "The standard of living, as well as poverty, is a relative thing...the right to housing, for example, no longer means simply a roof over one's head, but also a roof that does not leak (unlike many public housing units)."[68]

Some countries—as noted above—refuse to declare a poverty line, probably because they are afraid that people beneath the line would then demand help. Some years ago something like this happened when the newly-appointed head of the social welfare department of an Israeli city widely (but unwisely) disseminated written information regarding all the financial help to which people were entitled under the law. The resultant legitimate demands for money and services almost immediately used up the department's annual budgeted resources. (The department head was summarily fired).

For similar reasons some countries use proxies, such as the number of people receiving social welfare benefits, as an indication of poverty. Of course, the latter is a beautiful tautology that hides the basis for welfare help—people receive benefits because they are poor, and the number of poor consists of those receiving benefits, but the basis for receiving benefits remains purposefully obscure.

Still other countries use a modified absolute measure, in that they base the poverty level directly on the cost of a previously-determined amount and kind of food, often referred to as a "food basket," which obviously varies over time. However, "developing and costing what is considered to be an acceptable basket of goods is in practice very difficult, and involves the exercise of considerable judgment,"[69] not to mention political complications.

The use of an absolute measure of poverty has many advantages for government policy makers, and not just for statistical and comparative purposes. Once a low poverty line is established, it becomes very difficult for anyone to change the system or raise the measure. That is probably why President Johnson is said to have resisted setting the initial poverty threshold at what he regarded as too high.[70]

In Australia, for example, the 1954 poverty line established in New York State is still used. As Cox points out: "Why the relative cost of living...which applied in New York in 1954 would resemble the (in any case diverse) Australian situation in 1975 or 1996 is a mystery."[71] Robert Reich, the former Secretary of Labor, observes that during his term: "Whenever the question of the poverty data came up informally the consensus was not to change the standard for fear the poverty rate would look worse," although the present poverty figures, "are almost meaningless."[72]

If the United States absolute poverty line were to be used by nine other OECD nations, Australia and the United Kingdom would lead the way in the number of the poor, with the United States third among ten.[73] The inadequacy of the official poverty line in the United States is often attested, although inadvertently, by government sources themselves. For example, school vouchers are given in Cleveland to families ostensibly living under the poverty line (although not to all of them—they are chosen by lottery). They are called "indeed poor," although their median income is about $20,000,[74] as contrasted with the poverty line of $13,650 for a family of three.

Further, as concerns absolute poverty measures, some countries deal with incomes before social welfare transfers such as Food Stamps, publicly provided medical insurance and reduced-rent housing assistance, and some measure income after such payments. Some countries disregard housing costs, medical costs, work expenses, and so forth, in calculating income poverty. Although such differences in definitions make comparisons between countries difficult, many researchers simply use poverty as it is defined by each government as an adequate comparative measure.

Relative Measures

> *"With one foot in a hot stove and one foot in a cold refrigerator you are, on the average, comfortable."*
> Anonymous

For the above reasons, many countries use relative measures of poverty. In such cases, people are not considered poor in terms of their own situations, but only in relation to other people. One way of doing this is to define those in the bottom tenth, or fifth, or some other percentage of the general income structure, as being poor. Another way is to use a percentage of the average income or wage, or the minimum wage, plus or minus some items, as the poverty line. In Israel, for example—as noted previously—50 percent of the median income constitutes the poverty line.[75] In Australia the poverty line was originally set as the minimum wage plus family benefits for a one-earner family with two children, and then amended to exclude housing costs.[76] In Britain the widely used definition of poverty is based on 50 percent of average income after housing costs,[77] and this has been made official as concerns child poverty.[78]

The Canadian system uses a different kind of relative measure. This is the point at which families "spend a disproportionate amount on essential food, clothing and shelter, leaving little or no income for transportation, health, personal care, education, household operation, recreation or insurance."[79] Ireland also uses a relative measure,[80] as do many other countries. The United Nations and the World Bank use the lowest fifth of the income spread as a relative poverty measure.[81]

For the countries concerned, there are advantages in seeing poverty as relative. On the one hand, it can become a cop-out for the very existence of poverty. As long as poverty is measured in relation to other persons' incomes and assets, it can be argued that poverty can never be eradicated—unless society becomes completely equal in terms of money and possessions, there will always be some people with more and some with less. A presidential candidate in the United States is quoted as saying: "Efforts to eliminate poverty are as futile as greyhounds chasing a mechanical hare. You will never catch up. There will always be a lowest one third or one fifth."[82] Hence, efforts to wipe out poverty are posited as self-defeating, and activities should, at best, be merely incremental—that is, just to reduce it somewhat.[83]

Relative measures also lend themselves to rationalizations (a rationalization being defined here as a good reason in place of the real reason), *e.g.,* "These are only statistics and everyone knows that statistics lie. Nobody here is actually starving. And look how much better off our poor are than even rich people in Uganda, or Bangladesh, etc." An approach even more radical than rationalization is denial. In Britain, for example, from 1979 to 1997 there was no official concession that poverty existed and no definition of it was accepted.[84]

Further, relative positions are said to change with the general economic situation. As a country prospers—so goes the argument—the relative poverty line may remain the same, but in absolute terms, poor people are better off. For example, one publication of the World Bank says, "Average incomes of the poorest fifth of society rise proportionately with average incomes,"[85] but another points out that, "Finding that the share of income going to the poor does not change on average with growth does not mean that the growth raises the incomes of the poor as much as for the rich. Given existing inequality, the income gains to the rich...will of course be greater than the gains to the poor. For example, the income gain to the richest decile in India will be about four times higher than the gain to the poorest quintile; it will be 19 times higher in Brazil."[86] In fact, as will be documented later, there is plenty of evidence that the position of the poor actually deteriorates as the economy improves.

A poverty line based on average income may reflect a small number of enormous incomes at the top of the distribution, balanced by large numbers of extremely small ones at the bottom. One of the most controversial economic trends of the last two decades has been the soaring increases in pay for top business executives, and enormous severance payments—not referred to as "golden handshakes" and "golden parachutes" with no basis. During the year 2000, Chief Executive Officers in the United States received an average of 22 percent in raises, while the typical average worker received a 3 percent raise, and investors lost 12 percent in the worth of their portfolios.[87] The amounts paid to top officials are often referred to as "obscene," "absurd," and "totally unjustifiable." In 2000, business executives were given, on the average, $1.7 million in stock and handed an average of almost fifteen million dollars in stock options, in addition to their princely—nay, kingly—salaries.[88] Wall Street bonuses rose from $4.1 billion in 1991 to $11 billion in 1999.[89] Although the pay of executives was "only" forty times more than that of an average worker a generation ago, today it is more than 400 percent greater. However, this may be an underestimate, given "the tricks used to camouflage (the) exorbitant pay"[90] such as stock options, forgiven debts, pre-paid life insurance, and so forth. These are cold and impersonal figures, so in order to add human interest, pity the reported plight of Christos M. , who was forced by his investors to give back $21 million of his 2001 compensation: $800,000 salary, $4.1 million bonus, $29.3 million in stock, $9.9 million in retirement money, $15 million forgiven company loan, $1.6 million to pay taxes on the above, and $1.3 million new stock options.[91] Or L. D. Kozlowski, who received a guaranteed salary so large that it cost his company a tax deduction.[92] In order to rationalize such salaries, companies had to report that their highly remunerated executives were responsible for the realization of enormous profits. Now there is question as to whether the prosperity of the 90s was not simply a chimera created by fictitious reporting of overblown profits, often by the very executives whose excessive remuneration had been so justified.[93]

Add to these obscene payments the astronomical amounts paid to sports stars, to performers and to former politicians who write their memoirs as only a few examples, and recognize how each of these raises the average income—and thus the poverty line—without necessarily changing the position of the bulk of the poor.

There is a further problem with relative poverty lines. Determining averages or medians requires quite precise data-gathering and statistical handling, as well as methods of constant updating, and these are not always available, even in countries that use relative poverty measurements. Consequently, a good deal of guesswork—and official bias—is often involved in deriving the poverty line. Further, relative poverty definitions tend to become overextended, including categories like social deprivation, or exclusion, or other non-economic items to which poverty may be a contributing cause, but which are not officially recognized to be poverty as such by definition.[94]

As an example of the differences between absolute and relative measures of poverty, envision ten people making $100,000 a year and ten people making $5,000 a year, for a total of $1,050,000, or an average of $52,500. With a poverty line of 40 percent of average incomes, this would be $21,000, putting the people making $5,000 sixteen thousand dollars below the poverty line. Now say a prosperous economy results in raises of 50 percent in all incomes (which it never actually does). Ten people now making $150,000 a year and ten making $7,500 equals $1,575,000, or an average of $78,750, of which 40 percent is $31,500. The poor, who are 50 percent better off than they were in absolute terms, are now $24,000 below the poverty line; that is—if one insists on relative measures— much worse off (and there are probably now many more of them). As Anelauskas points out, when the incomes of the rich are five times or more the incomes of the poor, the median or the average is an increasingly unreliable indicator of the well-being of the typical person in a society.[95]

There is a technical positive feature to relative definitions of poverty, and that is the fact that they allow for measures of income gaps. When a bottom portion of the economic stratum of the population is compared with a top portion over time, it is possible to discern whether the gap is narrowing or widening. Like other methods of drawing the poverty line, this does not necessarily entail any action to change the situation. However, using relative measures of both 40 percent of median income and 50 percent of median income, the United States comes off badly. Among fifteen industrialized nations, the United States leads the way in relative poverty.[96]

The difference between measures of relative and absolute poverty is graphically demonstrated by the case of Hungary. Using a relative definition the proportion of people in poverty during the so-called transition period increased by 1.5 percent. However, using an absolute measure, the increase was 2.5 times.[97] Thus, defining poverty in relative terms has many advantages for governments, but does very little in terms of helping people leave or escape the poverty trap.

Subjective Measures

"Who, being loved, is poor?"
Oscar Wilde

In addition to countries that define poverty in terms of absolute figures or relative to other groups, there are also countries that use subjective measures, e. g., feelings of being poor. This approach has deep roots. A portion of the ancient *Talmud* ("Ethics of the Fathers") asks: "Who is rich?" And replies: "He who rejoices in his lot."[98] Conversely, the subjective approach says, in effect, that anyone who feels poor *is* poor.

One type of this approach asks people about their own situations—in effect, "Do you think of yourself as poor?" Another asks about hypothetical families—"Would you call such a family poor?" Another variant asks people what things they consider necessary to have in order not to be poor. Still another asks people what they consider to be the poverty line, or what they think the poverty line should be.[99] Many researchers have used these methods to assess poverty for various reasons, but few countries use the results as an official poverty line.[100] For example, in public opinion polls, most Americans say that a family of four needs about $20,000 a year not to be poor, as contrasted with the official poverty line for such a family of $17,052 (as of September, 2000). On the other hand, the Indiana Economic Development Council estimates that a family of four needs at least $25,000 annually to afford the basics.[101]

In the Netherlands, the National Social Minimum is determined politically and the Subjective Poverty Line arises from interviews with heads of families. It will come as no surprise that from 1985 to 1990, the Subjective Poverty Line—reflecting peoples' feelings—shows more people below the poverty line than does the politically derived National Social Minimum; in some years, almost twice as many.[102]

The use of subjective criteria—hopes, frustrations, satisfactions and sense of well-being[103]—to determine poverty has many difficulties. Responses may be based upon reference groups—my brother, my family, my ethnic group, my neighborhood, or any number of other past, present, or future reference points—compared to whom I feel better off or worse off, without regard to my actual situation. Then there is the fact that satisfaction is a function of expectations.[104] If I don't expect much, I may be easily satisfied with very little, and thus not subjectively poor. But if I am afflicted with Caesar's "vaulting ambition," then I may feel poor no matter what I achieve. There is also the fact that it is not pleasant to label oneself as poor, regardless of feelings, and many public opinion surveys founder on this fact. Finally, there are entire groups—sometimes large groups—who do not consider themselves to be poor regardless of income or life-style, because their focus is on other values—for example, religion. As has been noted in Israel: "The ultra-Orthodox do not recognize that (they are in) poverty. It isn't that they lack for nothing, or are in the upper decile—they are actually in the lowest decile—but they do not feel poor and do not call themselves poor."[105]

It should be emphasized once again that no country or program uses people's own evaluation of their situation as a basis for a poverty line, let alone action.

Normative Measures

"There is nothing stronger than human prejudice."
Wendell Phillips

Some groups are considered poor in the public mind because of their stereotypes, without regard to exceptions or measurements. For example, new immigrants—and especially migrants, illegal immigrants and refugees—are seen as penniless. This may not include a commitment to help them; it is simply an observation. Similarly, the old (and especially the very old), children, the mentally retarded, and physically disabled persons are often lumped indiscriminately among the poor population. Persons in institutions such as prisons and hospitals for the mentally ill are similarly regarded, as are residents of inner cities, as ghettos are now called. Even medical interns, young artists and priests are generally regarded as poor. In fact, 6 percent of the poor are full-time students.[106] Sometimes farmers are indiscriminately seen as poor, with sharecroppers and stoop laborers in an even more abject position. Entire ethnic groups may be looked upon as poor—for example, Romas and Aborigines. Some people belong to more than one normatively poor group—immigrants who are in jail, for example.[107]

The view of people as normatively poor has political advantages. If certain groups are *expected* to be poor, and are regarded as poor regardless of their actual circumstances, there is no real imperative to help them. In fact, many of these are—in the public eye—incapable of being helped.

Take refugees (as distinct from immigrants and migrants), for example. Most of them are objectively poor, leaving their homes with only what they can carry. It is estimated that in the next fifty years the European Union countries will have to accept seventy-five million refugees from other areas.[108] This will greatly increase their number of poor people, but help given refugees, as distinct from residents and/or citizens, is invariably much weaker. In Britain, for example, a very popular TV program—called, for an unfathomable reason, "Red Nose"—mounted an appeal for funds to help refugees in England. The response was quite good, until it became clear that the funds were to help the refugees stay in Britain, rather than to be used to repatriate or resettle them elsewhere. The funds immediately dried up.

Then there are people who are perceived of as only temporarily poor. With time the intern will become a doctor, children will become wage-earners, immigrants will become citizens and (rarely voiced) the elderly will die. In the long term, they will not be poor. It might be well for social planners and politicians to remember that when President Franklin Roosevelt proposed Social Security as a measure that would alleviate poverty in the long run, his advisor, the social worker Harry Hopkins, said, "But Mr. President, people *eat* in the short run."

Finally, as regards poverty lines in general, there is certainly a moral dimension involved.[109] The choice of a poverty line, the method of arriving at one, the items to be included, images of the poor and assumptions about them, all stem from ideological backgrounds, whether these be economic, religious or idiosyncratic. Choices that allow millions of people to be absolutely, relatively, subjectively or normatively poor are not ordained by Heaven nor by the forces of nature. They are societally-derived or—more simply—human decisions.

Informal Indices of Poverty

> "Life wasn't meant to be easy."
> Malcolm Fraser, Former Prime Minister of Australia

When one moves away from income-based definitions of poverty, whether absolute, relative, normative or subjective, categories begin to take the place of formulae. The International Labour Organization speaks of basic needs as food, shelter, clothing, safe drinking water, sanitation, transport, health and education.[110] Life expectancy and infant mortality are also used as indications of poverty. Even lack of personal safety can be defined as a kind of poverty, and there are those who speak of poverty of the imagination,[111] poverty of the spirit, etc.

Among these informal definitions of poverty is the question of inclusion and exclusion from the larger society, or from certain specific groups. Some writers speak of poverty in terms of individual and group empowerment; living as a member of a community within which he or she is able to take part and contribute to normal social activities.[112] Another speaks of humiliation as a form of poverty, and poverty as a form of humiliation.[113] Still others speak of a life that is tolerable according to working-class life-styles (why not middle-class?!).[114] There are other forms or indices of poverty. In the 1970s the expression "fuel poverty" became popular. In the 1980s there was talk of "water poverty." In the 1990s, talk of the "unphoned" has shifted to the "digital divide"—between those who have computers and those who don't.[115] Others speak of the "milk indicator" of poverty, in which the farm mother must sell all the milk produced, leaving none for her children. Then there is the "third world egg indicator," when farmers must sell their fowl rather than keep them as egg producers. [116]

The latter designations raise the whole question of rural poverty. It is very difficult to categorize farmers as poor or not, especially in those cases where some of the farm produce is consumed at home, and/or family members contribute unpaid labor. It is, however, normative to think about farmers as being poor (despite such notable exceptions as Jimmy Carter in the United States and Arik Sharon in Israel). In the developing countries, at least, this is true. In those areas urban poverty is only about 30 percent of the total. However, with the growth of urbanization—from 38 percent in 1995 to a projected 52 percent in 2020—the poverty rate will rise to 40 percent in urban sectors. And by 2035, when it is projected that 61 percent of the poor in developing countries will live in urban areas, the poverty rate there will be 50 percent.[117]

There are, however, more tangible and measurable aspects of poverty. Some of these are lack of education, health, nutrition, reproductive health, family planning, safe water and sanitation.[118] Infant mortality should be added to this list and—perhaps surprisingly—transportation, which has been described as one of the "most unyielding barriers to self-sufficiency."[119] Drawing such examples from lack of income poverty can easily be dismissed as "conceptual inflation," but the problems nevertheless remain.

Counting the Poor

"If I called the wrong number, why did you answer the phone?"
James Thurber

Despite the differences in methods of determining and (not) applying the poverty line, it is nevertheless possible to count the poor, using the methods that have been adopted by the countries themselves. In 1998, in nine countries usually thought of as developed, poverty ranged from 7 percent in the Netherlands to 25 percent in the United Kingdom. Among developing countries, Zimbabwe reported 62 percent as poor.[120]

On a more overall basis, it is estimated that 830 million people in the world are undernourished.[121] In the former Communist countries 160 million people—40 percent of the population—live in poverty, including 50 million children. In Kyrghyzstan alone, 88 percent of the people live below the poverty line.[122] In the developing world as a whole, about 1.2 billion people live on less than one dollar a day.[123]

Different methods of counting give different results concerning the poor in the United States. According to the Census Bureau's official standard, 11.25 percent of the American population was officially poor in 2000[124] and this rose to 11.8 percent in 2001.[125] In fact, using the nine measures published by the Census Bureau, mentioned previously, poverty ranged from 11.7 percent to 14.4 percent.[126] If medical expenses are deducted from countable income, the poverty rate in 1997 would have increased from 13.3 percent to 16.3 percent.[127]

Further, the standard of living has increased considerably since the 1960s, when the cost of food was the basic item. If one were to factor in rent increases since that time, increases in social security premiums, and expenses related to child care, health and work, another 7.4 million people would be under the poverty line—and half of these would be in families where the primary earner worked at least forty-eight hours a week.[128] Anelauskas points out that if poverty were measured at the 50 percent of the median income standard, which many countries use, the poor in the United States would be almost 20 percent, or one in five of the population. If the 60 percent level were used, one in four Americans would be in poverty.[129]

Viewed differently, in 1973 15.8 percent of Americans had incomes that were below 125 percent of the (very low) poverty line, and twenty-seven years later this was still 15.8 percent. Similarly, the proportion who had incomes between the poverty line and 125 percent of that amount was 4.4 percent in 1988, and 4.5 percent in the year

2000.[130] After all the efforts that have gone into poverty programs, and after so many years, these people "have wherewithal for only a bare existence and nothing more."[131]

It should be noted that the poverty line includes people with no income at all, as well as those right under the poverty line. It is salutary to notice, therefore, that in 1976 3.3 percent of the poor had incomes below 50 percent of the poverty line and—again—twenty-four years later this had *risen* to 4.4 percent.[132]

Others find that:

> In 1998, 7.2 million families and 8.5 million unrelated individuals (in the United States)—in all, about 34.5 million people, or 12.7 percent of the population—had pretax cash incomes below the official poverty threshold. The average family in this group had an income that was only 54 percent of the poverty threshold. This family would need $5,350 in extra annual income to reach the poverty line...one out of five Americans is poor, and one in six remains poor after being helped.[133]

Again, it would be a mistake to think of these figures as "mere" statistics. Of the people under the poverty line in the United States, almost 40 percent have incomes of *less* than half the poverty line by one estimate,[134] and 50 percent by another.[135] These are people whom even the Census Bureau calls "severely poor." They constitute 6 percent of the American population.[136] In addition, another 40 percent are termed "near poor"—that is, just above the absurdly low poverty line.[137]

Many researchers and observers have concluded that the current poverty line in the United States is utterly unrealistic. One estimate of a minimally adequate income for a family of four is given as $27,000, which—according to the Orshansky formula—comes to about two dollars a meal, and there are sixteen million jobs that do not pay this much.[138]

Poverty and inequality are higher in the United States than in some countries with much lower average incomes. An American citizen who is in the lowest 10 percent of the United States income distribution has a disposable income that is about 35 percent of the median income—that is five to seven points lower than similarly placed citizens in fifteen other Western industrialized countries.[139]

To summarize, in the year 2000 over 11.25 percent of Americans were below the poverty line. This compares to 1977 when the figure was 11.6 percent—a decrease that is hardly significant. If, however, one uses that which Anelauskas calls a common sense definition of the poor, then "One-third of the population in this country are destitute and perhaps another one-third are in constant danger of being thrown into poverty at any moment."[140]

Insofar as informal indices of poverty are concerned, it should be noted that in the year 2001 one billion people (that's one out of six human beings) did not have access to safe drinking water.[141] By mid-2002 another million people had joined the waterless group.[142] Some 2.4 billion lack adequate sanitation, and 3.4 million die each year from water-related diseases.[143] Indices in the developed world are different, but in 2001, 25,000 people were estimated to be homeless in New York City alone,[144] of whom 10,000 were children.[145]

It should be added that official poverty figures, like official unemployment figures, are always understated. They do not include people who do not apply for assistance, clandestine immigrants, people in institutions, the homeless, and individuals who are poor despite what appears to be adequate household or family incomes.[146]

WHO ARE THE POOR?

> *"...Your tired, your poor, your huddled masses*
> *yearning to breathe free."*
> Emma Lazarus

People in poverty can be categorized in many ways: according to age, degree of poverty, racial/ethnic groups, employment status, and others. These categories obviously overlap each other. Consequently, one can only say that in general, the poverty population is made up of children, the aged, non-working (often single) mothers of young children, the unemployed (all of whom have been disparagingly referred to as the "non-productive population")[147] and the working poor. In presenting the numbers in each group in this manner there is—as noted—inevitably some overlap, as non-working mothers may also be classified as unemployed, and there are undoubtedly some elderly persons who are still working full- or part-time. Similarly, "children" are usually considered those eighteen years or younger, while the Census Bureau has, at various times, used fourteen years, fifteen years, and at present sixteen years as the cut-off point for statistics concerning children at work.[148] On the other hand, it would be a mistake to assume that *all* unemployed people, part-time workers, or the aged are poor.

Children

> *"There was an old woman who lived in a shoe,*
> *She had so many children she didn't know what to do."*
> Anonymous

Children are more likely than any other group to be living in poverty. One source holds that more than one in three children (4.4 million) were living in poverty in 1997/98 in the United Kingdom.[149] This figure is based upon a poverty line of 50 percent of the median income. Under the American poverty formula, 20 percent of children in the United States are poor, followed by (under their own formulae) those of Australia, Canada and Ireland[150]—some of the most "developed" countries in the world. Looked at from another viewpoint, between 32 percent and 38 percent of the poor in the United States are under eighteen years of age.[151] Comparing programs affecting children in the United States with those in France, Bergmann says that the present American system keeps millions of American children deprived.[152]

Of course, child poverty is regrettable, but it has its usefulness—it is highly marketable. People and organizations that are not troubled by overall poverty figures become involved when child poverty figures are published. This is rather curious, because all of the proposed solutions to child poverty involve helping the parents. Children as such are almost always poor. That is normative. They have no incomes, do not work, and do not receive social welfare into their own hands. But instead of speaking of overcoming or alleviating poverty as a whole, or even the poverty of parents, public relations demands that the rhetoric deal with children. For example, the current Prime Minister of Britain has declared that he will halve child poverty in twenty years. How? By increasing benefits (to families); by promoting paid work (of adults); and tackling the problems of the disadvantaged (adults and children).[153] Actually, even if this program were to be enormously successful, only two-thirds of child poverty would be abolished in 20 years, and the extent would be no lower than it was 20 years ago in 1979.[154] In the United States the child poverty rate in 1999 was slightly *higher* than that in 1979,[155] and even current and proposed efforts to raise the incomes of low-wage workers would not be sufficient to reduce child poverty substantially.[156]

In short, child poverty is often used as a public relations gimmick to stimulate efforts to reduce poverty. One possible reason for the emphasis on children is that they are not seen in the same light as the adult poor—they are not lazy, shirking work, drinking beer, and laughing at society as they live off its largesse. They are, in short, *ipso facto*, part of the deserving poor.

The Aged

> *"Grow old along with me!*
> *The best is yet to be"*
> Robert Browning

The largest single group among the poor in most countries is the elderly population.[157] The elderly constitute 57 percent of the poor in England, 40 percent in Australia and 35 percent in Israel, and 10 percent in the United States, according to the various governmental definitions.[158] However, if 60 percent of the average wage is used as the poverty line, then the number of the aged in poverty ranges from 6 percent in the Netherlands and 15 percent in Sweden to 34 percent in the United States and 58 percent in Australia.[159] Countries like Sweden and the Netherlands still come out as the most equal societies in economic terms, while the United State remains the most unequal of wealthy societies, with the highest proportion of older people (and other groups) with relatively low incomes.[160]

During the next thirty years, the number of older adults in the United States will grow from 12 percent of the population to 22 percent,[161] which means that—other things being equal—the number of the aged poor will also grow. Similarly, between 1986 and 2040 the number of people over 65 in most OECD countries is expected to double, amounting to 20-25 percent of their populations (and about half of these will be over 75).[162] In the United States, the over-75 group will grow by 40 percent and the over-80 group will double by 2040.

The aged in America have not fared too badly during the last few decades. Due to Social Security and Medicare, the number of the elderly under the poverty line has diminished since 1960. Nevertheless, the current level is still higher than in any major democracy, and although the overall rate of aged poverty, as noted above, is about 10 percent, it is almost 20 percent among widows over sixty-five, and 25 percent among elderly Americans of African descent.[163] Not only do the aged constitute 10 percent of the American population, they also make up about 10 percent of the poverty-stricken.[164]

Part of this poverty arises from the inability of most of the aged to acquire income outside of social insurance payments. Although since 1970 the upper ranges show steady gains in income from private sources, the lower 40 percent of the income distribution have increased their non-Social Security income only slightly.[165]

Of course, there will be differences even among the poverty-stricken aged. Of non-married elderly women (widowed, divorced, never married), 17.3 percent are now living in poverty.[166] The risk of poverty for widows is clearly much higher when their husbands had life-long low earnings. Indeed, in 1991, 20 percent of recent widows, 35 percent of long-term widows and nearly 50 percent of divorced or separated women were near-poor, even after taking their home equity into account.[167] At age 67, divorced women are more likely to be in the bottom part of the income distribution than any other group.[168] As noted previously, some of the poor could probably sell their homes and invest the proceeds for income, but they would not net enough to pay for long-term residential care for any length of time.[169] The poor, including the elderly poor, have problems other than those brought on by poverty, of course—health, family, social exclusion, and so forth—but although younger people tend to see the problem as loneliness, as age increases economic factors become more important as the basis of problems.[170]

The Unemployed

"Oh, why don't you work like other men do?"
"How the hell can I work when there's no work to do?"
Hallelujah, I'm a Bum

Before looking further at the unemployment figures that impinge upon the poor, it might be instructive to see how such figures are derived. In some countries, the unemployed are counted as the number of people applying for unemployment compensation. This method leaves out those who have already exhausted their benefits (after twenty six weeks in most states),[171] those whose work record is so short they are not entitled to benefits, those within the "waiting time" required before payments can begin, and those whose payments are withheld for various administrative, bureaucratic, and legal reasons.

Most programs require "waiting time" before the unemployed person is eligible for compensation. It is hard to find a reasonable rationale as to why someone who loses his or her job today cannot begin to be compensated until a later period, and must suffer the loss of both salary and compensation while waiting, but this is the practice in even the most liberal of welfare states, such as Sweden.[172] In Britain, the waiting time is four weeks.[173]

In addition, in many countries the unemployed must report regularly in person to the employment office; and in some countries, each time they are scheduled to receive their compensation. In Israel, at present, the unemployed must line up three times a week in order to maintain their unemployment compensation. Presumably, this is to make sure the applicant is not working. Others require a one-time appearance, and then payments are sent by mail. Those who cannot get to the employment office in either of these cases—due to illness, lack of transportation, household duties, and acts of nature, such as snowstorms—not only do not get their compensation, but they are left out of the unemployment figures. Those who are considered uncooperative, or who refuse to accept certain types of work, or who refuse to work for the salary offered, also lose their compensation and their status as unemployed.

In the United States, the unemployment rate is derived from a household survey of fifty thousand families. The head of the household is asked only two questions: "Did you work last week?" If the answer is negative, the second question is: "Did you look for work?" Only people who did not work, but who looked for work, are considered unemployed. It should also be noted that under this formula the criterion for having worked is *one hour per week*. Thus, one who baby-sits for pay for an evening is not included in the unemployment figures, nor is someone who is paid for running a time-consuming errand. This method of counting also omits people who could not get out to look for work, those who worked only part-time or temporarily, and discouraged workers who have found that no work is available and have ceased trying to find what doesn't exist.

Just as every government tries to downsize the number of people in poverty, so there are attempts to find formulae that will indicate the smallest number of the unemployed. During the 1980s the government of Britain proposed twenty-nine different measures of unemployment—each of them designed to minimize the number of the unemployed.[174] In addition to various methods of fudging the figures, there are other ways of reducing the reported number. The OECD reports that "simply requiring claimants for unemployment benefits to attend an interview at the employment office will cause between 5 percent and 10 percent to drop off those rolls. The more letters they have to answer or forms they have to fill in, the more opportunities they have for failing to comply."[175] Perhaps as a direct consequence, 22 percent of Americans and 11 percent of Australian claimants for unemployment compensation are disallowed, although they have not refused to stay at work, to accept work offered, or to look for work.[176] In Germany the federal labor office was found to be exaggerating the number of new jobs created, leading to an investigative commission.[177]

Due to these and many other methods of downsizing the unemployment figures, many experts hold that published unemployment figures, everywhere in the world, should be increased by 50 percent to 300 percent to properly represent the real proportion and number of the unemployed.[178] Hence, the purported 4.2 percent unemployment achieved in the United States in the year 2000—one of the lowest rates on record—actually means that from six to twelve of every hundred members of the labor force were unsuccessfully seeking work during a period widely viewed as one of almost unparalleled prosperity.

It should also be mentioned that the unemployment figures are drawn only from those who are in the labor force. There are many others, technically not part of the labor force, who would like to work. The United States Department of Labor estimates that in 1999 these averaged over four and a half million persons.[179] If these were included in the unemployed figures, there would be a ballooning of the unemployment rate. For example, unemployment figures ignore incarcerated persons, although they are clearly not employed. If the incarcerated who were not working when incarcerated are included in the unemployment figures, the 1995 rate would have risen from 5.6 percent to 6.2 percent. If all the incarcerated were to be included as unemployed, the figure would have risen to 7.5 percent.[180]

Approximately three-quarters of family income in the United States comes from the labor market, and even families in the lowest fifth of the income distribution rely more upon labor income than on any other source.[181] Consequently, of Americans who did not work at all, almost 20 percent were poor.[182]

Given all of these explanations, qualifications and caveats, the United States Census Department reports the following breakdown of the officially poor in the year 2000, along the employment-unemployment axis as:

Children or armed forces	32 %[183]
Holding job	22 %
Unemployed	4 %
Not in labor force	41 %
	99 %[184]

It will be recognized from the above that insofar as popular voice and political programs focus on putting the *unemployed* poor to work, they are exerting a great deal of effort and resources on a very small part of the poverty population. Even if successful, the savings in unemployment compensation would be far over-shadowed by the costs of training courses, unemployment counseling, job search, and employer subsidies. From a rational economics point of view such efforts are self-defeating, but the assumed immorality of people being supported without their working overcomes logic.

The Working Poor

"Load sixteen tons and what do you get?
Another day older and deeper in debt"
John Henry

The common image of the poor as unemployed, and therefore employ-ment as the best antidote for poverty, is hard to shatter. And it will come as a surprise to many that—as noted above—the Census Department finds that only *four percent* of the poor are unemployed. The fact that 22 percent of the poor hold jobs but are nevertheless poor is an indication of part-time, temporary, and low-paid employment, which is a much more potent cause of poverty than unemployment. Indeed, 12 percent of the poor worked full-time and year round,[185] but remained in poverty. These facts, and the fact that most of the poor are outside the labor force (aged, children, the disabled), no matter how often repeated, does not seem to have much of an effect. Indeed, if we leave the official poverty line and use what has been termed "economic reality," the number of year-round full-time American workers who live in poverty is three times that which official census figures hold.[186] However, the public does not *want* to recognize the fact that one may work and still be poor. This goes against the grain of the "get 'em back to work" attitude, and the image of the poor as lazy loafers.

In truth, almost 30 percent of American workers earn only poverty-level wages and almost nine million Americans stay out of poverty only by holding more than one job. Half of the latter report they have to do so in order to meet their regular household expenses, to pay off debts, or to buy things they cannot afford on one salary.[187] The problem is not so much lack of work as such—it is lack of decently paid, full-time, long-sustained employment.[188] Without that, there will always be many people who work, but are nevertheless poor.

Single Parents

"Alone, alone, all, all alone"
The Ancient Mariner
Samuel T. Coleridge

As a consequence of the figures above, efforts to get the poor into employ-ment are not centered on the unemployed poor, but on groups presently outside the labor force. These include single parents whose childcare responsibilities make it difficult for them to go to work and spouses whose partners work but are nevertheless poor.

About 11 percent of the poor in the United States are single house-holders.[189] It should be noted—again—that there is some overlap between these figures and other categories of the poor. A single householder can be over sixty-five, or under eighteen. They may be parents and still be considered single householders. The single householder may be among the unemployed, the underemployed, the fully employed or outside the labor force.

Despite such statistical difficulties, the lot of the single householder, with no additional wage-earner present, is usually difficult. In fact, the original impetus for the Aid to Dependent Children Program (ADC) was the public image of the preacher's widow with two tow-haired children taking in sewing or giving piano lessons to try to eke out a living. The program was designed to help her raise her children decently. When the public image of the ADC recipient changed to an unmarried adolescent American of African descent with—perhaps—more than one child, the program was abandoned. Incidentally, this is a good example of the social work dictum: "Feelings are facts." The fact is that AFDC (to which the name was changed) was never a majority-Black program,[190] but it was widely seen as such and consequently terminated. But the difficulties remain and—leaving aside other categories—more than one in ten of poor people are single householders.

The situation of single parents (as opposed to householders) is widely recognized as acute. In the 1990s, 56 percent of children living with single mothers were poor in the United States and Australia. This varied by more than 40 percent from those living with married mothers.[191]

Given the number of single parents (women, in the very great majority) who are poor, much of the anti-poverty effort is aimed at getting these women into employment. The efforts use the carrot of training courses, employment counseling and wages as well as the stick of cutting off welfare payments. Where the problem is childcare, facilities to that end are sometimes offered. However, the need for childcare facilities far exceeds the resources made available for the purpose.

There is also the ideological question as to whether professional—usually group—childcare can equal family care. Since this is so hard to evaluate, and so many variables intervene, there are more opinions than data. As one example, however, take the Israeli *kibbutzim*, where the cost of childcare was not a factor. For generations, children were raised in their own living quarters by professionally trained educators. Both the philosophy and economic factors changed and today, there is hardly a *kibbutz* in which the children do not live at home, despite the cost of enlarging houses and impairing parents' work hours.

The great thrust to get single parents into the labor force does not arise from a conviction that nurturing children outside the home is more desirable, or to raise them out of poverty, but is an attempt to cut the costs of welfare, as detailed below. Consequently, many of the jobs being offered such women are minimum-wage or less, which, given the fact that they have children, will not raise them above the poverty line.

It might be well to note that there are also adults without dependents among the poor. Nearly five million of these able-bodied adults from 25 to 49 without children or disabilities have incomes at or near the poverty line. Eighty percent of these hold jobs (60 percent full time) and 20 percent are in training.[192]

SUMMARY

"A decent provision for the poor is the true test of civilization."
Samuel Johnson

The shamefulness of governments—especially rich governments—countenancing the existence of citizens who cannot afford decent housing, enough food for themselves and their children, and medical care, among other things, leads each of them to engage in semantic shilly-shallying, statistical subterfuge, corrupt counting, and fudging facts. Nevertheless, regardless of how poverty is defined or how the poverty line is derived, hundred of millions of people, including children, the aged, single parents, the working poor, and the unemployed are in poverty throughout the world. This not only results in immense personal suffering, but also destroys the very foundations of society. The results of such individual and societal degradation make up the subject matter of the next chapter.

ENDNOTES

[1] Tuchman, B., *The Proud Tower.* New York: Ballantine, 1962, p. 374.

[2] *Overview of Entitlement Programs.* Committee on Ways and Means, House of Representatives. Washington: GPO, 1996, pp. 437-438, 446-448. Quoted by Stoesz, D., *A Poverty of Imagination.* Madison: University of Wisconsin Press, 2000, pp. 25-26.

[3] Schorr, A. L., *Welfare Reform: Failure and Remedies.* Westport: Praeger, 2001, p. 18.

[4] Edin, K., and L. Lein, *Making Ends Meet: How Single Mothers Survive Welfare and Low-Wage Work.* New York: Russell Sage, 1997, p. 38.

[5] Parker, H., *Low Cost but Acceptable Incomes for Older People.* London: Policy Press, 2000, p. 19.

[6] Silburn, R., "United Kingdom," in Dixon, J. and D. Macarov, (Eds.), *Poverty: A Persistent Global Reality.* London, Routledge, 1998, pp. 204-288.

[7] Veit-Wilson, J., "Setting a Governmental Minimum Income Standard—the Next Steps," *Poverty*, 105, Winter 2000, pp. 11-14.

[8] *Standardized and Unstandardized Experimental Poverty Rates: 1990 to 1999.* Washington: United States Census Bureau, 2001.

[9] MacPherson, S., "Hong Kong," in Dixon and Macarov, *op cit.*, p. 84, see endnote 6.

[10] *Ibid*, p. 88.

[11] Edin and Lein, *op cit.*, p. 2, see endnote 4; see also Newman K. S., *No Shame in My Game: The Working Poor in the Inner City.* New York: Knopf, 1999, p. xiv.

[12] *Ibid.*

[13] Uchitelle, L., "How to Define Poverty? Let Us Count the Ways." *New York Times*, May 26, 2001, internet edition, p. 1.

[14] Yaniv, G., *Annual Survey 1997/98.* Jerusalem: National Insurance Institute, 1998, p. 38 and p. E3.

[15] Sinai, R., "Drawing the Poverty Line." *HaAretz*, February 13, 2002, internet edition, pp. 1-4.

[16] Anelauskas, V., *Discovering America As It Is.* Atlanta: Clarity, 1999, p. 68.

[17] "Progress Reports," *Poverty*, 108, Winter 2001, p. 2.

[18] Ajzenstadt, M., and Z. Rosenheck, "Long-Term Care in Israel," *Journal of Social Policy*, 29, 2, 2000, pp. 247-262.

[19] Dhanani, S., and I. Islam, "Poverty, Vulnerability, and Social Protection in a Period of Crisis: The Case of Indonesia." *World Development*, 30, 7, 2002, pp. 1211-1231.

[20] Dixon and Macarov, *op cit.*, see endnote 6.

[21] Orshansky, M., "How Poverty is Measured," *Monthly Labor Review*, 92, 2, 1969, pp. 37-41.

[22] Pear, R., "Number of People Living in Poverty Increases in U.S." *New York Times*, September 25, 2002, internet edition, p. 1.

[23] Kilborn, P. T., and L. Clemetson, "Gains of 90's Did Not Lift All, Census Shows." *New York Times*, June 5, 2002, p. 1., internet edition.

[24] *Social Security Bulletin—Annual Statistical Report—1999.* Washington: Social Security Administration, 2000, p. 155.

[25] Dancoff, J., "Done Deals," *Modern Maturity*, 45, 1, January/February, 2002, p. 13.

[26] *Historical Poverty Tables.* Washington: U. S. Bureau of the Census, Current Population Survey. Poverty and Health Statistics Branch/HHES Division, Table 22, 2002.

[27] Segal, J. M., "What We Work for Now," *New York Times*, September 3, 2001, p. A15.

[28] Scarpaci, J. L., "The Theory and Practice of Health Services Privatization," in Scarpaci, J.

L. (Ed.), *Health Services Privatization in Industrial Societies.* London: Jessica Kingsley, 1991.

[29] "Spending Patterns by Age," *U. S. Department of Labor.* Washington: Bureau of Labor Statistics, August, 2000, p. 2. It should be noted that this analysis does not take income into consideration, although Engel's law says that the poorer the household the higher the proportion spent on food. See Deaton, A., and J. Muellbauer, *Economics and Consumer Behavior.* Cambridge: Cambridge University Press, 1984.

[30] Flanders, S., "Admired Welfare Plan in Connecticut Meets First Test in Hard Time," *New York Times*, 13 August 2001, internet edition, p. 2.

[31] Rowntree, S., *Poverty: A Study of Town Life.* London: Longmans Green, 1901.

[32] *Poverty Watch*, "Poverty," 106, Summer, 2000, p. 20.

[33] Parker, H., "Tackling Poverty—An Acceptable Living Standard." *Poverty*, September, 1999, pp. 12-15.

[34] Rimmer, A., "Power and Dignity: Women, Poverty and Credit Unions," in Sweetman, C. (Ed.), *Gender and Poverty in the North,* Oxford: Oxfam, 1997, pp. 26-34.

[35] MacPherson, S., and R. Silburn, "The Meaning and Measurement of Poverty," in Dixon and Macarov, *op cit.,* p. 17, see endnote 6. See also *Overcoming Human Poverty.* New York: United Nations Development Programme, 1998, p. 15.

[36] In 1990 the World Bank used $275 in 1985 prices for countries like India, and $370 per year for countries slightly better off. *World Development Report 1990: Poverty.* Oxford University Press: Oxford, 1990, p. 25.

[37] Bearak,, B., "Bangladeshs Sipping Arsenic as Plan for Safe Water Stalls." *New York Times*, July 14, 2002, p. 1., internet edition.

[38] *Saigon Times*, March 5, 2001, p. 4.

[39] *USNews and World Report*, March 6, 2001, p. 3A.

[40] Herbert, B., "Hunger in the City," *New York Times*, November 22, 2001, internet edition, p. 1.

[41] Forty years after that experiment I met an ex-student who said she remembered me because I had caused her to starve for two weeks!

[42] MacPherson and Silburn, *op cit.,* p. 17, see endnote 6.

[43] Leonhardt, D., "Leaving Shareholders in the Dust," *New York Times*, April 1, 2001, internet edition, p. 1.

[44] There were actually two budgets, one published by the Department of Agriculture, called the "low cost budget," and one published by the Department of Labor, called the "economy budget." Orshansky's formula is based on the latter, which is the lowest of these. See Macarov, D., *Incentives to Work.* San Francisco: Jossey-Bass, 1970.

[45] Uchitelle, L., *op cit.,* see endnote 13.

[46] The caloric total of Orshansky's food budget does not seem to have been published anywhere. In fact, it has been impossible to locate either of the two original budgets. I rely for the caloric content on my 1968 conversation with Orshansky in Washington, where she gave me this information.

[47] Doron, A., "Definition and Measurement of Poverty," *Journal of Welfare and Social Security Studies.* 2, 1990, pp. 27-49.

[48] Gerdes, K. E., and K. L. Pehrson, "Philippines," in Dixon and Macarov, *op cit.*, 171-203, see endnote 6.

[49] Millman, S. R., and L. F. DeRose, "Food Deprivation," in DeRose, L., E. Messer, and S. Millman (Eds.), *Who's Hungry? And How Do We Know? Food Shortage, Poverty, and Deprivation.* New York: United Nations University Press, 1998, pp. 131-163.

[50] *Statistical Yearbook 1999.* New York: United Nations, 2000, p. 101.

[51] Millman S. R.,and L. F. DeRose, "Measuring Hunger," in DeRose, Messer and Millman,*op cit.*, pp. 20-52, see endnote 49.

[52] McPherson, Stewart, "Hong Kong," in Dixon and Macarov, *op cit*, 74-92, see endnote 6.

[53] Gerdes and Pehrson, *op cit.*, see endnote 6.

[54] Lipton, M., *Successes in Anti-Poverty.* Geneva: International Labour Office, 1998, p. 13.

[55] Ringen, S., and P. R. DeJong, *Fighting Poverty: Caring for Children, Parents, the Elderly and Health.* Brookfield: Ashgate, 1999.

[56] For an argument in favor of using assets rather than income, see Sherraden, M. W.,

Assets and the Poor. New York: Sharpe, 1991.

[57] Liebling, A. J., *The Press.* New York: Ballantine, 1964.

[58] *How Can They Be Poor—They've All Got Videos!* London: Child Poverty Action Group, 1994.

[59] Hancock, R., "Housing wealth, income and financial wealth of older people in Britain," *Ageing and Society,* 18, 1998, pp. 5-33.

[60] *Annual Statistical Supplement, 1990.* Washington: Social Security Administration, 2000, p. 377.

[61] Goodin, R. E., *Reasons for Welfare: The Political Theory of the Welfare State.* Princeton: Princeton University Press, 1988.

[62] Macarov, D., *The Design of Social Welfare.* New York: Holt, Rinehart and Winston, 1978.

[63] Maslow, A. H., *Motivation and Personality.* New York: Harper Bros., 1954.

[64] Margalit, A., *The Decent Society.* Cambridge: Harvard University Press, 1998.

[65] Jencks, C., "Foreword," in Edin and Lein, *op cit.,* pp. *ix-xxvii,* see endnote 4.

[66] Macarov, 1978, *op cit.,* see endnote 62.

[67] Viet-Wilson, *op cit,,* p. 105, see endnote 7.

[68] Maor, A., *Knesset Proceedings, 2001,* Jerusalem, Israel. (parentheses in the original).

[69] MacPherson and Silburn, *op cit.,* p. 10, see endnote 6.

[70] Uchitelle, I., "Devising New Math to Define Poverty." *New York Times,* October 18, 1999, internet edition, p. 1

[71] Cox, D., "Australia," in Dixon and Macarov, *op cit.,* p. 24, see endnote 6 (parentheses in the original).

[72] Reich, R. B., *The Future of Success.* New York: Knopf, 2000.

[73] Smeeding, T., L. Rainwater and G. Burtless, "United States Poverty in a Cross-National Context," *Focus,* 21, *3,* Spring, 2001, pp. 50-54.

[74] Steinberg, J., "Cleveland Case Poses New Test for Vouchers." *New York Times,* February 10, 2002, internet edition, p. 1.

[75] Yaniv, G., *op cit.,* p. 38, see endnote 14.

[76] Cox, D., *op cit.,* pp. 20-44, see endnote 71.

[77] "Poverty Watch," in *Poverty,* 106, Summer 2000, p. 20.

[78] Veit-Wilson, *op cit.,* see endnote 7.

[79] Shewell, H., "Canada," in Dixon and Macarov, *op cit.,* pp. 45-73, se endnote 6.

[80] Callan, T., and B. Nolan, "Ireland," in Dixon and Macarov, *op cit.,* pp. 93-115, see endnote 6.

[81] *Overcoming Human Poverty, op cit.,* see endnote 35.

[82] Dirks, L. E., "The Poor Who Live Among Us," in Shostak, H. B., and W. Gomberg (Eds.), *New Perspectives on Poverty.* Englewood Cliffs: Prentice-Hall, 1965.

[83] Completely equal societies are not mere chimeras. The Israeli *kibbutz,* in existence now for almost a century, is—in its pure state—a society in which no one is richer or poorer than anyone else. Almost all property is communally owned, and everyone is ensured satisfaction of basic needs, and many wants. See Macarov, D., "Constructing and Deconstructing Utopia: The Israeli Kibbutz as a Case in Point," in Shostak, A., *Utopian Thinking in Sociology.* New York: American Sociological Association, 2001. For a more theoretical approach to equality, see Dworkin, R., *Sovereign Virtue.* Cambridge: Harvard University Press, 2001.

[84] Piachaud, D., and H. Sutherland, "Child Poverty in Britain," *Journal of Social Policy,* 30, *1,* 2001, pp. 95-118.

[85] Dollar D, and A. Kraay, *Growth is Good for the Poor,* Washington: World Bank, 2001.

[86] Ravallion, M., *Growth, Inequality and Poverty: Looking Beyond Averages.* Washington: World Bank, 2001.

[87] Leonhardt, D., "For the Boss, Happy Days Are Still Here," *New York Times,* April 1, 2000, internet edition, p. 1.

[88] *Ibid.*

[89] Eaton, L., "2001 Bonuses on Will Street Decline 30 percent, to $10 Billion." *New York Times,* December 11, 2001, internet edition, p. 1.

[90] Krugman, P., "The Outrage Constraint." *New York Times,* August 23, 2002, p. 1,

internet edition.

[91] Leonhardt, D., "E*Trade Chief Accepts a Cut in Compensation." *New York Times*, May 10, 2002, internet edition, p. 1.

[92] Leonhardt, D., "An Example of Anything-Goes Executive Pay." *New York Times*, June 4, 2002, p. 1., internet edition.

[93] *Ibid.*

[94] See Tabone, C., "Malta," in Dixon and Macarov, *op cit.*, p. 119, see endnote 6.

[95] Anelauskas, *op cit.*, p. 69, see endnote 16.

[96] Smeeding, Rainwater and Burtless, *op cit.*, see endnote 73.

[97] Henderson, J., D. Hulme, R. Phillips and L. Andor, *Economic Governance and Poverty in Hungary.* Paper delivered at the Conference on Globalisation, Growth, and (In)Equality, Warwick University, Coventry, UK, 2002.

[98] *Pirke Avoth.* New York: Academy Photo Offset, 1940, p. 66.

[99] See Miller, D., "Distributive Justice: What the People Think," *Ethics*, 102 (1992), pp. 555-593.

[100] For more detail on subjective measures, see Know, P. L., "Subjective Social Indicators and Urban Social Policy: A Review," *Policy and Politics*, 7, 3, 1979, pp. 299-309.

[101] Uchitelle, L., "How to Define Poverty? Let Us Count the Ways," *op cit.,* see endnote 13.

[102] Dirven, H-J., D. Fouarge and R. Muffels, "Netherlands," in Dixon and Macarov, *op cit.*, pp. 136-170, see endnote 6.

[103] Knox, P. L., "Subjective Social Indicators and Urban Social Policy: A Review," *Policy and Politics, 7, 3,* 1979, pp. 299-309.

[104] For a more detailed explanation of reference groups and expectations, see Paim, L., "Definitions and Measurements of Well-Being: A Review of Literature," *Journal of Economics and Social Measurements*, 21, 1995, pp. 297-309.

[105] See Rubinstein, A., "Ultra-Orthodox Poverty." *Ha'aretz*, March 28, 2001, internet edition, p. 1.

[106] Blank, R. M., *It Takes a Nation: A New Agenda for Fighting Poverty.* Princeton: Princeton University Press, 1997, p. 20.

[107] There are over 20,000 immigrants in 225 jails and prisons in the United States, and they make up the fastest growing segment of the country's prison population. It is not clear how many of them are incarcerated simply because they are illegal immigrants. Hedges, C., "Policy to Protect Jailed Immigrants is Adopted by U.S.," *New York Times*, January 2, 2001, internet edition, p. 1.

[108] *Leta Daily Press Review*, October 2, 2000, p. 2.

[109] MacPherson and Silburn, *op cit.*, p. 3, see endnote 6.

[110] Danker, S., "Global Cohort of Poverty Increases," *Earth Times*, 8, *15*, August 16-31, 1999, pp. 22-23.

[111] Stoesz, *op cit.,* see endnote 2.

[112] *Ibid.*

[113] Margalit, *op cit.,* see endnote 84.

[114] In MacPherson and Silburn, *op cit.*, p. 7, see endnote 6.

[115] "Does 'Public Utilities' Mean Anything Any More?" *Poverty*, 108, Winter 2001, pp. 6-9.

[116] Yoon, S-Y., "A Beginner's Poverty Index." *Earth Times*, October 16-31, 1999, p. 25.

[117] Ravallion, *op cit.*, see endnote 86.

[118] Danker, *op cit.*, see endnote 110.

[119] Singupta, S., "In New York Millions Pile Up While Welfare Programs Wait," *New York Times*, May 5, 2001, internet edition, p. 1.

[120] Dixon and Macarov, *op cit.,* see endnote 6. For British figures see also "Poverty Watch," *Poverty*, 106, Summer, 2000.

[121] Cone, J. T., "Millions Still Affected by Hunger," *Earth Times*, January, 2001, p. 5.

[122] *New York Times*, October 23, 2000, internet edition, p. 1.

[123] Ravallion, *op cit.*, see endnote 86.

[124] *Current Population Survey March 2001.* Washington: U.S. Census Bureau, 2001.

[125] Pear, *op cit.,* see endnote 22.

[126] *Standardized and Unstandardized Experimental Poverty Rates: 1990-1999, op cit.,*

see endnote 8.

[127] Burtless, G., and T. M. Smeeding, "The Level, Trend and Composition of Poverty," *Focus*, 21, *2*, Fall, 2000, pp. 4-9.

[128] Chamberlain, S., "Gender, Race and the 'Underclass': The Truth Behind the American Dream," in Sweetman, C., *op cit*, p. 19, see endnote 34.

[129] Analauskas, *op cit.*, p. 68, see endnote 16.

[130] *Historical Poverty Tables, op cit,* Table 6, 2002, see endnote 26.

[131] Anelauskas, *op cit.,* see endnote 16.

[132] Historical *Poverty Tables, op cit.,* Table 22., 2002, see endnote 26.

[133] Burtless and Smeeding, *op cit.,* 4-9, see endnote 127.

[134] "Poverty in the United States 1999," *Current Population Reports.* Washington: U. S. Census Bureau, 2000, p. vi.

[135] Morris, J. M., "Chronic Homelessness Among Working-Age Adults: Personal Problems and Public Assistance.*" Journal of Social Distress and the Homeless*, 6, *1*, 1997, pp. 57-69.

[136] *Ibid.*

[137] *Poverty in the United States 1999, op cit.,* p. *vi*, see endnote 134.

[138] Schwarz, J. E., *Illusions of Opportunity: The American Dream in Question.* New York: Norton, 1997, quoted in Schorr, *op cit,* p. 52, see endnote 3.

[139] Smeeding,. Rainwater and Burtless, *op cit.,* see endnote 173.

[140] Analauskas, *op cit.*, p. 65, see endnote 16.

[141] Bird, M., "Dried Out." *Time Magazine,* 157, *18*, May 7, 2001, pp. 48-51.

[142] Swarns, R. L., "Lack of Basics Threatens World's Poor." *New York Times,* August 2002, p. 1, internet edition.

[143] Bird, *op cit.,* see endnote 141.

[144] Bernstein, N., "Family is Stranded at Gates of New York Shelter System," *New York Times*, March, 2001, internet edition, p. 1.

[145] *Ibid.*

[146] Room, G., *Anti-Poverty Action-Research in Europe.* Bristol: SAUS Press, 1993.

[147] Sinai, R., "The Freeloaders." *Ha'Aretz*, January 16, 2002, internet edition, p. 1.

[148] Schorr, *op cit.*, p. 137, see endnote 3.

[149] "Poverty Watch," *Poverty*, 106, Summer, 2000 (second parentheses added).

[150] Bennett, W. J., *The Index of Leading Cultural Indicators.* New York: Broadway Books, 1999, p. 225.

[151] *Poverty in the United States 1999, op cit.,* see endnote 134.

[152] Bergmann, B. R., *Saving Our Children from Poverty: What the United States Can Learn from France.* New York: Russell Sage Foundation, 1996.

[153] Piachaud and Sutherland, *op cit.,* see endnote 84.

[154] Kleinman, M., "'Include Me Out?' The New Politics of Place and Poverty," *Policy Studies,* 21, *1*, 2000.

[155] *Poverty in the United States. op cit.,* p. vii, see endnote 134.

[156] Plotnick, R. D., "Child Poverty Can be Reduced," *The Future of Children,* 7, *2*, Summer/Fall, 1997, pp. 72-87.

[157] Dixon and Macarov, *op cit.,* see endnote 6.

[158] Macarov, D., "Poverty Has a Rich Future," in Didsbury, H. F. Jr. (Ed.), *Future Vision: Ideas, Insights and Strategies.* Washington: World Future Society, 1996, pp. 56-75.

[159] Whiteford, P., & S. Kennedy, *Incomes and Living Standards of Older People.* London: HMSO, 1995.

[160] *Social Security Bulletin*, 57, *3*, 1994, p.118.

[161] Mays, N., "Fostering a Continuum of Care for Older Adults," *Links*, Spring, 2000, p. 2.

[162] Park, N-H., and N. Gilbert, "Social Security and The Incremental Privatization of Retirement Income," *Journal of Sociology and Social Welfare*, 26, *2*, June, 1999.

[163] Bok, D., *The Trouble with Government.* Cambridge: Harvard University Press, 2001, p. 118.

[164] *Poverty in the United States, op cit.,* p. vi, see endnote 134.

[165] Park and Gilbert, *op cit.,* see endnote 162.

[166] *Annual Supplement, Social Security Bulletin.* Washington: Social Security Administration, p. 13.

[167] *Social Security Bulletin*, 60, 4, 1997, p. 49.

[168] Butrica, B. A., and H. M. Iams, "Divorced Women at Retirement: Projections of Economic Well-Being in the Near Future." *Social Security Bulletin,* 63, 3, 2000.

[169] Hancock, R., "Housing, Wealth, Income and Financial Wealth of Older People in Britain," A*geing and Society,* 18, 1998, pp. 5-33.

[170] Beri, M., "Who Takes Care of the Elderly?" *Dorot*, 46, July 2000, pp. 20-21. (Hebrew) (Translated from *Age and Attitudes. Eurobarometer Survey).*

[171] *Statistical Abstract of the United States 2000.* Washington: US Census Bureau, 2000.

[172] Mishra, R., "Globalization in Comparative Perspective: Sweden, Germany and Japan" in Mishra, R. (Ed.), *Globalization and the Welfare State.* Toronto: York University, 1999, pp. 75-93.

[173] Field, F., "Making Sense of the Unemployment Figures." In Field, F. (Ed.), *The Conscript Army.* London: Routledge and Kegan Paul, 1977.

[174] Atkinson, A., and J. Micklewright, "Turing the Screw," in A. Dilnot and I. Walker (Eds.), *The Economics of Social Security.* Oxford: Oxford University Press, 1989, pp. 17-51.

[175] Goodin, R. E., "False Principles of Welfare Reform." *Australian Journal of Social Issues*, 36, 3, August 2001, pp. 189-209.

[176] *Ibid.*

[177] Erlanger, S., "Seeking Votes, German Leader Endorses Plan to Aid Jobless." *New York Times*, August 18, 2002, p. 1., internet edition.

[178] See, for examples, Field, F., "Making Sense of the Unemployment Figures." In Field, *op cit.,* 1977, see endnote 173; Kogut, A., and A. Aron, "Toward Full Employment Policy: An Overview," *Journal of Sociology and Social* Welfare, 7, 85-99, 1980; Levinson, A., *The Full Employment* Alternative. New York: Coward, McCann & Geoghehan, 1980; Schwartz, G. G., and W. Neikirk. *The Work Revolution.* New York: Rawson, 1983; Yankelovich, D., H. Zettenberg, B. Strumpel, and M. Shanks, *Work and Human Values: An International Report on Jobs in the 1980s and 1990s.* New York: Aspen, 1983 ; Schneiderman, L. *The American Welfare State: A Family Perspective.* Paper delivered at the International Conference on Social Welfare, Seoul, Korea, 1992.

[179] "Labor Supply in a Tight Labor Market," *Issues in Labor Statistics.* Washington: U. S. Department of Labor, Bureau of Labor Statistics, Summary 00—13 June 2000.

[180] Western, B., "Incarceration, Unemployment and Inequality," *Focus*, 21, 3, Spring, 2001, pp. 32-36.

[181] Freeman, R., "The Rising Tide Lifts...?" *Focus*, 21, 2, Fall, 2000, pp. 27-31.

[182] *Ibid.*

[183] It is not clear why children and soldiers are considered to be one category.

[184] Despite the seminal importance of this figure, it does not seem to be published anywhere. Much library research, and requests for it from several think tanks, statistical data banks, and governmental bodies were in vain. Even the US Census Bureau had to do a custom tabulation at my request (and expense) to produce the proportion of the total poverty population who were laid-off and unemployed. *Custom Tabulation*, Current Population Survey, March, 2001. Washington: United States Census Bureau, 2002.

[185] *Poverty in the United States, op cit.,* see endnote 134.

[186] Schwarz, J.E., and T. J.Volgy, *The Forgotten Americans.* New York: Norton, 1993, pp. 33-37, quoted in Anelauskas, *op cit.,* p. 63, see endnote 16.

[187] *Statistical Abstract of the United States 2000, op cit.,* p. 413, see endnote 171.

[188] Schorr, *op cit.,* p. 153, see endnote 3.

[189] *Poverty in the United States, op cit.,* see endnote 134.

[190] Schorr, *op cit.,* p. 12, see endnote 3.

[191] Rainwater, L., and T. Smeeding, "Doing Poorly: The Real Income of American Children in Comparative Perspective." *Working Paper.* Syracuse: Maxwell School of Citizenship and Public Affairs, 1995.

[192] *Poverty in the United States, op cit.,* see endnote 134.

CHAPTER 2

The Results of Poverty

"I've been rich and I've been poor, and believe me—rich is better."
Sophie Tucker

Living in poverty destroys individuals, creates dysfunctional families, and raises societal problems of immense importance. The direct cost to poor people and the indirect costs to society are almost incalculable, and a number of these costs are not even usually associated with poverty in the public mind. As Levitan, *et al*, say: "The poor tend to suffer more than their share of most social ills—family breakup, teen pregnancy, inadequate housing, ill health, drug and alcohol abuse, child and spouse abuse, juvenile delinquency, and involvement as either victims or perpetrators of crimes."[1]

Others concur:

> Increased poverty results in homelessness, begging, repossession of homes and appliances, electricity disconnections, reappearance of sweat shops and casual labor, including illegal child labor, rising number of accidents and deaths at work, loss of employment rights and different forms of work security, deterioration of housing, a sharp increase in theft and crimes of violence, deterioration in the public's health and vandalism.[2]

Thousands of poor people cannot afford to visit a dentist or an optician. They are forced to hunt through charity shops for bargains. They cannot afford to go to the movies or engage in any organized recreation. Vacation trips or stays are out of the question for them.[3] In addition, they pay more for many things than do those who can pay cash, buy in quantity, or take advantage of deals.[4]

Some of the results of poverty are hard and clear. For starters, take hunger:

HUNGER

"Let them eat cake."
Marie Antoinette

From an individual point of view, hunger, of course, is the most terrible of all poverty results. According to findings by the Department of Agriculture and the Community Childhood Hunger Identification project, 4.1 million households in America and approximately 4 million children under the age of twelve go hungry because of insufficient funds during some part of the year.[5] Others give the number of those Americans who do not have enough to eat as twenty to thirty million,[6] including five and a half million children.[7] Throughout the world poverty kills over eleven million children a year. Malnutrition, one of the most extreme forms of poverty, is implicated in over half of these deaths.[8] Further, more than forty thousand people throughout the world die of hunger *every day*.[9] It should not be assumed that widespread hunger arises from an insufficiency of agriculture. Available land and water resources are sufficient to meet the food needs of the estimated nine billion population that is expected by the year 2020,[10] and although the world's population has grown sixfold in the past two centuries, food production has grown faster.[11] Indeed, it has been shown that massive crises of widespread hunger and increased mortality often occur despite aggregate food supplies that are no less adequate—and sometimes even more abundant—than usual.[12] Not only is the distribution factor to blame here, but there are many instances of food-stuffs actually being exported to gain foreign currency while the domestic population starved. Speaking of the situation thirty or forty years ago, one authority says, "The pain of poverty endures and in some ways is worse. For instance, the rule of thumb used to be that one shouldn't pay more than 25 percent of your income on housing. Now in New York people sweat blood to pay 40 percent and 50 percent. Add the cost of prescription drugs and you wonder what's left for, say, food."[13]

HEALTH

"Look to your health; and if you have it, praise God"
Izaak Walton

One of the most visible of the effects of poverty is on health. The severity of this problem, and the long-term implications, are apparent in the fact that—unlike the rest of the population—life expectancy for the poor has ceased rising and, as a matter of fact, has begun to fall. In Great Britain, growing inequality in health in the 1980s produced a fall in the overall life expectancy of men and a fall in life expectancy of women after childhood.[14] This is the first time in the peacetime history of Britain since the Victorian era that life expectancy has stopped being extended, and—as noted—the fall in life expectancy is among the worst off.[15] In Africa, there has been a decrease in life expectancy during the last ten years in no less than seventeen countries. It has also decreased in two Asian countries, in two European countries, and in one Western Hemisphere country.[16] The drop in life expectancy in the countries of the former Soviet Union is pronounced—life expectancy for men in the Soviet Union in 1985 was 62.87 years; in the Russian Federation in 1995 it was 58.27 years.[17] In Belarus alone, men's life expectancy dropped from 64.60 in 1989 to 62.87 in 1998.[18] During 1990 and 1996 life expectancy in Latvia dropped by 3.4 years for males. This has been explained as the "rapid move from etatist paternalism to neo-liberal philosophy."[19] It is of particular significance as a telling social indicator of the effect on general public well being of the economic system left behind compared to that which has now been embraced.

In addition, although the percentage of premature deaths is declining in most countries, during the last fifteen years it has risen in poor countries like Burkina Faso, Congo, Madagascar, and Albania; and it rose in Russia recently.[20] Even in developed countries, children in the manual social class are twice as likely to die in an accident as those in non-manual classes, and there is still a strong relationship between low birth weight and social class.[21] In one area in Los Angeles with the highest percent of poverty in the county (37 percent), people have the highest number of deaths due to diabetes, heart disease and lung cancer. More than 17 percent of mothers give birth with no prenatal care, 25 percent of adults have no regular source of medical care and 47 percent of adults and nearly 28 percent of children have no health insurance.[22] In general, poor people suffer from four to twenty-eight times more health conditions attributable to living conditions than do the non-poor.[23] They go to hospitals more often and stay longer—80 percent more in one study. The average number of days a person is bedridden increases as income comes down, and work-related injuries are more common among the worst paid.[24]

There is a circular relationship between poverty and health. Squalid living conditions, lack of medical care, the high cost of medicines and other such situations connected to lack of money make people sick; and sick people cannot hold jobs, cannot pay health insurance premiums, and must nevertheless pay for costly medicines and attention, thus becoming—or remaining—poor.

However, the effect of poverty on health is only one side of the coin. Poverty not only creates ill-health; ill-health creates and perpetuates poverty.[25] As has been pointed out in relation to AIDS, there are diseases that are not only caused by poverty, but that cause poverty.[26]

Poor health conditions condemn many people to a life of poverty. Indeed, if health costs were to be deducted from countable income, the poverty rate in the United States in 1997 would have increased from 13.3 percent to 16.3 percent.[27] It is clear that the cost of medical attention is a serious problem, and not only for the poor. One source says that in the United States 14 percent of the population, or 38.7 million people, are without health insurance coverage,[28] while another source estimates that 43 million people have no health insurance,[29] among them 11 million children.[30] One-third of all working age adults earning less than $20,000 have no health insurance. Nearly 30 percent had a medical problem during the year but could not afford to see a doctor,[31] and 30 percent of American children have never seen a dentist.[32]

A large part of their problem is the lack of health insurance among most of the poor, and the rising costs of health care in general. January 2001 saw the biggest surge in medical inflation since the early 1990s. In 1998 there were 44.3 million people without health insurance, and rising costs may lead to an increase in the number of people without insurance. In general, the American public is in for a shock—"they have no idea how much health care costs have increased over the last five or six years."[33] A large part of health costs is contained in prescription drugs and one-third of American Medicare recipients have no prescription coverage.[34]

At the time of this writing, it is reported that doctors are charging people large sums over and above their insurance coverage in order to give them better service than other people. The defense offered by doctors is that they are "just trying to give patients more attention." They do not remark that the time taken for this better service is taken away from those who cannot pay the extra cost.[35]

In health, as in economics, trickle down has become bubble up: "The care of the poor once was supported by the wealthy and the insured, but now the opposite is happening…it is the people who are most provided for who get the benefit…the system is brutal and inhumane."[36] Even among the poor there is a racially-created imbalance in health and health care, especially where chronic conditions are concerned: "Socioeconomic conditions, not health risk behaviors, are the primary origins of the racial stratification of health…Black Americans live fewer years than whites and live more years with chronic health problems."[37]

This growing inequality in health care, further documented in the section on privatization, which follows, has been termed the worst inequality of all by the former British Health Secretary:

> There is no more serious inequality than knowing that you will
> die sooner because you are badly off. There is an eight-year

gap in life expectancy between the affluent outer wards of Sheffield and the more deprived inner city. There is now a gap of nine and a half years between professional men and their unskilled counterparts.[38]

Not only does poverty lead to illness—the factors making for poverty play a direct role in increased sickness and disability. As mentioned previously, the number of contingent workers is growing as a result of both privatization and globalization, and the health conditions of such workers are almost always worse than those of full-time, year-round workers. In one study it was found that injuries in the informal sector exceeded those in the formal sector by a factor of ten; and illness by a factor of a hundred.[39]

One article which purports to find little connection between income inequality and health was bitterly assailed by other researchers on the basis of its assumptions, methodology and conclusions.[40] An Israeli paper headlined a surprising finding, to wit, "Study finds poor children more likely to suffer chronic illnesses."[41] The surprise is that it took a study to come to that conclusion, and that the paper felt it was unusual enough to warrant a headline and a story.

The ultimate end-results of poverty have been summarized thus: "Ill-health, disability, and premature death have been linked to material and social deprivation. In short, poverty kills."[42]

Mental Health

> *"No man [sic] can live with the terrible knowledge that he is useless."*

The concept of mental health ranges from actual mental illness to negative self-images, all of which may have a connection with economic situations. For example, the poorest two-fifths of the economic spectrum are one-and-a-half times as likely to be at risk of a mental illness than the richest two-fifths.[43] Mild retardation is fifteen times more likely to occur in impoverished areas.[44] Minorities, including the poor, suffer a disproportionate burden of mental illness—they have less access to services and receive lower quality care.[45] Another, previously mentioned, impact of poverty on health is the need to hold more than one job in order to survive, and what this does to health, mental health, and social conditions. The number of Americans who need to hold down more than one job has been growing for decades. In 1965 fewer than four million Americans held multiple jobs; in 1979, about five million; in 1999, this was almost nine million. This factor should be seen in the light of the fact that job stress (even from one job) has been found to be one of the most serious health issues of the twentieth century. More heart attacks occur between 8:00 and 9:00 on Monday mornings than at any other time during the week.[46]

Almost all the poor suffer mentally—one way or another—from being poor. As one ex-poor person puts it: "Poverty has a way of leaving an indelible stamp of insecurity and low self-esteem. I sometimes wonder whether I will ever totally shake off the damaging consequences of poverty. In many ways I will always feel poor."[47] Another says,

> The inescapable impact of being born in a condition of poverty that this society finds shameful, contemptible, and somehow deserved, has had dominion over me to such an extent that I

have spent my life trying to overcome or deny it. I have learned with great difficulty that the vast majority of people believe that poverty is a voluntary condition.[48]

Poverty determines many aspects of its victims' behaviors:

Poverty is a subculture, and people are stuck in the vicious cycle of ever-recurring poverty. Poverty makes its own norms, which are marked by very short-term objectives and a 'live for the moment' tendency. It is essentially a demeaning and disempowering condition. Few social factors diminish and demean people more than being caught in the vicious cycle of poverty.[49]

To be known as poor is to be stigmatized: "To many the term is synonymous with welfare moms, urban blight and undereducation."[50] One aspect of the mental suffering attached to poverty is recounted by an interviewee who used food stamps:

(In the grocery store) everybody sees where we get our money. Even his playmates, he goes to a nice school. You have all these professor children going there, and all this stuff. When I run into his friends with their parents (in the store), I get totally embarrassed. I don't even want to show them the stamps. And I have, at a point—I didn't buy the food (at that store). That's how embarrassed I can get.[51]

The stigma attached to poverty is well described by Gagnier, who also points out that the amount of money distributed to the poor through various programs in 1982 roughly totaled the amount distributed to wealth holders through high interest rates. Money given the poor raised endless debates about whether they were deserving—but nobody asked if the wealthy who benefited from government policies were deserving.[52]

For many people, poverty is not a one-time or short-term incident—even if a traumatic incident—but a long term, perhaps lifetime experience, and one which they communicate to their children. "Parents teach children a felt jeopardy, vulnerability, and soon enough, those boys and girls are quite aware of their uncertain, if not grim prospects—to the point that they foresee clouds on the horizon, not only for themselves but for their own children."[53]

Nor is "a taste of poverty" necessarily stimulating, uplifting, or a reason for changes in behavior, as the popular myth sometimes has it:

I grew up poor, hated, the victim of physical, emotional and sexual violence, and I know that suffering does not ennoble. It destroys. To resist destruction, self-hatred, or lifelong hopelessness, we have to throw off the conditioning of being despised...to refuse lying myths and easy moralities.[54]

Poverty may also lead to a behavior that the non-poor view as unmotivated or even apathetic, but which is actually a self-survival device. Offered advice and sometimes opportunities, poor people who do not take up these leads are viewed as not even wanting to change their situation. However, this behavior may arise because the poor person has little margin for error. He or she has managed to survive, somehow, under present conditions, and there is always the danger that any change may worsen, not improve, the situation. People living on the edge develop a basic conservatism. This is akin to the reaction of many poor rural farmers. Shown new methods, seeds, fertilizers, etc., they stick to the old ways. This is not stubbornness or lack of imagination. They, too, have managed to survive with familiar methods. There is no guarantee that the proposed new methods will not ruin them (which in many cases it has).[55]

Although the mental health of people constantly under financial strain is clearly a national health problem, Congress has consistently voted down plans to include mental illness under health plans or programs, mainly because it would increase costs for employers.[56]

HOUSING

> *"Show Me the Way to Go Home."*
> Folk song

Although homelessness sounds like an unambiguous term, distinctions have been made between those who literally have no roof, those who are unhappy or unsatisfied with their living quarters, and those who are "culturally" homeless.[57] Despite such semantic difficulties, the United States Department of Housing and Urban Development says that 5.3 million households in 1995 consisted of very low-income renters who received no federal housing assistance and either lived in severely substandard houses or paid half or more of their reported income for rent.[58] In the year 2000, there were said to be over 280,000 homeless people in the United States—up from about 230,000 in 1990. However, the difficulty of locating the homeless to count them has caused the Census Bureau to abandon its counting efforts.[59]

One report says that people are remaining homeless longer than heretofore, and that an increasing proportion of the homeless are families with children. In many cases families have to be broken up for their members to be accommodated in shelters. It is also reported that the number of homeless will continue to rise.[60]

Although demands for privatization of public housing often rests upon the supposed inadequacy of such housing, research indicates that most persons in public housing are fairly well satisfied with what they have, and the elderly, in particular, express themselves as quite well satisfied with their housing and their neighborhoods.[61] The attempt to privatize such housing, therefore, does not arise from an altruistic desire to help people, since the benefits of selling public housing rarely accrues to the tenants, but rather to "exchange professionals, estate agents, solicitors and others whose economic interests are closely tied to the further extension of home ownership."[62]

For many years the axiom in American housing policy was that "urban renewal means negro (sic) removal." Public housing tenants were induced or forced to leave while the premises were "refurbished," only to find that the rents were then so high they could not return. A graphic description of this process in Israel has been recorded,[63] in which low-income people were moved out of their slum homes, which were then rebuilt into a very exclusive artists' quarter. This process has been repeated in many other places throughout the world.

The life of the homeless has been documented in many places, but Vanderstaay gives a graphic picture of people who, in essence, must keep continually moving:

> Ushered out of department stores, bus stations, libraries, even churches and synagogues, asked to move along by local police after a moment's respite on a park bench, homeless people with nowhere to go are often forced to spend their day getting there. Walking, remaining upright, and endlessly waiting become all-consuming tasks, full-time work.[64]

EDUCATION

"A little knowledge is a dangerous thing."

Poverty unmistakably contributes substantially to differences in school performance.[65] For example, efforts to increase educational equality in Europe have been nullified by the fact that children of the working class are drawn disproportionately to what has been called the "less noble" tracks.[66] In the United States a bill to make up for inequalities in school funding was passed in 1965. Thirty-five years later "the gap between majority and minority children…hasn't been closed in any significant way."[67] A government inquiry in Britain found that if one father's earnings are double the level of another, his son's math scores will be 5 percent higher than the son of the other, and 2.7 percent higher on reading. The difference for a daughter will be 5 percent in both cases.[68]

Similarly in less developed countries: In Vietnam it was found that the richer elements of the society more-or-less appropriated the subsidies for education, and—not surprisingly—poor communities tend to have lower quality schools.[69] An American observer found that, "Specific educational structures, operating within the school, perpetuate the cycle of poverty by determining educational outcomes and limiting the economic ability of less-advantaged students."[70]

CRIME

"Only fools fear crime: We all fear poverty."
G. B. Shaw, *Major Barbara*

There is a general tendency to equate poverty with crime—or, at least, with a propensity for crime. As a British police officer put it: "Social deprivation can be linked to most areas of crime."[71] This attitude has been challenged by those who put the blame for crime on the absence of family values,[72] the structure of society and other factors. To what extent poverty is linked to crime requires detailed examination.[73] On the other hand, there is also the fact that poor people are more often the victims of crime than its perpetrators.

It is almost impossible to find a correlation between poverty and crime, let alone to prove causality, because so many definitional and practical difficulties intervene.[74] For one thing, there is in general a gap between crimes committed, crimes reported, and crimes adjudicated. Actions that would be reported as crimes in one setting may be overlooked, or dealt with internally, in another. An expensive private school or summer camp would tend to deal with offenses by students or campers—even technically criminal offenses—through internal disciplinary methods, or through discussions with parents, or even ouster, whereas children in public schools committing the same offenses might be turned over to the police. Similarly, in Israeli communal villages called *kibbutzim* (plural of *kibbutz*) there is almost no crime, since any anti-social action is dealt with by the organs of the *kibbutz* itself. Some years ago, when some *kibbutz* youngsters were accused by the police of raping a girl member, the horror of the incident was almost overshadowed by the members' indignity that the police had been called in.

Or take another example: In a suburb of Lòs Angeles in the 1970's a new community center was opened with the hope that it would result in a diminution of juvenile delinquency in the neighborhood. As police records subsequently indicated, this did indeed happen. However, it was not known to the general public that the director of the center had reached an agreement with the police that all first-time juvenile offenders were to be referred to the center rather than be booked. Consequently, the neighborhood experienced a noticeable drop in *recorded* juvenile delinquency. To what extent the center actually reduced juvenile crime—or recidivism—is not known. In Britain, it has been charged that only one in fifteen crimes is punished.[75]

Such is the difficulty of determining the crime rate that governments usually choose the method that results in reports of less or lessening crime. The Prime Minister of Britain has been accused of picking and choosing among crime rates.[76]

Further, poor people are more likely to be found guilty of crimes because of the inadequate and/or uncaring attorneys appointed for them by the courts. Wealthier people can hire better lawyers. Although indigent defendants are entitled to legal representation without cost, New York City, for one, offers representation to the poor that is said to routinely fall short of even the minimum standards recommended by legal experts: "No part of the indigent defense systems functions as it was intended." And on appeals, "the poor fare no better." [77] Even given adequate representation, it is no secret that "the higher social groups benefited from the differential implementation of the law."[78] In some countries it has been found that legal aid is given only to the poorest of the poor, leaving many poor people without representation in court.[79]

Some of the difficulties in measuring crime across localities, through time, among groups or in relation to other factors have been discussed in detail elsewhere,[80] and it should be constantly borne in mind that the vast majority of poor people do not engage in crime. Nevertheless, from 1979 to 1995 poverty in the United Kingdom more than doubled—from 5 percent to over 13 percent—and at the same time the notifiable offences recorded by the police rose by approximately 70 percent.[81] Braithwaite summarizes:

> For both women and men, being at the bottom of the class structure, whether measured by socioeconomic status or socio-economic status of the area in which the person lives, being unemployed, or being a member of an oppressed racial minority, increases rates of offending for all types of crime apart from those for which opportunities are systematically less available to the poor (i.e. white collar crime).[82]

Although the usual assumption is that if poor people engage in crime, it would be crime against property—for example, stealing food or items that can be converted into cash—the reality seems to be that poverty-related crime is greater in the area of violence than goods or money. It is the foreclosure of opportunity, rather than greed or need, that leads to most poverty-related crime.[83]

Social Security Misrepresentations

There do seem to be three areas in which crimes are concentrated amongst the poverty population. One of these is social welfare fraud. Although there are undoubtedly non-poor people who fiddle their reported incomes (or have unreported incomes) the bulk of social security fraud cases—reported and/ or detected or not—arise from the poor. If welfare benefits are not adequate to meet even elementary needs, then fooling the social security system is seen as less illegal, as it were, than other criminal activities, such as stealing property. These personal crimes must be distinguished from organized schemes to cheat the system, which even most of the poor regard as unacceptable.[84]

Even if there is some social welfare fraud, the amount is highly overstated by governments. Insofar as social security fraud in England, for example, is concerned, Sainsbury points out that official figures include "suspected (but unproven) fraud;" that the amount *recovered* from this so-called fraud is not published anywhere; and that the amount lost through so-called fraud was not far distant from the amount of benefits unclaimed by those eligible.[85]

In the interests of perspective, it might be wise to take a look at white-collar crimes. These have been characterized as crimes by the firm and against the firm. Offenses by the firm include income-tax fraud, violations of labor laws, invasion of privacy and illegal spying on rival companies. Fraud against the firm includes embezzlement, thievery, false working records, and so forth. As opposed to general attitudes that regard welfare fraud as a punishable crime, only one in twelve employees in one study considered stealing from the company a crime.[86] Further, investment houses that engage in illegal practices are reported by the media as simply over-enthusiastic in meeting their performance targets, but

> It is unlikely that social security claimants who defraud the system by working on the side would be regarded as just 'over-enthusiastic' in their efforts to make ends meet. It seems that the pressure to *succeed* is regarded as an understandable justification for the crimes of the rich, but pressure to *survive* is regarding as insufficient to justify many crimes of poverty.[87]

Although minor frauds engaged in by people with no other way to live (read: poor people) have always created titillating news items and resulted in anger and resentment among the non-poor public, this has been heavily overshadowed by the recent exposures of widespread—almost global—fraud by corporations and their executives. The enormous losses fraudently hidden by Enron, WorldCom and others were certainly caused by greed, rather than need. These CEOs, directors of boards, and heads of auditing firms were not protecting their children from hunger, but padding their ways of life to obscene proportions. Indeed, one is tempted to wonder to what extent the growth and prosperity reported during the Nineties was an artifact of such false reporting of profits, stock values, etc.

Not only have recent exposures led to suspicion of Big Business, its methods and goals as such, but they have been accompanied by an increase in suffering among hundreds of thousands of people. These include those left without paid-for or worked-for pensions, or left with worthless stock, and the workers who were fired by "downsizing" as these and similar corporations sought to increase their (paper) profits.

Fraud committed by social welfare recipients and others in the same position fades to insignificance in the face of the corporate fraud now being exposed. In this context, to complain vociferously about the former is like equating the effect of the ant and the elephant crossing a swaying bridge together.

Prostitution

The other crime almost entirely attributable to poverty is prostitution.[88] Very, very few prostitutes enter the profession because they enjoy indiscriminate sex. In almost every case examined, poverty plays an important causal role. Nor do many prostitutes manage to rise above the poverty level for any length of time—the profits, so to speak, go to pimps, organized crime, and corrupt officials.

Violent Resistance

Another area in which poverty plays a part is in generating an impetus towards certain types of violent resistance to civil authority, whether occurring as an expression of the non-cognitized frustration of individuals, or as the result of resistance by organized political groups. Not all who engage in politically-related violence are poor, of course, as witness Bin Laden, or indeed the leaders of the Communist revolutions of the twentieth century. Nor should we discount the impact of government-initiated violence directed against downtrodden populations or the nonviolent protest movements which seek to represent them, resulting in the slaughter of tens of thousands of innocent villagers and committed activists and intellectuals in Latin America, Asia and elsewhere, which in turn has contributed to the escalation to violence by the victimized communities.

Nor do all acts of violence arise from poverty in a directly class-related sense. Much anti-poverty struggle also carries an ethnic component, where both politico-legal and socio-economic discrimination has led a national ethnic group to suffer disproportionate impoverishment—where poverty may not be viewed as the greatest of the injustices it suffers—but which nonetheless feeds participation in liberation movements by various oppressed nationalities. There is also the violence that arises from sectarian differences, xenophobic attitudes, national rivalries, and Hitler-like obsessions such as that directed by German skinheads against Slavic, Muslim or African immigrants, where once again, poverty may play a role in relation to the competition between ethnic groups for scarce jobs.

Ecological Spoilation

*"I think that I shall never see
a poem lovely as a tree."*
Joyce Kilmer

In many other ways, poverty disrupts society. Despite efforts to achieve a sustainable environment and to safeguard the ecology, many poor people have no choice but to slash and burn forests, or to overfish rivers and lakes, or to hunt animals that are an important part of the food chain. In the Ukraine, the fertile black earth that made the Ukraine the "breadbasket of Europe" is being dug up and exported to richer countries to acquire foreign currency. The ultimate result of this rape of the earth will be evident in the agricultural statistics in years to come.

As Indira Gandhi one said: "Poverty is the greatest polluter...As long as people are poor, the immediate issue is survival. Caring for the future is a luxury."[89]

OTHER DISCRIMINATORY PRACTICES AGAINST THE POOR

Although one tends to think of the poor as hungry and homeless—and perhaps ill—there are many other aspects of life in which they are discriminated against and which rarely enter into the public conscience. For example, even in the matter of voting, the votes of poor people and minority members are more than three times as likely to go uncounted as the votes of more affluent people.[90]

In as small a matter as check cashing, the poor have no standing at banks. One out of every five Americans pays a fee for cashing a check,[91] and these obviously are not the wealthy. In Indiana alone, over five hundred payday lenders allow workers to write postdated checks for an interest fee, and the average loan is outstanding for six months, which means that interest rates hit triple digits. The courts have now limited interest to a *mere* 36 percent![92]

There is no legislation in Britain to prevent anyone from becoming a money-lender, and no limits upon the amounts of interest they can charge. Reputable companies may charge 50 percent or more interest, while loan sharks are known to have charged up to 400 percent. People living on low income have access only to high-interest loaners.[93] In one study it was found that more than 90 percent of businesses in low-income neighborhoods were refusing to accept ATM cards issued by the state for welfare, were refusing to allow them to be used to retrieve cash, or were applying a surcharge for every transaction.[94]

Further, the Internal Revenue Service is more likely to audit the returns of poorer rather than richer people.[95] On a more serious note, it has been found that the more welfare recipients (read: poor) in a state in the U.S., the higher the rate of serious errors in decreeing the death penalty.[96]

For the poor, the basic facilities most Americans take for granted such as financial services or quality retailers are largely out of reach. "They are...served ...by predatory institutions delivering much–needed services at a hefty price."[97] Indeed, over forty years ago an inquiry into exploitation of the poor by merchants, money-lenders and others led to a book with the descriptive title: *The Poor Pay More*,[98] and until this day, they do.

COPING WITH PENURY

How do people manage as they sink deeper and deeper into such poverty? One study found the following progression:

> People look for better-paid work or full-time work; spend their savings; claim social welfare benefits; sell their non-essential possessions; use more credit; delay paying bills; take casual badly-paid jobs; cash their insurance policies; pawn their valuables; sell their essential possessions; ask for charity; beg; and finally engage in petty crime.[99]

Another study found a slightly different progression, but the same end result: People acquire income from additional payments; income from other household members; casual earnings; saving, credit and loans; sale of goods; help from family and friends; and stolen goods.[100]

Another researcher lists six ways that the poor seek to augment their incomes, ending with "taking from others," and seven ways that they try to cut down expenses, including tolerating poor health and minimizing recreation.[101] People who exhaust their emergency benefits—especially during a recession—find themselves in deep trouble. In the early 1990s, almost of quarter of them were unable to find a job for three years. Six percent of those whose benefits ran out filed for bankruptcy, and 26 percent were receiving some kind of public assistance.[102]

A more graphic description is Dear's: "Some welfare mothers ransack supermarket garbage bins (called 'garbaging')...to get enough food for their children. Others sell their blood plasma twice a week for about $10 a pint to gain some desperately needed additional income. Still others pilfer Good Will drop-off bins to get clothing for themselves and their children...Some mothers, in absolute desperation, resort to prostitution to get money."[103] As noted previously, thousands are unable to afford to visit the dentist or optician and are forced to hunt through charity shops for bargains. Leisure activities, such as the cinema and pub, are also beyond the reach of many and all but the cheapest holidays are completely out of the question.[104]

Social welfare covers about three-fifths of the expenses of welfare-reliant mothers. They make up the gap by generating extra cash, garnering in-kind contributions, and purchasing stolen goods at below market prices.[105] In a recent study, all welfare mothers reported that their combined benefits ran out before the month was over. Speaking of the welfare program, a typical mother said:

> "Me myself, I just got back on and I been off for about six years because I was working. But I had some health problems and needed some medical insurance so I had to get back on the program. It's just not enough. You just can't live off it especially with three kids or two kids. It is impossible, the things you have to do to last you until the next month. Me myself, I get $380 in cash for three kids, plus food stamps. The rent I pay is just impossible plus my other little bills."[106]

In short, poor people live a hand-to-mouth, scrabbling, trying to make-do, existence. Although the existence of a universal "culture of poverty" has been generally disproved, most poor people spend the major part of their time dealing with the fact and results of their poverty. Far from being the happy, lazy, exploiters of society as portrayed by some popular myths, most poor people are desperately trying to move out of poverty, or, at least, to manage to live with it.

ENDNOTES

[1] Levitan, S. A., G. L. Mangum and S. L Mangum, *Programs in Aid of the Poor*, Baltimore: Johns Hopkins, 1998, p. 24.

[2] Townsend, P., *The International Analysis of Poverty*. New York: Harvester Wheatsheaf, 1993.

[3] McCallum, I., and G. Redhead, "Poverty and al Performance," *Poverty*, 106, Summer, 2000, p. 14-17.

[4] Caplovitz, D., *The Poor Pay More*. New York: Free Press, 1963.

[5] Bok, D., *The Trouble with Government*. Cambridge: Harvard University Press, 2001, p. 37.

[6] Chamberlain, S., "Gender, Race and the 'Underclass': The Truth Behind the American Dream," in Sweetman, C. (Ed.), *Gender and Poverty in the North*. Oxford: Oxfam, 1998, pp. 18-25.

[7] *Poverty and the Environment*. New York: United Nations, 1995, p. 7.

[8] Talal, B. B., "Investing in the Rural Poor: A Challenge for the 21st Century." *UN Chronicle,* 3, 2000, pp. 4-5.

[9] Mehta, S. L., *Globalization, Food Security and the Social Implications*. Paper delivered at the 28th International Conference, International Council on Social Welfare, Jerusalem, Israel, 1998.

[10] *Ibid.*

[11] "Farm Aid: The Kindest Cut." *International Herald Tribune*, June 15-16, 2002, p. 8 (quoting *The Economist*, London).

[12] DeRose, L., and S. R. Millman, "Introduction," in DeRose, L., E. Messer and S. R. Millman, (Eds.), *Who's Hungry and How Do We Know It? Food Shortage, Poverty and Deprivation*. New York: United Nations University Press, 1998, pp. 1-19. M65

[13] Gupte, P., "The Pain of Poverty Endures, and Is Even Worse..." *Conference New Daily,* July 28, 2001, p. 5.

[14] "Fall in Life Expectancy Among the Worst Off." *Poverty*, 99, Spring, 1998, p. 20.

[15] *Ibid.*

[16] *Demographic Yearbook 1990*. New York: United Nations, 1992; *Demographic Yearbook 2000*. New York: United Nations, 2000.

[17] *Demographic Yearbooks, 1985, 1995*. New York: United Nations, 1985, 1995.

[18] *Ibid.*

[19] Rajevska,, F., *Poverty and Exclusion Issues are Coming on Agenda in Latvia*. Paper delivered at the 28th Conference of the International Council on Social Welfare, Jerusalem, 1998.

[20] *Demographic Yearbooks*. New York: United Nations, 1983, 1989, 1999.

[21] "Poverty Research in 2000," *Poverty,* 108, Winter, 2001.

[22] Steingold, J., "Los Angeles Inner City Beset by Chronic Health Problems." *New York Times,* May 4, 2002, internet edition, p. 1.

[23] Colborn, D., "Who is Poor?" *Washington Post*, July 28, 1992, p. 12.

[24] Colborn, D., "Medicaid: A Safety Net with Some Holes." *Washington Post*, July 28, 1992, p. 19.

[25] Brundtland, G. H., "Healthy People for a Healthy Planet," *International Herald Tribune*, June 7, 2001, p. 12

[26] Quoted by Sander, D. E., *New York Times*, June 27, 2001, p. 1, internet edition.

[27] Burtless, G., and T. M. Smeeding, "The Level, Trend and Composition of Poverty," *Focus*, 21, 2, Fall, 2000, pp. 4-9.

[28] "Number of Uninsured Drops for 2nd Year," *New York Times*, September 9, 2001, p. 1, internet edition.

[29] Freudenheim, M., "Patients' Rights: What's at Stake?" *New York Times*, 19 August 2001, internet edition, p. 1.

[30] Herbert, B., "Sneak Attack," *New York Times*, February 4, 2002, internet edition, p. 1.

[31] Bok, *op cit.,* p. 37, see endnote 5.

[32] Roper, R. H., *Persistent Poverty: The American Dream Turned Nightmare*. New York: Plenum, 1991, p. 39.

[33] Freudenheim, M., "Consumers Facing Sharp Rise in Health Costs." *New York Times*, December 10, 2000, internet edition, p. 1.

[34] Brock, F., "A Health Care Revolt, Remembered," *New York Times*, April 7, 2002, internet edition, p. 1.

[35] Belluck, P., "Doctors' New Practices Offer Deluxe Service for Deluxe Fee," *New York Times*, January 14, 2002, internet edition, p. 1.

[36] Kolata, G., "Medical Fees Are Often More for Uninsured," *New York Times*, April 2, 2001, internet edition, p. 1.

[37] Hayward, M. D., E. M. Crimmens, T. P. Miles, and Yang, Y. " The Significance of

Socioeconomic Status in Explaining the Racial Gap in Chronic Health Conditions." *American Sociological Review*, 65, December, 2000, pp. 910-930.

[38] Quoted by Bok, *op cit.,* see endnote 5.

[39] Quinlan, M., C. Mayhew and P. Bohle, "The Global Expansion of Precarious Employment, Work Disorganization, and Consequences for Occupational Health: Placing the Debate in a Comparative Historical Context," *International Journal of Health Services*, 31, 3, 2001, pp. 507-536.

[40] Mellor, J. M. and J. Milyo, "Reexamining the Evidence of an Ecological Association Between Income Inequality and Health," *Journal of Health Politics, Policy and Law*, 26, 3, June, 2001, pp. 487-522; House, J. S., "Relating Social Inequality in Health and Income," *Journal of Health Politics, Policy and Law*, 26, 3, 2001, pp. 523-532; Kawachi, I., and T. A. Blakely, "When Economists and Epidemiologists Disagree," *ibid*, pp. 533-541.

[41] Shadmi, H., "Study Finds Poor Children More Likely to Suffer Chronic Illnesses," *Ha Aretz,* February 27, 2002, internet edition, p. 1.

[42] Townsend, *op cit.,* see endnote 2.

[43] "Fall in Life Expectancy," *op cit.,* see endnote 14.

[44] Mandelbaum, A., "Mental Health and Retardation," in Turner, J. B. (Ed.), *Encyclopedia of Social Work.* New York: National Association of Social Workers, 1977.

[45] Satcher, D., *Mental Health: Culture, Race and Ethnicity*, paper presented at the American Psychological Association meeting, San Francisco, 2001. Quoted by Goode, E., "Minorities' Care for Mental Ills is Called Inferior." *New York Times,* August 27, 2001, internet edition, p. 1.

[46] Fox, M., *The Reinvention of Work: A New Vision of Livelihood for Our Time.* San Francisco: Harper, 1995.

[47] Dass-Brailsford, P., "Resolving to Tame the Beast," *Journal of Poverty*, 5, 1, 2001, pp. 113-114.

[48] Allison, D., "A Question of Class," in Coles, R., and R. Testa (Eds.), *Growing Up Poor: A Literary Anthology.* New York: New Press, 2001, pp. 75-86.

[49] Sonn, F. A., "Social Development for the New Millennium: Visions and Strategies for Global Transformation." *Social Development Issues*, 22, 1, 2000, pp. 4-8.

[50] Fattah, H., "The Rising Tide," *American Demographics*, April, 2001, pp. 48-58.

[51] Kalil, A., H. Schweingruber, M. Daniel-Echols and A. Breen, "Mother, Worker, Welfare Recipient: Welfare Reform and the Multiple Roles of Low-Income Women." In Danziger S., and A. C Lin, (Eds.), *Coping with Poverty: The Social Contexts of Neighborhood, Work, and Family in the African-American Community.* Ann Arbor: University of Michigan, pp. 201-223.

[52] Gagnier, R., *The Insatiability of Human Wants: Economics and Aesthetics in Market Society.* Chicago: University of Chicago Press, 2000, p. 206.

[53] Coles, R., "Introduction," in Coles, R., and R. Testa (Eds.), *Growing Up Poor: A Literary Anthology.* New York: New Press, 2001, pp. xv-xxiv.

[54] Allison, *op cit.,* p. 86, see endnote 48.

[55] See Macarov, D., and G. Fradkin, *The Short Course in Development Training.* Ramat Gan, Israel: Massada, 1973; also published as *El Curso Corto de Entrenamiento Para el Desarrollo.* Santo Domingo, Republica Dominicana: Solidarios, 1974.

[56] Pear, R., "Drive for More Mental Health Coverage Fails in Congress." *New York Times*, November 19, 2001, internet edition, p. 1.

[57] Chamberlain, D., and G. Johnson, "The Debate about Homelessness." *Australian Journal of Social Issues,* 36, 1, February 2001, pp. 35-50.

[58] Bok, *op cit.,* p. 37, see endnote 5.

[59] Holmes, S. A., "Bureau Won't Distribute Census Data on Homeless," *New York Times,* June 28, 2001, p. 1, internet edition.

[60] Belluck, P., "New Wave of the Homeless Floods Cities' Shelters." *New York Times*, December 18, 2001, internet edition, p. 1.

[61] Weicher, J. C., *Privatizing Subsidized Housing.* Washington: AEI Press, 1997, pp. 25-26.

[62] Forrest, R., and A. Murie, *Selling the Welfare State: The Privatisation of Public Housing.* London: Routledge, 1991, p. 252.

[63] Jaffe, E. D., *Yemin Moshe: The Story of a Jerusalem Neighborhood.* New York: Praeger, 1988.

[64] Vaanderstaay, S. (Ed.), *Street Lives: An Oral History of Homelessness in Contemporary America.* Philadelphia: New Society Press, 1991, p. 81; quoted by Gagnier, *op* cit., p. 213, see endnote 52.

[65] McCallum and Redhead, *op cit.,* see endnote 3.

[66] Ambler, J. S., and J. Neathery, "Education Policy and Equality: Some Evidence from Europe." *Social Science Quarterly*, 80, 3, September, 1999, pp. 437-456.

[67] Clymer, A. and L. Alvarez, "Congress Reaches Compromise on Education Bill." *New York Times*, December 12, 2001, internet edition, p. 1.

[68] Callincos, A., *Equality.* Polity: Cambridge, UK, 2000, p. 100.

[69] Niimi, Y., P. Vasudeva-Dutta and L. A. Winters, *Trade Liberalisation and Poverty Dynamics in Vietnam.* Paper delivered at the Conference on Globalisation, Growth and (In)Equality. Warwick University, Coventry, UK, 2002.

[70] Ansalone, G., "Schooling, Tracking and Inequality." *Journal of Children and Poverty*, 7, 1, March, 2001, p.44.

[71] Cook, D., *Poverty, Crime and Punishment.* London: CPAG, 1997, p. 1.

[72] See Howard's comment in Cook, *ibid.*

[73] Using unemployment as a proxy for poverty, surveys of surveys do not indicate a clear correlation between unemployment and crime. See, for example, *Economic Crisis and Crime*. European Commission on Crime Problems, Council of Europe, 1985 (cited by Cook, *ibid.*).

[74] For a detailed examination of the difficulties of correlating poverty with crime, see Cook, *ibid.*

[75] "Goodchild, S., "Only One in Fifteen Crimes is Punished." *The Independent.* June 16, 2002, p. 1.

[76] Ford, R., "Prime Minister Makes a Careful Choice of Crime Statistics." *The Times of London*, March 14, 2002, p. 11.

[77] Fritsch, J., and D. Rohde, "Legal Help Often Fails New York's Poor." *New York Times*, April 8, 2001, internet edition, p. 1.

[78] Sutherland, W., *White-Collar Crime.* New York: Holt, Rinehart and Winston, 1949.

[79] Alon, G., "The Price of Justice." *HaAretz*, February 18, 2002, internet edition, p. 1.

[80] Findlay, M., *The Globalisation of Crime.* Cambridge, UK: Cambridge University Press, 1999.

[81] "Poverty Watch," *Poverty*, 106, Summer, 2000; and Cook, *op cit.*, p. 51, see endnote 71.

[82] Braithwaite, J., *Crime, Shame and Reintegration.* Cambridge, UK: Cambridge University Press, 1989, quoted by Findlay, *op cit.*, p. 27, see endnote 80.

[83] Findlay, *op cit.*, p. 70, see endnote 80.

[84] Cook, *op cit.*, p. 39, see endnote 71.

[85] Sainsbury, R., "Getting the Measure of Fraud," *Poverty*, 108, 2001, pp. 10-13.

[86] *Ibid*, p. 60.

[87] *Ibid,* p. 62 (emphasis in original).

[88] In many countries prostitution as such is not a crime, although living on the profits of prostitutes, soliciting, and renting premises to prostitutes often is. On the other hand, some countries—like The Netherlands—license and supervise prostitutes.

[89] Brundtland, *op cit.*, see endnote 25.

[90] Stout, D., "Study Finds Ballot Problems Are More Likely for the Poor." *New York Times*, July 9, 2001, p. 1, internet edition.

[91] Fattah, *op cit.*, see endnote 50.

[92] "Indiana Court Limits Payday Lenders." *New York Times,* August 16, 2001, internet edition, p. 1.

[93] Rimmer, A., "Power and Dignity: Women, Poverty, and Credit Unions," in *Gender and Poverty in the North.* Oxford: Oxfam, 1997, pp. 26-34.

[94] Gupta, S. S., "State Rethinks Deal to Provide Extended Welfare via ATM." *New York Times*, July 14, 2001, internet edition, p. 1.

[95] Schorr, A.L., *Welfare Reform: Failures and Remedies.* Westport: Praeger, 2001, p. 85.

[96] Herbert, B., "The Fatal Flaws," *New York Times*, February 11, 2002, internet edition, p. 1.

[97] *Ibid.*

[98] Caplovitz, *op cit.*, see endnote 4.

[99] Kempson, E., A. Bryson, and K Rowlingson. *Hard Times? How Poor Families Make Ends Meet.* London: Policy Studies Institute, 1994.

[100] Roper, *op cit.,* see endnote 32.

[101] Gilliat, S., *How the Poor Adapt to Poverty in Capitalism.* Lewiston: Edwin Mellen, 2001, p. 65.

[102] Eaton, L., "For 100,000 Without Jobs, Time and Aid Are Almost Up." *New York Times*, June 10, 2002, p. 1., internet edition.

[103] Colborn, D. "Medicaid: A Safety Net With Some Holes." *op cit.*, p. 19, see endnote 24.

[104] McCallum and Redhead, *op cit.,* see endnote 3.

[105] Edin, K., and L. Lein, *Making Ends Meet: How Single Mothers Survive Welfare and Low-Wage Work.* New York: Russell Sage, 1997, p. 43.

[106] *Ibid.,* p. 39.

CHAPTER 3

What Causes Poverty?

POPULAR NOTIONS OF WHAT CAUSES POVERTY

The roots of poverty can be traced to the beginnings of history, and they probably go back to pre-history. The provisions for care of the poor promulgated by even the most ancient religions and civilizations testify to the ubiquity of poverty. As early as 2370 BC in Sumer there were actions to curb the oppression of the poor.[1] The Bible contains explicit instructions about not reaping the corners of produce fields and not gleaning fruit trees in order to leave something for the poor. In fact, provisions for poor relief are explicit.[2] The Egyptian *Book of the Dead* records acts of charity. About 500 B. C., Buddha spoke of poverty.[3] Similarly, the Byzantine Empire was said to be, "characterized by its many works of practical philanthropy." [4] In the Islamic world, the fifth pillar of *zakat* was instituted as an effort at income-redistribution and poverty relief. Throughout the Dark and Middle Ages, poverty (and usually extreme poverty) was the lot of the common people.[5] In fact, for many centuries poverty was actually considered a national asset. Only poor people worked, and the more there were, the more the wealth of the country (but not of the workers) increased.[6]

Much later, in the 1880s, Chancellor Bismarck in Germany felt impelled by political considerations to deal with the poverty of working people by instituting a social insurance plan.[7] In Britain in 1924 Sir William Beveridge had poverty in mind when he advocated "insurance for everyone against everything," and in the United States in 1964 President Johnson felt it necessary to declare war on poverty. Nor is poverty a new phenomenon in the United States. Indeed, it is coeval with the establishment of the state, and almost a hundred years ago "estimates of minimum 'health and decency' budgets ran from $1820 to $2080 a year; but average earnings of workers never rose above $1500 at any point in the decade. And there were many below average."[8] Even if there were times when the world did not produce enough for all its population[9] (which, except in very specific locales and times, was probably not true),[10] why did the differences between the haves and the have-nots continue?

Before going into the causes of poverty, it should be noted that the causes and the results of poverty are in a dynamic interaction. Poverty leads to bad education and bad education leads to poverty. Poverty causes illness and illness causes poverty. Such examples could be multiplied. Consequently, there is some overlap between this chapter and the previous one.

Poverty As Deviance

One presumption concerning the cause of poverty is that it results from pathology or deviance.[11] In other words, the fault lies within the poor person who is somehow abnormal as regards the rest of the population. He or she may be lazy (the most prevalent concept), unmotivated, rebellious, apathetic, stubborn, uneducated, unskilled, illiterate, disabled, ill, or a sociopath in these or other ways. The person is the problem, and the solution lies in changing the person.

Traditionally, this approach held that the poor could be helped to enter the mainstream through ethical conduct and moral values.[12] Diligence, sobriety and thrift would reduce the poverty of the individual—the important thing was that poverty reduction should not reduce the self-reliance of the poor.[13] This approach—that poverty was the fault of the poor—led to opposition to any structural modifications in their favor.[14] Catholic Charities USA, for example, is said to have tried to help the poor to enter the mainstream by "emphasizing ethical conduct and moral values."[15] In short, the way out of poverty lay in individuals practicing the virtues.[16]

What these "virtues" might consist of—taking the rich as examples—include stinginess as a major component. As one writer puts it, "It's a sad truth that the vast majority of very rich people got that way because of their own spectacular meanness...the richest 20 percent of households in Britain give less than 1 percent of their income to charities, while the poorest 10 percent give 3 percent."[17]

One factor underlying this approach is a kind of unreasoning fear—the fear of (other peoples') dependency. It is felt more important to oppose avoidable dependency than to reduce material poverty,[18] or, to put it another way, it is better for people to be poor than to be dependent on others. The horror with which dependency is viewed arises from two elements. The first is what seems to be the manifest unfairness of independent people having to support dependent ones. The second is a deep-lying feeling that dependency is not only bad psychologically and emotionally, but is actually immoral. This attitude, carried to excess, prevented relief efforts to mitigate the effects of the great Irish famine. Britain, as the colonial power, decided that help extended to the starving Irish farmers would undermine their moral character. Hence, no help was given and millions did starve. This might be called the immorality of morality

Social workers are trained to help their clients to become as independent as they possibly can. Since they are also trained to help clients to achieve their own goals, they rarely see the paradox in insisting that someone who wants to be dependent, likes to be dependent, and is achieving dependency should be coerced to become independent. (I am reminded of a social work student of mine, dealing with a paralyzed person who wrote with extreme difficulty, refusing to write letters for the client so that the latter would not feel dependent!).

And yet, the prosperous classes are dependent on their inherited place in the social order, and their influence on the police, government, law, and many other factors. Tawney put this graphically long ago:

> Few tricks of the unsophisticated intellect are more curious than the naive psychology of the businessman, who ascribes his achievements to his own unaided efforts, in bland unconsciousness of a social order without whose continuous support and vigilant protection he would be as a lamb bleating in the desert.[19]

So ingrained is the fear that people will become dependent that one of the catch-words of welfare reform is to overcome "welfare dependency." The phrase is so laden with moral and ethical implications that it is difficult to begin to determine if and/or why some people might truly be dependent on welfare through no fault of their own.

Poverty As Accident

The second reason adduced for poverty is "poverty as incident or accident."[20] The Twin Towers tragedy impoverished many people through no fault of their own. The same reasoning applies to those who sink into poverty through the death or withdrawal of a bread-winner, or as a result of war or a natural catastrophe. In these cases there is no blame attached, and poverty is seen as one of the exigencies of living to which anyone may be subjected. In most discussions of poverty or its reasons this aspect is neglected or completely overlooked. There seems to be a tacit understanding that poverty arising from accident will be rather quickly overcome. In any case, there are very few governmental programs in place to deal with this aspect of poverty, and it is mostly left to voluntary organizations, such as the Red Cross.[21]

STRUCTURAL CAUSES OF POVERTY

The third reason for poverty that is put forth is structural.[22] The way society and the economy operate, people are made poor or kept poor. It is the thesis of this book that the overwhelming majority of poor people are in that situation because of structural reasons—it is not their fault, nor have they undergone a traumatic experience. However, it is in the best interests of those who make policy, govern, and/or enjoy a prosperous lifestyle to maintain the present structure, if not to increase its inequalities. In a wider sense, the structure of the economy—in particular—demands that there be a poverty group. Adam Smith said, "The oppression of the poor must establish the monopoly of the rich, who by engrossing the whole trade to themselves, will be able to make very large profit...For one very rich man, there must be at least five hundred poor."[23] Whether this is stated as an observation or a prescription, it is indicative of societal structure.

The maintenance of the texture of society and the economy that dooms many people to undergo poverty lies in part in the attitudes and ideologies that were and are prevalent in society, and in changes of ideology. Inequality, for example, was "pushed off both domestic and international agendas, replaced by theories of self-help, and the notion that individuals and poorer countries should take responsibility for their own choices and actions."[24] As noted below, the ideology or attitude that greed is the only dependable motivation for human actions has led to many of the frightful activities that are now taking place in the name of social planning and welfare.

Ideologies and Attitudes

> *"Things perceived as real are real*
> *in their consequences."*
> Kluckholm

The question of the origin of ideologies and attitudes goes far back in history, even further back than the discussions of innate tendencies versus education /socialization debated by Locke, La Metrie, and other philosophers in the eighteenth century and even earlier. However, the nature versus nurture controversy no longer relates to ideologies and attitudes. Ideologies, in particular, are now generally considered as taught rather than inherited and the discussion tends to be framed in other terms: "If you are for it, it is education; if you are against it, it is indoctrination."

Ideologies are created and perpetuated by the same forces that structure the educational system, the economic system, and societal beliefs in general. Although Bok feels that few Americans have been committed to any ideology,[25] attitudes toward poverty are a contrary example.

The fact that there has been poverty "since the memory of man runneth not to the contrary"—as noted above—means that it has become normative. The idea that there could or should be no poverty simply does not even arise in the imaginations of most people. That is the way the world is, and that is that. Nothing can be done about it, and nothing should be. Except for a few individuals and small groups that inveigh against poverty, an unequal world is the accepted *status quo*. At this particular historical juncture, those who speak seriously of wiping out poverty are considered either impractical "bleeding heart liberals," Communists, or ignoramuses.

The very idea of a world without poverty is simply inconceivable to most people.[26] And yet, such civilizations have existed. In ancient Greece, citizens did not work and they knew no poverty. Unfortunately, they exploited slaves for all the necessary work, but the production was shared equally among citizens. Slavery is reprehensible, but visions of a modern workless society have machines, technology, and robots doing the work—which have no moral implications—and could result in a world without poverty.[27] Incidentally, the result of the Greek no-work experience was an outpouring of creativity—drama and philosophy, poetry and literature, mathematics and logic—that has never since been equaled.

Another example: During a visit to Communist China, when it first allowed visitors from abroad, I continually asked about poverty, and almost invariably received the reply that everyone in that vast country had food, housing, clothing, and work, which seemed to be true. Although these were often on a level that others might judge to be poverty in an absolute sense, the fact that there was very little economic stratification meant that there was little relative poverty. Very few people were rich, but very few were poorer than their neighbors. To be sure, this situation was achieved at the expense of individual choice, liberty, and other human rights, but that does not contradict the fact that everyone had their most basic needs taken care of. Indeed, the opening of China to international influences was not brought about by the existence of widespread poverty but by a desire to become a world power. The lot of the average Chinese farmer has not improved as a result.

Another attitudinal factor that is rarely talked about is the feeling of superiority that the non-poor often acquire when considering the poor. As Tawney says, "The demonstration that distress is a proof of demerit…has always been popular with the prosperous."[28] There is also a certain feeling of righteousness that ensues—I must be doing something right, not to be like them. Or, as the New England merchant is said to have exclaimed: "God made me a rich man."[29]

Without the poor against which to measure oneself, there might be some difficulty in acquiring feelings of superiority and righteousness. One might be judged on other virtues, such as neighborliness, honesty, civic participation, or even a sense of humor—and be found lacking.

Another ideological/attitudinal factor might be entitled the "see no evil" approach. Norway's Foreign Minister speaks of the lack of empathy for poor people which he has observed.[30] In Hungary, too, welfare and poverty issues are said to be effectively ignored.[31] Then there are the Indian Dalits (Untouchables), the sight or touch of whom, for the upper class Brahmins, is an act of pollution. Lack of empathy is deepened when absolute denial takes place. Years ago the Finance Minister of Israel was taken to a shack in a development town in the

Negev in which a large family lived, obviously in deep poverty. On TV, the Minister took in the situation, and with the interior of the house and the condition of the family in full view, delivered his impression: "Such things do not exist in Israel." In other words, complete denial in face of facts.

Further along this range of reactions to poverty is the notion, often purveyed for self-serving motives by political figures (Ronald Reagan's "welfare queens", as an instance) that the poor are exploiting the rest of society—that they are parasites living on the labor of others. Consequently, as Jencks points out, social welfare policy cannot afford to be seen as offering the indolent something for nothing.[32] Even deeper is hatred of the poor. Tropman holds that not only does America hate the poor, but that this hostility is becoming deeper as time goes by.[33] In his view, the poor represent our own worst fears of downward mobility and we hate them for showing it to us. Hate also becomes a justification for the exploitation of the poor which feeds our economy.[34]

In short, not only does nobody love the poor, but most people don't want to be reminded of them, to have to acknowledge them, or even to see them, and rather than sympathizing with them, hate them for mirroring ourselves and our society.

Religion

> *Pity would be no more*
> *If we did not make somebody poor*
> *Mercy no more could be*
> *If all were as happy as we.*
>
> William Blake

While some religions have sought to alleviate the plight of the poor and sectors of believers within them have even radically aligned on the poor's behalf, organized religion has frequently played a part, if not in the creation, at least in the continuation of poverty, by providing dicta that legitimizes a refusal to pursue greater economic egalitarianism or resist existing authority. The New Testament phrase, "For ye have the poor always with you"[35] has come to be seen not only as a description, but as a prophecy, if not a prescription. Thus, for some people attempting to change the situation becomes tantamount to denying that which is written in the Bible, and close to heresy. In more extreme terms: If God had wanted a world without poor people He would have created it so. Thus, attempts to wipe out poverty become attempts to question, if not to defy, God.

Further, the existence of poverty is necessary for acts of charity, and charity is a universal virtue. In Christianity there is faith, hope and charity, and "the greatest of these is charity." In Judaism the central prayer on the Day of Atonement indicates that repentance, prayer, and charity (simply termed "righteousness") will avert an evil decree. Islam enjoins a tax (*zakat*) for the poor, and during Ramadan each Muslim is required to feed at least one poor person.[36] Buddhism takes the case even further—poverty is enjoined on priests so that people can gain merit by giving to charity. Were there no poverty, one could not perform the *mitzvah* of helping the poor, regardless of one's religion.   A world without poverty would be a world without charity, and how then would one merit heaven? In short, poverty is necessary so that the non-poor can become meritorious.

There is also the notion, explicit in some religions and implicit in others, that the poor must be sinners in some sense. If not, they would not be in their condition. A righteous God would not leave them in their situation without cause, and there must be something about them that we do not know to cause their suffering. Even the growing gap between the wealthy and the poor can be justified on religious grounds: "Unto everyone that hath shall be given, and he shall have abundance; but from him that have not shall be taken away even that which he hath."[37] It has been said of the Hoover administration, during the days of the Great Depression, "The administration seemed to have committed itself to 'the economics of original sin;' it had acted as if misery was foreordained and nothing could be done about it."[38]

Most people, even very religious people, do not consciously hold these thoughts, but their *weltanschauung*—their worldview—is colored by its unconscious acceptance. Consciously or not, they take seriously President Lincoln's humorous comment that God must love the poor people because He made so many of them.

Discrimination Against Minority Groups

"I have a dream."
Martin Luther King, Jr.

Most groups that are minorities within the states where they reside have become so as a result of some historical process: by conquest of their territory (indigenous peoples), by involuntary emigration (the African diaspora in the Americas) or as a result of redivision of territories resulting from wars or arbitrary creation of states after colonization. The result of these historic events have frequently left the groups concerned not only politico-legally powerless within a majority-dominated multinational state, but also facing socio-economic discrimination due to cultural differences with the dominant group and an enduring antipathy generated by and unresolved since the initial conflict.

As regards poverty, discrimination has two interrelated influences. The first is personal or attitudinal. When persons of different ethnic groups, or—in a western, particularly an American context, different skin colorings—are considered inferior by the dominant group, not only is their poverty unimportant—to the members of the dominant group—but again, to the dominant group, it is clearly caused by their inferiority. Their behaviors, their morals, their attitudes toward life—particularly as these may differ from those of the dominant group—keep them poor, and unless and until they change (which is manifestly impossible) they will remain an underclass. The second aspect is structural. Given the historical realities that led to their existence as a minority within the present state structure, minority groups have no ability (in majoritarian states which have not provided politico-legal means) to exercise structures of governance or law-making power that might permit them to effectively address their situation. As numerical minorities, they are unable to use standard democratic processes such as elections in order to make their policy needs felt. Equally, they exercise little control over the dominant institutions within the state related to education, the media, and so on. Rather, in such states, they are frequently confronted with a situation of forced assimilation, where their ability to conform to the norms of the dominant group are necessary—but not necessarily sufficient—to win them a place in majority-dominated institutions, either governmental or corporate. Failure or refusal to assimilate is viewed by the dominant group as a sign of inferiority: they cannot absorb the same education and hold the same values as the rest of the population, and therefore they cannot be trusted with important tasks, be given the same jobs, or paid the same salaries.

The results of this structural discrimination are present in such masses of economic and social evidence that it is hardly worthwhile to buttress it. Let us consider the situation of African Americans as an instance. Having first been captured and officially enslaved, then officially segregated under American law, it should come as little surprise that the 30 million African Americans, who make up fifteen per cent of the American population, constitute almost 26 percent of the poor, or three times the poverty rate for White, non-Hispanic Americans.[39] When the jobless rate in the United States was 5.8 percent in December, 2000, that of black workers was 10.2 percent—almost twice as much.[40] The poverty rate for African-Americans living in female-headed households was 42.8 percent, while those of white female-headed households was 30.7 percent. Of married couples in poverty, the black rate was almost double that of whites.[41] Indeed, the higher the percentage of Americans of African origin in its caseload, the lower a state's welfare benefits are.[42]

Similarly, ethnic groups such as Native Americans, Iluits, Hispanics and others find themselves in poverty because of prejudices against them, and a similar inability to institutionally address their needs. The Roma constitute 5 percent of the Hungarian population, and the proportion is growing. They are worse-off than ethnic Hungarians in most almost every poverty index.[43] In Israel, a clear correlation between ethnic and national divisions and poverty has been noted.[44] In the United States it has been shown that minorities get inferior health care[45]—a fact that will surprise very few people. That racism and ethnicity are important causations of poverty is indisputable.

Sexism

"The feminization of poverty."
Mimi Abramovitz

It is also indisputable that sexism contributes to poverty among women. On the one hand, women who work generally receive less income—even from the same work—than men. In addition, they more often hold low-paying jobs. They are more likely to be part-time and/or temporary employees and they are more likely to be laid off from permanent jobs.[46] In the United States, nearly 70 percent of women had entered the labor force by 1990, but in recent years, "many have been able to obtain only part-time jobs."[47] As a result of the socioeconomic configuration, women hold only 3 percent of the top jobs in the Fortune 500 companies.[48] On a more mundane note, over a third of female-headed households were in poverty in 1999.[49]

Recent efforts at so-called "welfare reform" have been said to be pushing women into the low-wage labor market without the support and training that makes employment possible.[50] Walby holds that insofar as women are concerned, the changes in the form of equality that are inherent in globalization and modernization simply "replace housework with low-paid employment," changing the inequality picture very little.[51]

Laissez-Faire Economics

Full steam ahead,
and let the devil take the hindmost!

While all of the factors mentioned above contribute to the creation and continuation of poverty, in truth they may be regarded as corollary components which assist in preparing the groundwork, the atmosphere, the rationale, and the on-going rush toward the phenomenon known as privatization: an entrenchment of extreme laissez-faire capitalism at the behest of corporate/financial power through the rollback of public institutions once intended to further public well-being. If it could be said that capitalism, as an economic system, is second to none in its capacity to create great wealth, it must also be said that capitalism both needs poverty in order to do so, and paradoxically, creates new poverty and further deepens existing poverty as a result. Privatization is but an exacerbation of these tendencies, as elaborated in the following chapter.

ENDNOTES

[1] *Encyclopedia Britannica*, 1965, Volume 11, p. 41.

[2] Levenberg, M., "On the Development of Philanthropic Institutions in Ancient Judaism: Provisions for Poor Travelers." *Nonprofit and Voluntary Section Quarterly*, 23, 3, 1994, pp. 193-207.

[3] Conze, E., *Buddhism: Its Essence and Development*. New York: Harper and Row, 1959.

[4] Constantelos, D., *Byzantine Philanthropy and Social Development*. New York: Rutgers University Press, p. 11.

[5] Manchester, W., *A World Lit Only By Fire*. Boston: Little, Brown and Company, 1993.

[6] Mizen, P. "'Work-Welfare' and the Regulation of the Poor: The Pessimism of Post-Structuralism." *Capital & Class*, 65, Summer 1998, pp. 35-54.

[7] Schottland, C. I., "The Changing Roles of Government and Family," in Weinberger, P. E. (Ed.), *Perspectives on Social Welfare: An Introductory Anthology*. New York: Macmillan, 1974.

[8] Schlesinger, A. M., Jr., *The Crisis of the Old Order*. Boston: Houghton Mifflin, 1957, p. 111.

[9] Throughout the so-called First World each country was food producing and even exporting. "First world hunger is not caused by a country's failure to provide sufficient food." Riches, G., "Hunger, Welfare and Food Security," in Riches, G. (Ed.), *First World Hunger: Food Security and Welfare Politics*. New York: St. Martin's Press, 1997, pp. 165-178.

[10] Mayer, J., "Toward a Non-Malthusian Population Policy," in D. Callahan (Ed.), *The American Population Debate* (Garden City: Doubleday, 1971, pp. 135-153), and *The Secret of Affluence*. Washington, D. C.: U. S. Department of Agriculture, 1976.

[11] Macarov, D., *Incentives to Work*. San Francisco: Jossey-Bass, 1970, pp. 28-30; and Jennings, J., "Persistent Poverty in the United States," in Kushnick, L., and J. Jennings (Eds.), *A New Introduction to Poverty: The Role of Race, Power, and Politics*. New York: New York University Press, 1999, pp.13-38.

[12] Johnson, D., "Charities of the Future," *The Futurist*, 36, *1*, January/February, 2002, p. 11.

[13] Schwartz, J., *Fighting Poverty with Virtue: Moral Reform and America's Urban Poor, 1825-2000*. Bloomington: University of Indiana Press, 2000, p. 3.

[14] Katz, M. B., "Reframing the 'Underclass' Debate," in Katz, M. B. (Ed.), *The "Underclass" Debate: Views from History*. Princeton: Princeton University Press, 1993, pp. 463-464.

[15] "Society: Charities of the Future," *The Futurist*, 36, *1*, January/February, 2002, p. 11 (quoting Magnet, M. (Ed.), *What Makes Charity Work? A Century of Public and Private Philanthropy*. New York: Dee, 2000).

[16] Schwarz, J.E., *Illusions of Opportunity: The American Dream in Question*. New York: Norton, 1997.

[17] Knight, I., "It Takes Money to be Mean." *Sunday Times* (London), June 30, 2002, p. 5.

[18] Schwartz, *op cit.*, see endnote 13.

[19] Tawney, R. H., "Economic Virtues and Prescriptions for Poverty," in H. D. Stein and R.

A. Cloward (Eds.), *Social Perspectives on Behavior.* New York: Free Press, 1958, p. 284.

[20] Jennings, *op cit.,* see endnote 11.

[21] For instances where government help is given directly to disaster victims, see Yanay, Y., "Assistance to Civilian Casualties of Hostile Actions." *Social Security (*Israel*),* 3, August, 1994, pp. 137-163; regarding crime victims, see Greer, D., *Compensating Crime Victims: A European Survey.* Freiburg im Breisgau: Max Planck Institute, 1996.

[22] *Ibid.*

[23] Smith, A., "Civil Government is for Defence of Rich Against Poor." *An Inquiry into the Nature and Causes of the Wealth of Nations.* London: Routledge & Sons, 1845; quoted by Andreski, A., *Reflections on Inequality.* London: Croom Helm, 1975, pp. 53-58.

[24] Woods, N., "Order, Globalization, and Inequality in World Politics," in Hurrell, A., and N. Woods (Eds.), *Inequality, Globalization and World Politics.* Oxford: Oxford University Press, 1999, pp. 8-35; quoted by Jones, B. G., *The Growth of Inequality: The Structural Determination of Need in the Era of Globalisation.* Paper delivered at the Conference on Globalisation, Growth and (In)Equality. Warwick University, Coventry, UK, 1999.

[25] Bok, D., *The Trouble with Government.* Cambridge: Harvard University Press, 2001, p. 175.

[26] See Milojevic, I., "From Utopia to Dystopia and Back." In Shostak, A. B., *Utopian Thinking in Sociology: Creating the Good Society.* Washington: American Sociological Society, 2001, pp. 46-47.

[27] Macarov, D., "Planning for a Probability: The Almost-Workless World," *International Labour Review,* 124, 1985, pp. 629-649. Also appears in French in *Futuribles,* 104, Novembre, 1986 and in *"Vers l'an 2000...et apres?" Les Cahiers Francais,* 232, Juillet-Septembre, p. 30; in Spanish in *Grupcaixa,* 11 Septembre-Octubre, 1986, pp. 62-58; and in Finnish in *Sosiaalinen Aikakauskirja,* 4, 1987, pp. 45-47.

[28] Tawney, R. H., "Economic Virtues and Prescriptions for Poverty," in Stein, H. C., and R. A. Cloward (Eds.), *Social Perspectives on Behaviour.* New York: Free Press, 1958.

[29] Amory, H., *The Proper Bostonians,* New York: Dutton, 1947.

[30] Gupte, P., "Sustaining Peace by Tackling Root Causes of Poverty is Essential," *Earth Times,* October 30, 2000, p. 30.

[31] Henderson, J., D.,Hulme, R. Phillips and L. Andor, *Economic Governance and Poverty in Hungary.* Paper delivered at the Conference on Globalisation and (In)Equality, Warwick University, Coventry, UK, 2002.

[32] Jencks, C., *Rethinking Social Policy.* Cambridge: Harvard University Press, 1992; quoted by Stoesz, D., "The American Welfare State at Twilight," *Journal of Social Policy* (forthcoming).

[33] Tropman, J. E., *Does America Hate the Poor? The Other American Dilemma.* Westport: Praeger, 1998.

[34] *Ibid.*

[35] *Matthew,* XXVI, 11.

[36] Dixon, J., "Social Security in the Middle East," in Dixon, J., (Ed.), *Social Welfare in the Middle East.* London: Croom Helm, 1987.

[37] *Ibid,* 29.

[38] Schlesinger, *op cit.,* p. 188, see endnote 8.

[39] *Poverty in the United States, 1999.* Washington: U. S. Census Bureau, September, 2000.

[40] Alstman, D., "Nation's Unemployment Rate Rises to 5.8 percent." *New York Times,* January 5, 2002, internet edition, p. 1.

[41] Danziger, S., and Lin, A. C., (Eds.), "Preface," in *Coping with Poverty: The Social Contexts of Neighborhood, Work, and Family in the African-American Community.* Ann Arbor: University of Michigan Press, 2000, pp. 1-16.

[42] Schorr, A. L., *Welfare Reform: Failure and Remedies.* Westport: Praeger, 2001, p. 13.

[43] Henderson, *et al, op cit.,* see endnote 31.

[44] Doron, A., "Social Welfare Policy in Israel: Developments in the 1980s and 1990s." In Nachmias D., and G. Menaham, (Eds.), *Public Policy in Israel.* London: Frank Cass, 2002, pp. 153-180.

[45] Stolberg, S. G., "Minorities Get Inferior Care, Even If Insured, Study Finds," *New York Times,* March 21, 2002, internet edition, p. 1.

[46] Abramovitz, M., "Question: Is the Social Welfare System Inherently Sexist and Racist? Answer: Yes." In Karger, H. G., and J. Midgely (Eds.), *Controversial Issues in Social Policy.* New York: Allyn and Bacon, 1993.

[47] Aaronowitz, S., and W. DiFazio, "High Technology and Work Tomorrow." *Annals of the American Academy of Political and Social Science.* 544, March, 1996, pp. 52-67.

[48] *Ibid.*

[49] Freeman, R., "The Rising Tide Lifts...?" *Focus*, 21, *2*, Fall, 2000, pp. 27-31.

[50] Albelda, R., "Farewell to Welfare: But Not to Poverty," *Dollars-and-Sense*, 208, November-December, 1996, pp. 16-19.

[51] Walby, S., "Analyzing Social Inequality in the Twenty-First Century: Globalization and Modernity Restructure Inequality." *Contemporary Sociology*, 29, *6*, November, 2000, pp. 813-818.

CHAPTER 4

The Privatization of Poverty

"Down went the owners—greedy men whom hope of gain allured;
Oh, dry the starting tear, for they were heavily insured."
W. S. Gilbert

A monstrous addition to all of the factors making for world poverty has cropped up during the last few decades, in the form of widespread privatization of former governmental and voluntary functions. Like many other concepts, privatization has been defined in various terms. One researcher lists twenty-one different methods of privatization;[1] another condenses privatization methods into eight;[2] and still another summarizes them as four.[3] However, the most common meaning of privatization is the shifting of governmental functions and services to non-governmental entities, either to voluntary not-for-profit organizations, or to for-profit businesses. The net result of privatization is more profit for some and less well-being for a vastly greater number of others; and purported efficiency at the cost of effective distribution among the population as a whole, with widening gaps, both socially and economically.

When governments shift services to voluntary organizations, the latter rarely have the resources that were available to the government, so they often need subsidies that equal or exceed the original cost of the service to the government[4]—which is hardly a testimonial to the greater efficiency of the non-governmental sector. Further, when services devolve to voluntary organizations functioning on a charity basis, services which once were regarded as public rights are thereby being redefined as matters of private charity—and thereby, optional.

In any case, the great majority of government shifts are toward for-profit organizations. Interestingly, this, too, often results in government subsidies to private enterprises. Thus, in New Zealand, half of the expenditures on private hospital services were public subsidies,[5] and it is in no way uncommon for an industry—especially a failing industry—to demand and receive governmental subsidies to allow it to stay in business.

It should be noted that there is a position that is in-between public auspices and complete privatization. This is called Purchase of Services (POS), or contracting out, in which governments pay private agencies to perform some of the functions that were formerly governmental, but retain overall control of the service.

Insofar as privatization of public services is concerned it has been noted that areas such as refuse collection, data processing and street light maintenance lend themselves to successful privatization. However, when it comes to "more complex, undefinable, long-range and 'subjective' services such as are characteristic of the social welfare field, the record of successful experience rapidly thins."[6]

The pace of privatization differs from place to place. Walford holds that "Britain has been one of those leading the way, the dramatic pace of privatization has gathered more momentum here than practically anywhere else."[7] It was in Britain that an "Assisted Places Scheme," in which the government paid for some students to attend private schools, was initiated. There were tax concessions for private medical insurance; more than one and half million publicly-owned housing units were sold; people were encouraged to opt out of state pensions; and public long-term residential care fell from over 60 percent to under 30 percent of the total.[8] However, after fifteen years of privatization activities, momentum in Britain seems to be slowing down. The "Assisted Places Scheme" has been abandoned,[9] and there is a move toward purchase of services instead of outright privatization. For example, in 1994 the British government dropped its plan to privatize the postal services.[10] The United States, on the other hand, has always been more reluctant to move toward outright privatization, in many cases using the purchase of services option instead.[11]

Historically, societies have moved between public and private services and back again a number of times. This is particularly true when it comes to contracting out certain services. Sclar, quoting Adler, says:

> Between the 1820s and 1890s common councilors (in New York City) would first conclude that contracted private street cleaning was less expensive. But, they soon concluded that the streets were not being cleaned and brought it back as a public service. Then they decided that, even though it was effective, public street cleaning was too expensive. The city then once more sought to contract out the work. Shortly thereafter, they again brought it back in-house because of contractual nonperformance. Each time they revisited the issue of contracting out, they asserted that this time they really knew how to write a foolproof contract, but they never really did...every single contemporary argument pro and con in the debate about privatization was used in the past...every single trick to overcome principal-agent problems has been tried. But then as now, no one found a way *not* to pay the contractors when the work was shoddy or nonexistent.[12]

The inability of public agencies to regulate private companies is exemplified by the employee of the security company who permitted weapons to be brought into the Chicago airport. The Chicago Department of Aviation wanted the worker dismissed. Instead, he was suspended. "Since we don't have control over the company or the workers, there's nothing more we can do," said the Department spokesperson.[13] This incident is illustrative of the inability to achieve responsible performance from private corporations whose focus is on profit rather than on the service to be provided or the need to be addressed. Air travel security was once a government responsibility, with Air Marshalls riding every plane. Then it was turned over to private firms as being not only cheaper, but more efficient. After the Twin Towers affair and subsequent experiences—such as the "shoe bomber"—the government is moving in again, as government and the media, which have long eulogized privatization, quickly recognize the pitfalls of private enterprise—though they do not generalize this recognition to other spheres where the specific well being of workers or the poor is affected. Private contractors and their "poorly paid inspectors" are being closely checked to make sure they are doing the job properly.[14] Similarly, the New York City Health and Hospital Corporation found that a health care company that had been awarded a $314 million contract to care for prison inmates had failed to provide adequate service in thirty of the thirty-three categories called for in its contract.[15] The more things change, the more they remain the same.

There are also reasons for opposition to privatization that do not arise from economic considerations. Part of the objection to Italy's turning over its museums to the private sector is "The sense that profit motives could obliterate the study and scholarly work," which have always been part of museums' *raison d'être*.[16]

REASONS FOR PRIVATIZATION

There is a multiplicity of reasons why governments pass their functions over to other bodies, and the decision usually involves more than one factor.

Avoiding Strife

One reason is the desire to get rid of strife-creating operations like welfare services, where benefits may be seen by recipients and/or the public as stingy half-empty cups rather than appreciated half-full ones, with consequent resentment taking the form of demonstrations, lawsuits, and sometimes violence. Formerly government-run youth services, for example, are being rapidly privatized, because politicians, eager to make the juvenile crime problem go away and unwilling to take the heat for trying new approaches, are rushing pell-mell to get rid of the activity.[17]

Conversely, services in which the seemingly non-deserving are viewed as being pampered, leading to resentment on the part of taxpayers, may be abandoned. This is part of the reason that the United States government ended the Aid to Families with Dependent Children (AFDC) program, which had been adopted with much public approbation in order to help widowed or divorced mothers raise their children under adequate financial circumstances.

Flexibility

Governments are also attracted to use of private agencies because there is greater flexibility in negotiating salaries—fewer constraints by civil service regulations and labor unions.[18] The fact that private agencies can pay lower wages than governmental ones is one of the reasons for the claimed efficiency of the former; wage depression under privatization has been documented in many cases. The impact on wage demands overall serves to drive down the cost of labor.

Cost Cutting

Then there are services that just prove too expensive to continue. The rising costs of medical care, for example, with sophisticated but extremely costly technology, may exceed a government's entire budget for social services. The problem of the welfare state, including its medical component, is said to be the confrontation of a limited system with an unlimited demand.[19] This is also one of the reasons advanced for proposing radical changes in the social security system—

that the government will simply not be able to meet its obligations as the latter mount. Such reasoning may result in selling or giving governmental institutions and services to business entities.

Privatization by Stealth

In this connection it should be noted that privatization is sometimes attained not by outright sales or transfer, but by deliberately allowing services to run down, by erecting barriers to access, by withholding information, and by making receipt of benefits so difficult and demeaning that the public has little alternative but to turn to the private sector. This has been termed "privatization by stealth."[20] As Goodin says: "We can reduce the welfare rolls, even without any changes in the rules or entitlement, merely by marginal adjustments in bureaucratic procedures. The more cumbersome the process, the more people will fail to satisfy some requirement or other and consequently be 'breached off' the program. The more times they are supposed to turn up for interviews, the better the chances they will miss one or more of them."[21]

"Least Government" Ideology

There is also often an ideological aspect to privatization. The belief that the best government is the least government calls for the government to divest itself of every service that can be performed by voluntary, private, or for-profit bodies, regardless of their efficiency or effectiveness. This is somewhat akin to the ideological stance known as subsidiarity, in which it is believed that services are best performed at the lowest level possible, and that the government should only serve as the instance of last resort. It also draws on the belief that people "on the ground," so to speak, are best able to both understand and deal with their own problems. The latter reasoning is sometimes used cynically, as when it is decided to "return services to the community," when the community doesn't want to provide the services or isn't able to do so. As Stoesz points out, "Thousands of psychiatric patients were discharged from state hospitals to often nonexistent community programs during the 1970s."[22] In Britain, "The *concept of community*, and its operational consequence, *care*, has been a highly valued idea for several decades, but has been unmatched by either a firm agreement on its meaning, or the economic support to give reality to either its potential beneficiaries, its carers, or to citizens at large."[23]

In the same vein, "returning to family values" has been exploited as an ideological code word for reforming, and almost abandoning, welfare programs. In the United States subsidiarity, although unnamed, is the reason for the "states' rights" controversy, and for the patchwork of programs that permit some states to give absurdly low help to the poor, as contrasted with more (relatively) generous states.

Stemming from the "least government" philosophy in a wide sense is the more narrow economic ideology of "laissez-faire"—that is, "let alone." This is the free market without bounds, and found its intellectual forefather in Adam Smith, who argued that if everyone would compete against everyone else with no outside interference, the result would be a perfect market—good quality at low prices. All economic history since that day has shown that Smith was wrong—but Reagan, Thatcher, and others of that ilk never claimed to be historians. Laissez-faire found its heyday in the time of the robber barons of American finances, the enormous trusts, monopolies, and anti-labor legislation, whose abuses were so blatant that they required the government to step in. (We are being told today that the government should step out—"we won't let these abuses happen again. Just trust us". One is reminded of the old adage: If someone fools me, shame on him. If he fools me again, shame on me).

Lack of Trust in Government

Related to the ideological stance mentioned above is the growing lack of trust in government as such. In 1970, 38 percent of Americans polled said they did not trust the government to do the right thing. By the year 2000, this had grown to over 68 percent.[24] In a study of attitudes toward poverty in Israel, over half the respondents said they would be willing to sacrifice financially if they could be assured that their sacrifice would eradicate poverty. However, 21 percent of the respondents commented—without being asked—that they doubted if the government would use their money to fight poverty.[25] Government was seen as either incompetent or venal or both. Such mistrust leads to alienation from government—not wanting to sacrifice for governmental aims, to serve on governmental bodies, to respect elected officials, or to believe that governmental services will perform as desired.

Government as Impotent

Then there is the belief that the state *cannot* do what is obviously needed, due to the nature of the political process, the pressures of interest groups, and the limitations of the administrative bureaucracy.[26] The self-serving role of government bureaus is one of the reasons given by several commentators regarding poverty. This view holds that poverty serves as a *raison d'être* for the broad infrastructure of parasitical public assistance bureaucracies and is necessary for the continuing careers of a wide array of bureaucrats within the social services and criminal justice system who administer services to or otherwise regulate the poor.[27] Should they succeed in their ostensible mission of eliminating poverty, it is argued, an entire echelon of professional employment would be eliminated.

Elimination of Bureaucracy

Bureaucracy is said to be the greatest problem of social democracies, and not only of totalitarian socialism.[28] A specific link between social welfare services and the bureaucracy that administers those services has been postulated by Margalit: "It is a fact that cutting the bureaucracy leads to a cut in services."[29] Nevertheless, the need to reduce the bureaucracy is constantly invoked in defense of privatization of the human services.

It should be said in defense of much-maligned bureaucracy that it was instituted in antiquity to prevent the very problems with which it is now charged. Rather than have people standing in line for hours, if not days, to have their complaints heard, Jethro said to Moses:

> "Thou wilt surely wear away, both thou and this people who are with thee, for this thing is too heavy for you, you cannot do it alone ...Provide ...able men...to be rulers of thousands, and rulers of hundred, and rulers of fifties, and rulers of tens. Every

great matter they shall bring unto thee, but every small matter they shall judge."[30]

Much later, but still long ago, the positives of bureaucratic management were pointed out by Max Weber.[31] These include equality of service to everyone, specialization by workers, immunity from outside pressures regarding decisions, an equitable division of the workload and accountability.

However, the paradox of bureaucracy in practice is that the average bureaucrat gets no credit for making correct decisions—that is expected of him or her—but there is a penalty for making mistakes. This is a no-win situation—there is no reward for being correct but there is a penalty for being wrong. In such a situation, logic dictates that decisions should be evaded in order to avoid the ever-present possibility of a mistake, since there is a penalty for being wrong. Thus decisions are delayed, shunted sideways to another worker, or kicked upstairs. In this manner as well, the public sector begins to be seen as "serving the values and meeting the needs of those who direct it and work within it,"[32] rather than the putative clientele.

As a result of such mismanagement of pure bureaucracy, there has grown up a public image that blames bureaucracy for all the faults of underfunding, political expediency, conflicting policies and unintelligible directives. "Bloated bureaucracies" and "faceless bureaucrats" are but two of the terms used to express these sentiments, and cutting the bureaucracy is one of the most-used reasons given for wanting to divest the government of its functions. Yet, as Demone points out, if military employees are excluded, the actual number of federal employees in the United States has remained roughly the same for more than thirty years and, as the population has grown, the ratio of government employees to the general public has in actuality been declining for about forty years.[33]

Part of the felt impotence of government arises from its reputed inability to attract competent people to government service. This is not because of anything inherent in public service, but arises from the market-driven version of society, that only good people are highly paid (which is questionable) and that only the highly paid are competent (which is even more questionable). This view was expressed by New York's post 9-11 mayorality candidate Bloomberg: "You are not going to get a lot of people from the private sector. Private-sector people tend to have a life style that they could not continue to support in the public sector."[34]

Unique Needs

Privatization also arises from unique group needs that require distinctions in services that governments cannot provide. As Kramer, *et al,* put it: "The state is more adept at striving for uniformity and equity, while voluntary organizations can be more responsive to cultural and religious diversity."[35] The emergence of many religious- and ethnic-based services stems from the prohibition (sometimes written into law) against governments discriminating—positively or negatively—concerning services to or for such bodies. For-profit protected housing restricted to, or emphasizing, a specific religio-ethnic group is one example. The existence of private schools is another evidence of this need, especially Catholic schools, Jewish schools, Islamic schools, African American schools, and—in some countries—Protestant schools. There are also other groups with needs so special that government services can hardly deal with them—such as the various Anonymous groups (Alcoholics, Overeaters, Gamblers, etc.), among others.

Payment for Services as Deterrent to Using Them

There is another, perhaps minor, basis for privatization. This is the expressed view that people appreciate more and therefore use more wisely anything for which they have paid. In New Zealand, for example, one of the reasons advanced for privatization is that "patients should be made to feel the costs of health care so that they will act in a fiscally responsible manner."[36] This belief is expressed in various settings. Many community centers hold, as a matter of policy, that "Everyone should pay something," believing that they will therefore attend more regularly, respect the property, and gain more from the services. In short, people moral enough to pay for services are moral enough to appreciate them. The fact that payment for services, similar to a flat tax, imposes an unequal burden on the poor, is rarely thought germane to this contention.

Not only is there no research which indicates that payment for services increases appreciation, but there is both experience and common sense which says that the exact opposite may be the case—having paid for something, people may feel free to abuse it, since it thus becomes, in a sense, their property. Again, there may be no relationship between payment and behavior. Many relatively expensive services to help people with problems—such as weight-loss clinics— have repeated experiences with people who, having made a hefty advance payment for the service, never appeared again. It is almost as though they felt that having made the sacrifice of paying, the desired goal should be theirs with no further effort. Or, having made their sacrifice to the appropriate deity, he or she should now take care of the problem. In any case, the effect of payment on human behavior remains to be investigated.

Efficiency

Together with all the previous arguments advanced for privatization, the most common reason advanced is that "Private sector operations outperform their public counterparts."[37] This has been phrased as, "Any programme performed in the private economy could be done more efficiently, more cheaply, and with greater satisfaction to the beneficiaries than its counterpart could achieve in the public sector."[38] In short, that business can do it better.

THE MARKET AS THE ENGINE OF THE ECONOMY

> *"Gross National Product is our Holy Grail."*
> Stewart Udall

> *"There is no poetry in money."*
> Robert Graves

Underlying this belief is the now blatantly expressed ideology that the desire for self-gain by individuals, and for profit by business entities, is not only the most reliable and strongest motivation for efficient operations, but the only one. In this view there is little room for altruism,[39] humanism, sympathy or human relationships, especially if these are seen to get in the way of more individual or corporate profit. This has been succinctly expressed by Luttwak:

Nothing should stand in the way of economic efficiency, neither obstructive government regulations nor traditional habits, neither entrenched interests nor feelings of solidarity for the less fortunate, neither arbitrary privileges of labor or the normal desire for stability. For nothing must hinder competition, which alone enforces efficiency by impoverishing less efficient individuals, firms, industries, localities or countries—and sometimes all of them at once."[40]

Indeed, money spent on any activity other than that which is profitable is viewed as friction in the smooth running of the profit-seeking economy. Greed becomes the guide, the goal and the god of the market-driven society. For example, President Bush declined to sign the Kyoto agreement on limiting air pollution and thus lessening global warming, because it would not be good for the United States economy. W. R. Grace chose not to label its asbestos-containing Monokote building material as such, although they knew that "the risk of liability to customers is heightened by the decision"—a decision the *New York Times* called "protecting the product."[41] Tuchman describes the market-driven society in the form of a question: "Why does American business insist on 'growth' when it is demonstrably using up the three basics of life on our planet—land, water and unpolluted air?"[42]

The ideology of a market-driven society marked as subversive anything seen as cooperative, collective, nationalized, or even governmental, and—conversely— placed a seal of approval on everything based on the profit motive.[43] It gained enormous credence with the collapse of the Soviet Union in 1991, which was widely hailed as proof of the greater efficacy of the capitalist system, irrespective of the numerous other possible factors, *inter alia,* the USSR's enormous human and material losses in World War II, the ill-conceived "virgin lands" project, the corruption endemic in the country, the enormously costly arms race forced upon it by the United States,[44] and the paranoia and hubris of various leaders. In the postwar period "talk of inequality invoked concerns about communism, statism, or at least fiscally imprudent populism."[45] Kelly calls this the "vilification of European collectivism after the totalitarian years," and "an over-reaction to a political deviation caused by singular circumstances."[46] Consequently, the very terminology used in the USSR during the Cold War fell into disrepute, and in the discussions of reconstruction of transitional states no notions of social planning of any kind, or abhorred terms like socialism, capitalism, Marxism, five-year plans, etc., were permissible. Ten years on, the term "capitalism" has again become respectable, especially in its negative sense, *i. e.,*"anti-capitalism," as used by anti-privatization and anti-globalization forces[47]—for lack not just of terminological but also of ideological alternatives.

Further, since the market as the fulcrum for all society *must* result in winners and losers, it paved the way for Social Darwinism, in which financial success became the hallmark of all the virtues, and in which the less wealthy were assumed to be the victims of their own failings.[48] The very entrance of governments into the realm of business through anti-trust legislation, wage-hour laws, and social welfare provisions was the result of the failure of *laissez-faire* economics to deliver, but the current resuscitation of this philosophy arises from various combinations of the causes mentioned previously.

The result has been the widespread privatization of former government services and industries, including—among others—automobile manufacturing, hydroelectric dams, bridges, railways, telecommunications, arms, mining, mills, ports, banks, electricity, farms, pensions, prisons,[49] and what are referred to as the social services—notably medicine, education and social welfare. The latter also includes privatization of residential homes for the elderly, bus deregulation, sale of council homes, and pensions.

The reason most often offered for privatization as a public good is that it results in better, cheaper items and services, thereby benefiting everyone. The response to such rationalizations was offered as long ago as the nineteenth century by a member of one of the most cut-throating organizations then existing—J. P. Morgan and Company, *viz*, "What underlies ruthless competitive methods? The desire to supply the public with better goods at a lower price? Is that the moving, impelling force behind it? Nonsense!"[50]

From all the arguments in favor of the market-driven society, one is conspicuously absent: that it will decrease poverty. Instead, "It is the most powerful who have automatic absolute advantage, contrary to the ideological portrayal of free trade and open markets in terms of fairness, efficiency and comparative advantage."[51] As a member of the Overseas Development Institute affirms:

> Evidently, privatisation of formerly publicly-owned enterprises, whatever its other merits, is likely to increase ownership inequalities. This is worst in cases of 'crony capitalism,' where divestiture is used to reward the government's friends, but even where transparency prevails it is obviously the rich who are best able to take advantage of the new investment possibilities. The poor may be disadvantaged in other ways, too: through short-term job losses, through price increases and through stricter sanctions against non-payment, for example, for utilities.[52]

RESULTS OF PRIVATIZATION

> *"We are a feelingless people.*
> *If we could really feel, the pain would be so great*
> *that we would stop all the suffering."*
> Julian Beck

Measuring Outcomes

Leaving aside the moral implications of the view that greed is the only reliable motivation for human actions, there are questions about and objections to each of the reasons for privatization mentioned above, and to privatization as a desirable move in total. However, the pragmatic question is whether and/or when privatization of former public goods and services results in more efficient operations. This question is complicated by the fact that efficiency can only be properly measured if effectiveness is held constant, and defining and measuring the effectiveness of non-profit organizations has been termed a "unique criterion problem."[53] The criteria used to evaluate for-profit organizations seem inapplicable to the non-profit sector. This makes it very difficult to compare results of for-profit and non-profit operations. As has been pointed out,

> Because there is very little empirical, tested knowledge...policy questions are often resolved largely on grounds of expediency, or on the basis of questionable assumptions regarding the virtues of non-government organizations.[54]

A small example: Immediately after Great Britain privatized its railway system on the basis that private industry would run it more efficiently, the most severe hurricane in a hundred years hit the island. Tens of thousands of tree-trunks fell on the tracks, preventing the trains from operating. What did efficient private industry do to cope? They demanded that the inefficient government call out the army to clear the tracks for them. Which they did. And the British railway system remained such a mess that it was, in effect, recently re-nationalized under the title "Network Rail." "Although nominally a private company...its foundations are in the state."[55] Railtrack (the previously monopoly private railroad operator)[56] left a system that requires massive upgrading of the railway system at a cost estimated at six billion pounds.[57] Recently, British Energy paid out large dividends to stockholders, and then demanded 410 million pounds sterling from the government in order to continue furnishing power.[58] In Poland, the privatization of the Szczecin shipyard resulted in such suffering among workers that the government has taken steps to re-nationalize the industry.[59],

Specifically, there is a lack of convincing evidence that the values and operating principles and methods of the market can be effectively transferred to the personal social services, particularly in meeting the needs of the poor, or in assuring some semblance of equality.[60] Indeed, so widespread is the belief that other entities can outperform government that there seems to be some resistance to even attempting to compare outcomes. As Smith points out:

> Contracting for child welfare residential services attracts the keen interest and support of private nonprofit and for-profit child welfare agencies...but for the most part these agencies resist performance measurement and evaluation.[61]

Despite lack of empirical evidence as to its results, and despite the presence of competing ideologies, privatization is undoubtedly a major economic and political movement throughout the world today, with the possibility of enormous harm to human well-being. Privatization is "more concerned about cutting costs rather than improving quality and reducing inequities."[62]

Since it is beyond the constraints of this volume to survey the entire area of privatization, which—as indicated above—covers a vast number of entities and is growing very rapidly, let it suffice to use the privatization of industries and the major social services—namely medicine, education and social welfare—as examples.

Industrial Privatization

Examples of privatization of industrial enterprises are as widespread as they are varied: the National Weather satellites in the United States; British Telecom and British Gas; Japanese telephone, tobacco and railway monopolies; a Spanish automobile manufacturer; French television channels, and a bridge over the Bosporus in Turkey,[63] among many others. In Mexico, conditions demanded by the World Bank for economic help resulted in more than a thousand of the 1,115 industries the government had administered in 1982 being privatized, leading to more poverty, unemployment and out-migration.[64] In Bolivia the World Bank tried to privatize the water system in favor of a multinational corporation in April, 2000. The result was a doubling of water prices. Popular protest was so effective that the effort was abandoned.[65]

Certainly one of the most visible effects of privatization is increased unemployment. Headline after headline announces the number of workers to be laid off (read: fired) when an industry or service is privatized. Companies have announced their intention to be "lean and mean"—that is, to keep only a skeleton staff on a permanent basis, and hire part-time and temporary workers[66] as the need arises. Concomitant with dismissing permanent workers is the depression of wages and loss of benefits which comes with privatization. Workers rarely gain anything from privatization of their employers, and usually lose a great deal.

Part-time and Temporary Workers

Growth in the number of such workers has been a phenomenon of recent years. When termed "casual labor" the impression is that of itinerant laborers on the road, so to speak. However, the casualness of this group is occasioned by employment opportunities, not choice. This phenomenon is sometimes called insecure employment, floating employment, contingent workers and precarious employment. Regardless of terms, as firms and services declare their intention to be "lean and mean," their purpose, as noted above, is to retain as small a permanent workforce as feasible, hiring only when necessary, in as few numbers and for as short a time as possible. Not only are part-time and temporary workers badly paid as a general rule, they also are ineligible for benefits, such as insurance, child-care arrangements, vacations, pensions, etc. They also build up very little "vestedness" in social security programs, and are almost never members of labor unions that might offer them help.

Many part-time and temporary workers are not even employed by the companies for which they do work. They are hired by manpower agencies of various kinds, who then "lease" them out to employers. Consequently, the latter are not responsible for paying or offering social benefits, and efforts to charge the manpower companies for these services is fraught with legal and practical difficulties. Rarely do such workers get organized, and then only if there is a strong union fighting for them. In February, 1999, nearly 1 percent of the U.S. work force, or 1.2 million employees, worked for "temporary help agencies," and another 0.6 percent worked for "contract firms." It is expected that this number will increase by at least 50 percent in the next few years.[67] Although in some countries part-time workers have finally won some social benefits,[68] in the United States the record is not encouraging: Three small attempts to organize part-time workers were successful in 2001, only to be decertified later. Some teaching assistants have succeeded in establishing locals, but no serious progress has been made.[69]

Part-time workers are officially defined as those who work less than thirty-five hours a week. Unfortunately, there is no further breakdown, so the category includes those who can find only a few hours of work as well as those who work almost thirty-five hours. In any case, the number of part-time workers in the United States was 8.5 million in 1965; 13.5 million in 1975; and 33 million in 1999.[70] Among the poverty-stricken, about 30 percent were part-time workers.[71] As Mead says, it is the lack of steady work, not the total lack of employment, that separates poor adults from non-poor adults.[72]

It should not be assumed that contingent or casual workers are only the unskilled, less-educated portions of the work force. It has been estimated that 40 percent of the workers in Silicon Valley, the epitome of high tech, are contract or temporary workers.[73]

Inefficiency and Corruption

Despite the mythology that government-run services are more inefficient and subject to corruption than private industry, the case of sugar mills in Mexico is instructive. Opened in 1937 as a government enterprise, the Zacatepec sugar mill was privatized in 1992, together with twenty-six other sugar mills. They were once more taken over by the government in 2001, since they had been ruthlessly exploited by their owners, who performed no maintenance and ran up debts of billions of dollars to the government, cane growers and others. "They just sacked the plants and made themselves millionaires."[74]

Reduced efficacy has accompanied the drive for efficiency on many fronts. The crash of a Swiss airliner has been generalized as airports "forced to give priority to productivity at all costs and to short-term capacity." The air traffic company, Skyguide, was recently privatized.[75]

Privatization has been accompanied by widespread corruption in many countries, especially those characterized as "transitional"—that is, moving from public to private provision of services. As countries (many in the former Soviet Union) are induced or coerced by institutions like the World Bank, or so-called aid organizations, to move from controlled to uncontrolled economies, the only people with any semblance of managerial experience are those who ran the controlled economy—often very corruptly. Consequently, the same people—with different titles—now run the privatized enterprises and, in many, many cases, continue the corruption. Nevertheless, the World Bank continues to call upon countries like Latvia to accelerate privatization as though this were a panacea for corruption.[76]

Such corruption is not just incidental to the tasks of fighting poverty. The World Bank estimates that corruption can cost the poor three times as much as it does the wealthy.[77]

THE PRIVATIZATION OF MEDICAL SERVICES

The area of medicine seems to lend itself to privatization efforts for a number of reasons. For one thing, medical services are expensive, which means there is money to be made. For another, the need for them is universal and timeless. Further, the need for some of them, like prescription drugs, is so urgent that many people will pay anything demanded to get them. Finally, some of the functions of these services do not require professional or specialized skills, and thus low-cost labor can be used (and exploited).

As long ago as the early fifties some auxiliary medical services in Britain, such as refuse collection and architectural services, were contracted out by district health authorities. However, the results were so unsatisfactory that by 1980 these services were returned to the previous authorities. Such decrease in privatization was not looked upon kindly by a government that had entered upon a privatization program, so despite the previous experience, in 1979 the government instructed health authorities to again contract out certain services.[78]

The expansion of privatization of medical services in Britain was further strengthened in 1989 when local hospitals were allowed to opt out of local control, and become self-managing.[79] This unrestrained development of private hospitals in England has directly contradicted the National Health Services' RAWP resource-allocation policy.[80]

Long-term Care

There is a tendency in the area of medicine, as in other areas, for private services to "cream" the potential clientele—that is, to pick those patients or clients who are easiest and most profitable to deal with. For these reasons, long-term care—for example—is very difficult to obtain. Such services are both demanding and open-ended, and the amount of money available to pay for them is very limited. Even the public sector shies away from providing such care. Thus, "despite the fact that long-term care requires little or no professional skill, and very little technology, it is still very difficult to get any kind of insurance that will pay for long-term care...Medicare, in the United States, specifically exempts nursing home and in-home medical expenses from coverage."[81]

Due to complicated regulations and explanations, the fact that Medicare does not cover long-term care is not known by a majority of Americans. In a recent survey, 31 percent of Americans felt they had long-term care insurance while actually only 6 percent had it.[82] Estes, *et al*, speak of gaps in private insurance protection and negligible long-term care insurance coverage.[83] Efforts by the Clinton administration to provide some sort of long-term health care under governmental auspices were resoundingly defeated in Congress, and there is reason to doubt whether current efforts will succeed, even if passed.[84]

Although one tends to think of long-term care as bedside services, much of the help tendered has to do with the activities and instrumental activities of daily living (ADL and IADL), of which forty components have been identified.[85] Over seven million Americans need help with their activities of daily living.[86] Nor is this help confined to the elderly—about half of community residents needing help with ADL are under sixty-five, and only 20 percent of them are in nursing homes.[87] Yet, "private insurance is for the most part unavailable, and governments have so far established no insurance mechanisms to fill this gap."[88] The consequence is that about half of home-care costs are paid by the users, often with catastrophic results.[89]

In Israel, the situation is somewhat different. The National Insurance Institute (the equivalent of the American Social Security Administration) provides a limited number of home-help hours to persons judged to be incapable of the activities of daily living, as evaluated by a registered nurse and a social worker. This service is not limited to the aged, being available to the disabled, the chronically ill, and others.

A considerable share of long-term care personnel in Israel comes from abroad. Entering Israel legally as foreign workers, they are employed by persons made eligible by their physical condition, and they are protected insofar as social security, salaries, severance pay, and health coverage are concerned. Since the first wave of such workers came from the Philippines, the word "Filipino" has become generic in Israel, meaning a long-term care worker, and it is not uncommon to hear someone refer to a "Filipino" from Thailand or Romania. In the United States such long-term care as is available is provided by social workers and nurses, who are increasingly being referred to as "geriatric care managers."[90]

Long-term care of the poor is contracted out in Israel to manpower-provider agencies. The government pays the agencies, who in turn hire and supervise the caretakers. There is much criticism of the profits made by the agencies, the low salaries paid the workers, the lack of effective supervision, and more, but the vision of homecare services being provided only under private auspices is so alarming that the present system, with all its faults, is retained.

Some private insurance companies do offer a type of long-term care policy, but the maximum length of coverage is generally three to five years, and is feasible only for relatively young clients, since it is terribly expensive for older people. Since elderly persons needing help may live for fifteen, twenty, and even twenty-five years after their condition develops, and the non-elderly handicapped even longer, this system is hardly adequate.

It is clear that although those who can afford to pay carers, through income, assets, or insurance, will do so, it is the poor who will suffer most from this lack in governmental services. They are and will continue to be dependent on family, friends, and the helpful—but sporadic and inadequate—services of voluntary organizations. And many will simply not get the help that they need. As former governor Dukakis learned, "The notion that the private sector can and will provide continuing care for severely and chronically mentally ill people is, in my judgment, a pipe dream... Community services can be provided largely by contracting, but long-term hospitalization is something the public sector should do—and do well."[91]

Hospitals

Throughout the world the results of privatization of hospitals have raised questions concerning the quality of care, access, costs, and social implications. Beginning in 1938 hospital care in New Zealand was delivered at no cost to the user, but in the 1950s the hospital system became increasingly privatized, especially long-term geriatric hospitals. This change did not result in improved care of the patients: "There is no conclusive proof...that the private provision of health services is any more efficient than public provisions were."[92] On a wider basis, Kronenfeld and Whicker summarize their review of studies, saying: "There is little evidence that for-profit hospitals have major secrets about how to run hospitals better or at a lower cost."[93]

Private sector growth as regards hospitals has been quite great throughout Asia, perhaps as a result of the public sector's inability to finance health care. Not only do many developing and transitional countries suffer from endemic poverty that prevents them from offering their people the services taken for granted elsewhere, but the requirements of international organizations often force them to use their resources in other areas, such as servicing loans. The role of the International Monetary Fund in dictating to countries what their priorities must be in order to qualify for help is a case in point. For example, in the early 1990s the IMF and Western donors "urged Zambia to open up its economy by dropping agricultural subsidies and scrapping a centralized marketing—steps rich countries are reluctant to take themselves... Result: 'A massive decrease in the area that farmers are planting',"[94] and—presumably—a drop in farmers' incomes.

Ninety-five percent of hospitals in the Republic of Korea are private, 67 percent in the Philippines, 57 percent in India, and 30 percent in Thailand.[95] However, it should be recognized that some of these hospitals and clinics are one-room, one-staff facilities.[96]

In Korea, privatization of health care is said to have resulted in "cost increases, a two-tier health care system, commercialized health care, dependency on high technology, low priority of primary health care, and the lack of a referral channel."[97] One study comparing for-profit and not-for-profit hospitals found that the major difference concerned access—already a problem with not-for-profit hospitals, which was found to be further exacerbated by the for-profit sector.[98]

Concern with the bottom line, couched in terms of competition and managed care cost imperatives in the United States, has also been said to result "not only in the shortest length of hospital stays in the industrialized world, but in massive reduction in expert nursing staff in almost all the hospitals in the country—and it is only just beginning."[99]   This has been described as "the abandonment of the sick and vulnerable in an increasingly cost-cutting, market-driven health care world."[100]

The development of a two-tiered medical system is in full-swing in many countries, including those with public health provisions. Public facilities, such as governmental and public hospitals and clinics, are used by doctors to treat private patients (or those who are willing to pay a hefty sum over and above their insurance coverage). In England, the result is not only felt in growing waiting lists of non-private patients, but in many kinds of preferential treatment offered to those prepared to pay, including a fully carpeted private room, complete with en-suite facilities and satellite TV. The average National Health Service patient in England has to wait six months for a heart bypass operation, but for those able to pay over $20,000, there are hospitals that guarantee almost immediate treatment.[101] Similarly, in Boston one can get round-the-clock cellphone access to doctors, same-day appointments, nutrition and exercise physiology exams at one's own home, and doctors to accompany one to a specialist—if one can raise $4,000 a year over and above the insurance coverage.[102] In February of 2002 the Attorney General of Israel finally outlawed the practice of doctors using public facilities for their private practice, as well as forwarding waiting lists of those patients who are willing to pay for it,[103] but in October it was found that the practice continued.[104]

Two other aspects of medicine should also be noted. One is the growth in the number of doctors' hospitals—hospitals owned by the doctors who practice therein, thereby getting both fees and a share of the profits. There is very little, if any, evidence that doctors are establishing their own hospitals simply to give better care to patients.

The second aspect has to do with alternative medicine. For a number of structural and ideological reasons, practitioners of alternative (sometimes termed "complementary") medicine are overwhelmingly found in the private sector. Public medical facilities have not opened themselves to these methods in a manner commensurate with public acceptance of the methods, although there has been some movement in this direction.

Although private hospitals base their existence on claims that they are more efficient and less costly than publicly-run hospitals, they are not so convinced of their own claims as to forego government subsidies. Under law as of this writing, federal disaster assistance can be extended only to state and local governments, individuals and nonprofit organizations. As an aftermath of the Twin Towers attack, the Federation of American Hospitals is lobbying to have "private nonprofit facility" redefined to include "private for-profit medical facilities," so they can get government help to increase their profits.[105]

Prescription Drugs

Then there is the effect of privatization on the availability and cost of prescription drugs, which are now the fastest growing part of America's health care costs[106]—and the most profitable.[107] Throughout the world, and particularly the developing world, the astronomical cost of drugs which cost only pennies to produce is playing havoc with the health of the populations. As a result, there is now a "titanic struggle going on between pharmaceutical companies and public health advocates over the cost of drugs and who has the right to produce and market them."[108]   Part of this fight for a share of the drug market are organizations that buy medical supplies in bulk for hospitals, in which corruption takes place as they "endorse" those products for which they get a share of the sales income.[109] In Korea's private clinics only one- and two-day prescriptions are provided during visits, to encourage patients to visit the clinic repeatedly for a single episode of illness.[110] As any reading of an issue of *Modern Maturity*—the journal of the American Association of Retired Persons (AARP)—will indicate, the cost of prescription drugs is one of the greatest problems of the elderly. If so, how much more difficult for the poor, elderly or not. Public fights over what should be included in a medical basket under health insurance and under HMO auspices have become routine, and a positive end is not in sight. As regards prescription drug aid, one commentator has said: "If you think this is bad, it is going to get more dramatic in 2003."[111]

Why should the cost of drugs be so problematical? Because that's where the profits are. A discussion in Israel as to the necessity to provide a vaccine against pneumonia in the HMOs' health baskets puts it clearly:

> What logical reason could there be...to reject including the vaccine in the basket, when it doesn't add any costs and at the same time saves lives and money? It turns out that one of the factors is concern about a drop in the number of hospital stays and the resulting loss of revenues to hospitals.[112]

The development of new drugs and techniques promises little for the poverty-stricken population. New contraceptives almost ready for the market at this writing may not be available to poor women. "Public clinics, like those operated by health departments and Planned Parenthood, may not be able to afford these new methods for the 6.5 million women, mostly poor and young, that they serve."[113]

A further consequence of the privatization of medicine is that for-profit agencies invest very little in training and research, and almost nothing in basic research. "The institutions that produce and train medical manpower and perform much clinical research are being forced, by a competitive marketplace, to forego the resources necessary to carry out their research and educational functions."[114]

Concerning nursing homes, higher quality has been reported in nonprofit nursing homes, which are more costly than for-profit homes, but this is because the nonprofit nursing homes pay higher wages to their employees and hire more staff per patient.[115] Similarly, a study of homes for the aged in England found that the government was more efficient in managing large establishments, but that small establishments were more efficient in private hands. However, the latter were often run as Mom-and-Pop operations, with the owners paying help less than the minimum wage, and with the owners themselves working up to ninety-six hours a week without pay, so to speak, so that their real labor costs were not reflected in the statistics.[116] Perhaps the largest-scale recent study of public and private nursing homes was reported by the American Public Health Association in 2001. After investigating the differences between 13,693 investor-owned and not-for-profit or public nursing homes, it was found, *inter alia*, that two-thirds of American nursing homes are investor-owned, although tax dollars pay for more than four-fifths of all nursing home bills. The conclusions concerning quality of service were unequivocal: "Investor-owned nursing homes provide worse care and less nursing care than do not-for-profit or public homes."[117] In addition, patient charges were from 17 percent to 24 percent higher in for-profit institutions.[118]

Insofar as hospices are concerned, little difference in costs or quality of service has been found to flow from sponsorship—government, voluntary, or for-profit. However, nonprofit hospices have been described as "patient maximizers,"[119] in contradistinction to "profit maximizers".

Although the privatization of hospitals will allow many of them to show profits, and to improve services for those who can pay for expensive procedures, there is no evidence to show that such privatization results in more or better care for the low-income population.

Mental Health

Turning to mental health services, the complexities of funding, administration, populations, and evaluation make comparisons between for-profit and not-for-profit operations very difficult.[120]   However, Dumont is very clear:

> Chain-operated, investor-owned hospitals, the 'lean, efficient' ones, have never assumed responsibility for low-income patients...Privatization ...generates much of the human misery from which human service entrepreneurs will squeeze whatever profit they can... Privatization means the dissolution of what is left of a thin and friable social infrastructure in American urban life...A society that turns its back on the poor and the mentally ill must learn to look over its shoulder.[121]

Findings of the *New York Times* are more direct and more dramatic:

> A series of articles...describing the neglect and abuse of thousands of mentally ill men and women warehoused in for-profit adult homes that are every bit as awful as the back wards of state hospitals were half a century ago...suicidal people left unsupervised have committed suicide, during summers residents in sweltering rooms with no fans have died of heat-related causes, poor screening allowed a dangerous resident to kill his timid roommate. And nearly 1,000 recent deaths have gone uninvestigated....[122]

Other observers are more general, simply holding that privatization leads to separate facilities or services for publicly funded clients and for those with private health insurance—in short, separating clients on the basis of income, thus reinforcing a two-tier system of mental health care.[123]

Still another distinction between for-profit and nonprofit health settings: Persons employed in the nonprofit sector report themselves as gaining more satisfaction from their jobs than their counterparts in business and management. Again, this is not surprising. The goals and activities of the nonprofit organization tend to synchronize with the impetus that leads people to undertake careers as carers of various sorts. Consequently, although the classic dilemma of the professional versus the administration has been documented many times,[124] the situation of the personal service professional within a business-oriented organization is much more difficult. Note, for example, that when factories were privatized in Slovenia the number of social workers employed there immediately dropped from four hundred to eighty.

Another aspect of privatized services, not confined to medical services, is that staff participation in issues other than direct care tends to be neglected. Advocacy, social action, organizing client groups to demand change—none of these are seen as within the assignment of the worker in the for-profit organization. Smith points out that, "Even though the staff are also interested in broader health care concerns including health care for the uninsured, it is very difficult for the staff to advocate aggressively for these other issues."[125]

Rural medical services seem to offer little hope for profit, and hence have not been privatized to any great degree. Indeed, in order to provide doctors to outlying areas, the American government offered bonuses intended to pay off student loans to those volunteering for such sections. Nevertheless, it is estimated that at least twenty thousand clinicians would be needed to provide adequate access to health care in such areas, compared to the nineteen hundred now in place.[126]

It might be well to begin a summary of the above by quoting Chan: "Given the economics of health care, there exists no country that can rely solely on the market to deliver necessary health and medical care to the bulk of its citizens."[127] Or, as Baer, *et al,* summarize:

> In our country (the United States), we have great faith in the ability of the marketplace and of competition to serve us and our loved ones. We believe, in spite of evidence to the contrary, that the private sector is more efficient in delivering its products. Perhaps health care is the ultimate testing ground of this mythical faith in the market.[128]

On balance, privatization of health services does not seem to have resulted in improved health. On the contrary, there is both widespread feeling and evidence that more people are being left out of the health services, and that the less affluent are receiving worse care and attention than heretofore. As a consequence, there are the stirrings of a movement back to government provisions rather than private auspices. As noted previously, attempts to bring about universal (read: governmental) health coverage are under way in several states—namely Maine, Oregon and Maryland—but seem to have little chances of success. Although a referendum in Maine passed by a narrow margin, it was purely advisory, and the chances of the legislature adopting it seem slim.[129] Even if these proposals were completely successful, they would affect only a small part of the poverty-stricken population, since most insurance plans are for those in the labor force, where the majority of the poor are not to be found.

In summary, there is abundant evidence that privatization of medical services results in a two- (or more)-tiered system, with the poor at the bottom of the tiers. As in every other case in which the poor are crowded into a section of services, the social work dictum proves itself: "Services for the poor become poor services."

THE PRIVATIZATION OF EDUCATION

Examining the relative merits of public, non-profit and for-profit education involves some very complex definitions, dimensions and details. One overarching question, which dates back to antiquity, concerns the goal of education. Currently, this has been formulated as the debate between communitarian and laissez-faire approaches.[130] The two positions, starkly stated, are that education should result in wisdom, self-awareness, a personal philosophy, societal functioning and adaptability to various life situations; or, in contrast, that the goal of education is to prepare one for a job (or jobs), occupation, vocation, or career, to become an efficient and effective member of the economic order.

There are, of course, various in-between positions emphasizing different mixes of these disparate goals, and evaluation of educational programs becomes difficult as the goals themselves differ from place to place, and change over time. The march of privatization into education, however, does not seem to be affected very much by the differences of opinion concerning the desired goals of education. Those forces emphasizing privatization seem to be saying that whatever the goals, private agencies can reach them better. There is, however, some bias towards the functional goals of education in privatization efforts, perhaps because those administering the efforts are themselves part of market forces.

The problems related to examining privatization in education are further complicated since they apply differently to various levels of education—elementary; high school; university with at least three different degree programs; continuing education; adult edication; in-service training; vocational schools and programs; correspondence courses; and—increasingly— education via television and the internet.

Further, the same definitional problems concerning privatization that affect more general areas also impact on education: public education that is completely provided by government, public education that contracts out certain services, such as catering and/or cleaning; public education that nevertheless derives income from students or parents of students; and public education that derives income from other in-house activities, such as renting out the auditorium or gym, charging admission to sports events, holding garage sales, etc.   Indeed, such fund-raising activities sometimes squeeze out the educational function for which the facility was devised.[131]

Then there are educational systems of non-profit bodies, primarily religious groups, that derive income from the activities enumerated above, from fund-raising among the membership and the public, and from government subsidies.

Finally, there are for-profit educational entities, which charge fees, and may also engage in all of the fund-raising listed above, as well as receiving government subsidies. In some cases, however, private educational bodies are forbidden to engage in other forms of fund-raising, in which case it is not unknown for them to engage in illegal activities,[132] including those mentioned above. Indeed, "private institutions are involved in disguised profit-making operations in almost all countries."[133] Tilak summarizes these educational patterns as the total private sector; strong privatization; moderate privatization; and pseudo-privatization. The latter are privately run institutions that receive almost their total budgets from government.[134]

Government subsidies to educational institutions may be direct block grants, or they may be based on the number of students or the number of classes. On the other hand, they may be for specific purposes, *i.e.*, hot lunches, school books, military training, etc. A rather recent, much-touted, method of indirect privatization of education in the United States comes through the use of vouchers, which presumably allow students to choose their own schools. Finally, although not strictly a form of privatization, "home schooling" should be mentioned, since it constitutes a move away from public education as such.

In addition to, or perhaps because of, this welter of forms and styles in education there are only a few scattered empirical studies that can be said to compare the overall results of non-profit and for-profit educational institutions in a clear-cut manner. A survey of these found that "The research literature contains no clear evidence that private schools are better than public schools."[135] There are, however, studies of specific activities. For example, the employment of outside psychologists in school systems can cost more than employing school psychologists.[136] As Tilak says, "Sophisticated arguments based on hard core evidence are rarely made in favour of privatization."[137] On the other hand, there are a number of positions, attitudes, and claims, some dealing with marginal issues, that are hotly debated.

Overall, however, it seems that there is now an international trend towards a manpower approach to educational policy. This began with the enunciated policies of Thatcher in Great Britain, Strauss in West Germany, Barre in France, Soleto in Spain, and Reagan in the United States.[138] Although none of these leaders remain in power today, their legacies remain. In Britain, for example, the privatization of public education can be said to have begun in 1980, with the above-mentioned Assisted Places Scheme that helped parents pay the costs for—and thus of—independent schools. It has been argued that one effect of the plan, intentionally or unintentionally, is to help independent schools with their financial problems. That students in the Assisted Places Scheme actually did score better academically was nullified by the fact that they were carefully selected for academic achievement in the first place.[139] In any case, about 250 private schools that applied for recognition in the Scheme were rejected for scholastic reasons, which casts some doubt on whether private schools are automatically better than public ones.

Looking now at the larger record, Ascher *et al* studied educational experiments in the United States. In Alum Rock, California, the use of vouchers did not raise the students' achievement levels. The Milwaukee voucher program actually resulted in the closing of several schools. In Chelsea, where Boston University undertook to run the school system, there was no apparent improvement in students' academic performance. Indeed, between 1969 and 1972 more than two hundred school districts were privatized, some of them offering to pay students for improved performance. "In none of the sites did performance contracting...improve students' test scores—in some cases the students did less well than corresponding groups of control students."[140] Another series of comparative studies found that so-called magnet schools were only slightly more likely than neighborhood schools to reach the rank of high achievers. Charter schools, which operate with fewer regulations than public schools and are usually free to select their students, were no more likely than neighborhood schools to excel.[141]

In comparing American public to private schools, Kronenfeld and Whicker found that the Catholic school system seems to provide a higher level of service than other systems, but qualify these findings since these schools generally have students of a higher socioeconomic status at the beginning, which is not controlled for in the research.[142] Lack of evidence that private schooling results in better education than public schools does not deter the pace of privatization. There is money to be made in privatized education. For example, a (false) report that Educational Achievement Inc.—which runs some of Baltimore's schools—had improved students' test scores caused its stock prices to shoot up.[143] Obviously, this was greeted with enthusiasm by the stockholders, but not because of the supposed improvement in educational methods. Fueled by consistent failures in public schools, the driving force in some places seems to be a feeling that anything would be better than the present situation, and is worth trying. Consequently, about fifty of the worst-performing schools in New York City are to be turned over to private companies or nonprofit agencies in the fall of 2001.[144] The short history of privatization of public schools is a classic case of denial. Despite failure after failure, the mythology of privatization continues to lure school systems into foredoomed experiments. For example, a program was tried in Texarkana, in which a private company undertook to raise school grades generally, but particularly in reading and math, as well as reducing the number of dropouts. In addition to changing teaching methods, they offered successful students radios and a television set as bonuses for improving. At the end of the third year—the termination of the contract—the dropout rate had *increased*, attendance had *declined,* and only 28 percent to 38 percent of the students had improved a grade level in reading and math.[145] In Hartford, thirty-two schools were turned over to private auspices. The experiment failed relatively quickly.[146]

In an even more definitive evaluation of privatized education, the Office of Economic Opportunity tested the effectiveness of so-called performance contracting by private educational companies in eighteen school districts across the country. The results? The differences between experimental and control students in reading and mathematics were minimal and in subjects not taught by the contractors, the control groups did better than the experimental group. "The achievement of the experimental students fell far short of the promises of the private companies."[147]

Unfortunately, results regarding students' grades seem less important than the savings to taxpayers when the government is relieved of the cost of education, and the gains to stockholders when private schools are run by corporations. The city of Philadelphia rammed through a proposal to privatize two-thirds of its schools as an amendment to a bill to provide loan assistance to nursing students, after thirty seconds of debate. The move has been called "brazenly undemocratic," and allows for creation of schools which would not be obligated to follow state civil rights, environmental and labor regulations.[148]

A recent issue that seems destined to become a serious bone of contention is the entrance of advertising into schoolrooms through the internet. In the United States there are a number of states in which students in classrooms are required to watch programs interspersed with advertising. As of now, only New York State bans such programs. In addition to such direct advertising of products in classrooms, there is also the undeclared goal of developing consumer loyalty to a specific computer company and/or internet provider by making its resources (and only its resources) available in the schoolroom[149]

Insofar as higher education is concerned, there has lately developed a booming business in correspondence, overseas, internet and limited-attendance courses, thick with MBAs and replete with Ph.D.s. Some of these are extended through well-respected universities of long standing, but the great bulk seem to be offered by little known institutions and—it is feared—by so-called universities established for just this purpose, leading to what has been described as "diploma inflation." For example, an e-mail message just received by this writer offers:

> Bachelors, masters, MBA, and doctorate (PHD) diplomas...no
> required tests, classes, books, or interviews...No one is turned
> down...Call now to receive your diploma within days!!!

The primary appeal of such educational businesses is to overseas students, often from countries in which higher education is difficult to attain due to scholastic or financial constraints. Entrance into the modern business world requires accreditation, and market forces are quicker to respond to such demands than is the academic world.

Whether such demands are justified by results is another question. In at least one survey, graduates of private universities did not receive higher rewards in the labor market, either in the form of lower unemployment rates, better paid jobs, or higher earnings.[150] In the developing world many countries—such as the Philippines, Thailand and Turkey—find that the unemployment rate is higher among private university graduates.[151] In addition, the heavy preponderance of management, manpower and economic courses in such programs reflects a more general privatized education—the neglect of the humanities as an area of study, and diminishing resources for educational research and innovation. Studies in the Indian state of Kerala, and in Bolivia, Peru, Colombia and Ecuador find that cheap commercial and vocational training results in neglect of research activities.[152]

This penetration of the market society into the schoolroom at all levels is graphically described by Walford:

> "Schools now have a 'senior management team', often with clear 'line management'. A curriculum is now 'delivered' or 'implemented'; the school is concerned with its 'public relations' and its 'image'. Children become 'inputs' and examination successes 'outputs'. 'Consumer research' is conducted and 'new markets' are sought." [153]

As Gewirtz puts it: "In education, parents are now seen as consumers and schools as small businesses, their income dependent on their success in attracting customers."[154]

New Right definitions of appropriate educational policies stress vocational and training content over types of curricula that are irrelevant to production and to industrial efficiency.[155] As a consequence of such privatization, public education is visibly being dismantled, both insofar as students are concerned and, inevitably, educational staff. Less than 50 percent of graduates with majors in education now enter the field, and of those, 25 percent soon leave.[156]

An additional but relatively unremarked aspect of the privatization of education is the fear that it will contribute to institutional racism, as governmental obligation to provide equal services in education is undermined, while wealthier sectors of the population, in disproportionately greater numbers from the dominant ethnic group, are free to access services dependent on their capacity to pay.[157] Discussions of market forces, consumer choices and privatization are usually "race-free," but the effects of the market-driven society on the marginal and excluded portions of society are very clear in the area of education. However, it should be noted that certain ethnic and religious groups, together with those that reject the general school system in favor of other methods of education, are—in some cases—attracted to private schools which reflect their philosophies.

In summary, the growing privatization of education at all levels is being prodded by the ideology of the market. Schools are becoming more like businesses, are serving commercial interests, and graduating students primarily prepared to become producer/consumers. The humanities are being abandoned and the necessity for research deprecated. An excluded underclass, rooted in inferior education, is being created. It is not necessarily true that lack of education leads to poverty, but it is certainly true that being poor increasingly leads to participation in an inferior educational system.

THE PRIVATIZATION OF SOCIAL WELFARE

Social welfare services have not been privatized to the extent that medicine and education have, perhaps because there is little money to be made from most social welfare services. Nevertheless, there are areas of privatization worth examining. Those that follow are only the ones that impact on poverty and the poor, although the cost-effectiveness and results of other privatized social welfare services—such as rehabilitation and substance abuse—are highly questionable.[158] In examining the chosen areas the same cautions offered previously should be kept in mind: comparison of methods is possible only if results are similar.

Unemployment

One of the most intractable of social problems facing governments is always that of unemployment. Although the level of "acceptable" unemployment varies from time to time and place to place, governments are constantly trying to keep the recorded number of the unemployed down.[159] As indicated later in Chapter Six, this often includes definitional deviousness, numerical namby-pamby, and statistical subterfuge. Since cost-cutting is the name of the game in privatization, firing workers is often the first action after a firm or service is privatized, thus making governmental obfuscation even more necessary.

Insofar as privatization is concerned, the bottom line impact is more unemployment, more underemployment, and lower wage levels.

Housing

The provision of housing for those who cannot afford to do so for themselves has been a government responsibility stemming back to the poorhouses of medieval times. With the phasing out of poorhouses, several methods have been used to make housing available and/or affordable. In some cases the government has built housing, or ordered that it be built. In others it has limited or frozen rents. Still another method is to subsidize either the building or renting of housing, or to provide low-rate loans or to guarantee such loans. In any case, for government housing in Britain the term used is "council houses"; in the United States, "public housing."

One attempt at solving the problem of homeless poverty-stricken single people in the United States was known as SORs—single occupancy rooms, in which buildings like hotels were provided for the needy. Insofar as the hotels were privately owned and the rents were paid by the government, generating a profit for the owners, this was a method of privatization. Attempts at increasing profits by cost-cutting devices, such as withholding heat, not making repairs, and neglecting general maintenance, led to deterioration of the properties, which became neighborhood eyesores. With the needy resisting being warehoused under such circumstances (in many cases preferring to sleep "rough"—*i.e*, on the streets), the tenants were increasingly drawn from hard-core social cases. Consequently, the level of decency in such housing fell to the point that they were closed, and few alternatives for the homeless remained.

The continuation of the need for low-cost decent housing is attested by the number of homeless people in almost all of the developed countries. It is true that a certain percentage of these have personal or emotional problems, but many are working at jobs that simply do not provide enough income for housing. There is no evidence at all that for-profit enterprises offer a solution to this problem.

Leaving aside the homeless, the push toward general privatization of housing has been most dramatic in Britain. However, funding for federally-constructed low-rent housing in the United States also dropped 90 percent between 1976 and 1986.[160] The sale of council housing in Britain is said to have benefited many people—some tenants, the government, and certainly real estate personnel and lawyers. "But for the homeless, the poorly housed in all tenures, and for a substantial marginalised minority, the policy has been irrelevant if not highly damaging. Even the most ardent advocates of council house sales have rarely claimed that the benefits go beyond those tenants able to take direct advantage."[161]

In short, as indicated by Forrest and Murie, "The privatization of housing will hurt many poor people because it forces them out of the protection of the government and the evidence indicates that the private market will not provide them with affordable shelter." [162]

Childcare

Although it is possible to add other categories, the care of children as a social service will be limited here primarily to adoptions, foster homes and daycare. Most foster home placements are made by social agencies, with the government paying the foster family (although there are a few altruistic families that take children in without payment). There have, however, been attempts to turn over the placement and supervision of foster children to for-profit agencies. Evaluation of one experiment in privatizing foster care in the United States found that the children were better off before privatization of the system. They stayed twice as long in their first placements and were subjected to half as much moving to other placements.[163] Under privatization, there is often disagreement about the standards of care, the social workers involved not accepting the level of care provided by the private agencies,[164] but the agencies having the final say.

One reason that private agencies are able to show a lower cost per child is that historically they have accommodated a less difficult or dependent clientele, with fewer dependencies, behavioral problems, handicaps, delinquent tendencies or whatever. This is certainly true of both of the two main areas of contracting-out: residential care for children and elderly persons.[165] Hence the caseloads of workers in privatized agencies are generally much lower than those in the public agencies, leading to fewer staff, and thus lower costs—at the expense of those denied the service.

There are many rather recent instances of employers providing childcare facilities and/or arrangements. This is mainly in areas of labor shortages, and the care is offered to induce, and make possible, women working. Such arrangements are almost always offered by large-scale employers. Small enterprises cannot afford to provide these services, and although there have been some attempts at "grouping" childcare facilities among several small employers, this is the exception rather than the rule. In Central and Eastern Europe it is reported that, "emerging small-scale businesses and private industry are not offering supports previously available to families. They can neither support long-term leaves nor provide subsidized daycare at the work place. Thus women working in these businesses do not have access to organized childcare."[166]

Critics of privatization of child welfare services point out that when it was tried in at least two states in America, "It has been a story of broken promises, of children's lives being further disrupted and of cost overruns."[167] In summary, it is clear that if state services do not respond adequately to the needs of poor families and minority groups, private capital will be less likely and able to do so, and it will be the poorest and most disadvantaged people who will generally bear the costs of such policies.[168]

Despite such reservations and warnings by critics, large for-profit chains providing childcare services are now preparing for an extended period of corporate growth and profits. As a result, lower-income families, childcare workers and women will face an even more restricted supply of affordable care. There will be only poverty level compensation for childcare workers and, of necessity, an increase in the unpaid work of care giving. These effects of privatization raise important questions about what values ultimately shape childcare policy.[169] As usual, when privatization offers good childcare facilities for a good price, the poor will be left with inadequate, undependable and largely unsupervised childcare.

Youth Care

Youth care, in both residential and non-residential settings—for delin-quents, the mentally retarded, youths with behavioral, learning and emotional disabilities, and the disabled—has become very big business. It is seen as an "almost bullet-proof profit spinner."[170] As one observer remarks, "Investors are pouring in money."[171] From boot camps to summer-camp-like facilities to actual youth prisons, for-profit corporations and chains of corporations are taking over previous mom-and-pop operations everywhere. In 1996 federal laws were changed to allow states to use federal money to contract with for-profit providers, and the latter are jumping at the chance. Insofar as delinquents are concerned, "the wave of tough anti-drug laws and the public's 'lock-em-up' attitude for juvenile offenders is now sweeping along the for-profits that focus on young people."[172]

Generally the for-profit operators prefer large-scale operations—five hundred- or more-bed facilities that offer economies of scale. In anything less than a hundred-bed facility they find it difficult to make a profit. They build in out-of-the-way places where labor costs are low and unions are weak, and often have government subsidies or tax forgiveness. In order to make a profit, they hire fewer employees and offer lower wages and benefits than government agencies. They often use temporary and/or part-time staff, leading to training problems, relationship problems, and lack of continuance in dealing with the youngsters.

The scale of the for-profits' operation is felt by many to be counter-indicated as compared to smaller settings, after-school and weekend reporting programs and other more traditional techniques. Some places, like Seneca, New York, have rejected such large-scale projects. In any case, the move of for-profit organizations into the youth care field is too recent to have undergone any large-scale long-term evaluations, so the question of efficacy is still untested.

Corrections

Etzioni points out that in the United States there are more than twice the number of private guards than police officers, and that although between 1990 and 1996 the prison population increased by 1.5 times, the number of adults in private prisons increased by 5.6 times. Further, "to enhance profits, private prisons have been hiring underqualified prison guards, using unsafe methods to transport prisoners, and allowing gross abuses of inmates." As a result, the government has already repossessed some of the private facilities.[173]

This being so, why are governmental agencies so positive about this privatization? One observer remarks that politicians see it as a way to divest themselves of programs that are visible and criticized, by diverting them onto others,[174] as well as getting out from under the criticism as to what more prison beds would cost the government.

The Refocusing of Social Work

From the earliest days of social work, when volunteers ("friendly visitors") carried most of the burden, through the professionalization of such services and up to recently, social work has been carried out as a non-profit enterprise. Although there has often been some conflict between administrators and workers—especially when the former were not social workers—it was understood that the condition of the client(s) was the determining factor in social work activities.[175] Social action on behalf of clients was at least taught as an important component of the job, although not always translated into practice. As social services and agencies become privatized, however, social workers find themselves working in settings whose goals are irrelevant, if not in conflict with, those of social work.[176] The National Association of Social Workers' Code of Ethics speaks of "preventing and eliminating discrimination, and expanding choice and opportunity for all persons"—activities that are rarely of concern for for-profit services.[177]

On the other hand, social work has been privatizing itself for years. More and more students opt for micro-concentrations in their studies, and more and more graduates seek opportunities to go into private practice. In the United States only 7 percent of social work students choose macro-concentrations such as community organization and planning, administration and management—the remainder want direct-practice or combination training.[178] Many social work schools are beset with the problem of students who want only those courses that will prepare them for eventual private practice—which often means only psychiatry- and/or psychology-based material.

Social Security

A great deal of concern is being expressed concerning the future of social security programs. Mainly because of lengthening life expectancy, the growth of future demand for benefits threatens to outstrip expected payroll deductions. Indeed, one report holds that life expectancy will grow further and faster than official government policy estimates,[179] substantially aggravating the dimensions of the problem. The extent to which this will happen, and when, is subject to many definitional and statistical discussions. However, the importance of the issue is demonstrated by the fact that even among recipients who are relatively well off now, social security payments provide nearly half of their total incomes, and if there were no social security, 50 percent of older people would be below the poverty line.[180] Regarding pension income from outside social security, over the last decades those in the lowest 40 percent of the income distribution gained very little, while those at the top had steady gains from private sources.[181]

Proposals to "cure" social security include changes in provisions—i. e., higher premiums, lower payments, longer vestment requirements, higher retirement age, caps on payments, removing the cap on premiums, changes in permitted post-retirement employment rules, taxing certain levels, and means tests. Another completely different approach has to do with the way social security funds are invested, how they are used by governments, and other such fiscal changes. Among the most widely bruited of these is the proposal to privatize social security by investing premiums in stock market shares, banks, insurance companies, and other financial institutions. In some of these proposals, the government would simply invest the sums received through the payroll tax, and make payments from the profits. In other cases, the investments would be made in the name of the individual beneficiaries. In still others, workers would be free to make their own investments with the funds they would previously have paid into the program; and in still others there would be a combination of investments and continuation of social security coverage. Senator Moynihan, for example, proposes to cut payments to the government, with recipients free to use the difference by engaging in private investment.[182]

All of these proposals are squarely based upon the market-driven society concept: Saving is bad—investment is good. Thrift, restraint, prudence, caution—all the traditional virtues—are not only to be abandoned but rejected, in favor of taking chances, gambling on the stock-market, and hoping to be a winner in a winner-loser society.

In this connection, there continue to surface studies which show how much better off the social security recipient would be if he or she had judiciously invested the money they paid into social security. Such studies rarely indicate what would have happened to people who invested injudiciously, or at the wrong time, or who sold their stock to meet an unexpected emergency, or who needed their profits just as a downturn in the economy and stock market were occurring. Take, for example, the Chilean experiment of turning all public and employer public pension funds into stock-market investments managed by private enterprise. This experiment attracted widespread attention, and was held up as an example for some years. While for fifteen years returns averaged a robust 12 percent, this declined to 2.5-4.7 percent between 1994 and 1997 and since then the Chilean stock market has lost 25 percent of its dollar value, with pension funds losing another 5 percent.[183]

Galveston County, Texas, also experimented with investing on behalf of its employees, opting out of Social Security in 1981. A private company was entrusted with investing the funds. The result: after fifteen years, Galveston's benefit was worth only 45 percent to 72 percent of Social Security's, depending on the earnings level of the worker. After twenty years, Galveston's benefit was down to 38 percent to 62 percent of Social Security's. The same result was found in two other counties that had elected to follow the same path.[184]

One alternative or supplement to Social Security instituted years ago in the United States was termed the 401(k) retirement plan. Under this plan people were enabled and encouraged to save for their own retirement income, and at present writing President Bush is exploring ways to permit Americans to even manage a portion of their Social Security benefits. Unfortunately, 401(k) funds are dependent upon the vagaries of the stock market—as Social Security is not—and in July, 2001, these funds began to shrink. The average account lost about $600 during the year 2000, and "the guaranteed retirement income provided to many at the end of World War II through the early 1990's is disappearing."[185] By 1998 the average amount saved in 401(k)'s by people now getting close to retirement was $57,000—less than four years of monthly pension payments in typical company plans.[186] R. Brady, former business correspondent of CBS News, asked a leading member of the movement to privatize social security whether he could guarantee an annual return to social security investors if they placed their money in the stock market. The reply? "You know I can't. You know I can't."[187] Indeed, informed opinion holds that it is impossible to privatize Social Security without huge cuts in benefits.[188]

Another example is found in the Enron Corporation's financial decline toward the end of 2001. Employees had been induced to put much of their 401(k) retirement plan investment in Enron shares. When these shares began to dive, Enron froze employees' assets and did not allow them to switch investments. The resulting situation pretty much wiped out every employee's savings plan, including those who lost up to $900,000. Similar retirement payments were wiped out for employees of Nortel Networks Corporation, Lucent Technologies, and Global Crossing Ltd.[189] In Britain, it is estimated that "a staggering" 50 percent of workers have had their secure pension programs threatened and millions of workers face destitution because of the government's reliance on private pension plans.[190] As noted elsewhere, the staggering fraud at Enron, Worldcom, and other "solid as Gibralter" corporations, resulted in immediate job losses by workers, and loss of accrued pension credits for them, and even for those who were not fired.

In short, it seems that while the stock market may be a place for some to make money, it is hardly a place to save money, and the latter was the underlying principle of most social security programs.

In viewing the effects of privatization, it is clear that in almost every case the poor are exploited, services offered them are inferior, and there are side-effects in terms of negative images and self-images that are created and/or reinforced. Admittedly, there are those who make a case for privatization as a social good, whose arguments have not been discussed here—because in no case has privatization been put forward as helping the poor, reducing their numbers, or improving services to or for them. Put in ideological terms, "The 'privatization revolution' is in essence the spearhead of a major international campaign to recapture for the capitalist class many of the resources won over generations of struggle by working people."[191]

ENDNOTES

[1] Pirie, M., *Privatization.* Aldershot: Wildwood Press, 1988.

[2] Liberman, M., "The Significance of Privatization and Choice for Education," in L. Myron (Ed.), *Privatization and Educational Choice.* New York: St. Martins, 1989, pp. 3-25

[3] Tilak, J. B. G., "The Privatization of Higher Education," *Prospects*, 21, 2, 1991, pp. 227-238.

[4] Kramer, R. M., H. Lorentzen, W. B. Melief & S. Pasquinelli, "Implications for Social Policy in the Welfare State," in Kramer, R. M., H. Lorentzen, W. B. Melief & S. Pasquinelli (Eds.), *Privatization in Four European Countries: Comparative Studies in Government-Third Sector Relationships.* London: M. E. Sharpe, 1991, pp.187-196.

[5] Barnett J. R., and P. Barnett, "The Growth and Impact of Private Hospitals in New Zealand," in Scarpani, J. L. (Ed.), *Health Services Privatization in Industrial Societies.* London: Jessica Kingsley, 1991, pp. 83-111.

[6] Liberman, M., "Should Government Buy or Make Education?" in Myron, L. (Ed.), *Privatization and Educational Choice.* New York: St. Martins Press, 1989, pp. 25-57.

[7] Walford, G., *Privatization and Privilege in Education.* London: Routledge, 1990.

[8] Hills, J., *The Changing Balance Between Public and Private Social Provision: Experiences in Britain.* Paper delivered at Paul Baerwald School of Social Work, The Hebrew University, Jerusalem, 1999.

[9] *Ibid.*

[10] Demone, H., Jr., "The Political Future of Privatization," in Gibelman, M., and H. W. Demone, Jr. (Eds.), *The Privatization of Human Services, Volume One.* New York: Springer, 1998, pp. 211-244.

[11] *Ibid.*

[12] Sclar, E. D., *You Don't Always Get What You Pay For: The Economics of Privatization.* Ithaca: Cornell, 2000; quoting Adler, M., "Been There, Done That: The Privatization of Street Cleaning in Nineteenth Century New York, " *New Labor Forum*, 4, Spring/Summer 1999, pp. 88-99.

[13] "F. B. I. Says Man Carried Knives Past Screeners," *New York Times*, November 6, 2001, internet edition, p. 1.

[14] Shenon, P., "At the Airport, Nothing Remains the Same." *New York Times,* December 28, 2001, internet edition. P. 1.

[15] Finkelstein, K. E., "City Says Inmate Care Fails in Most Contract Categories," *New York Times*, November 26, 2001, internet edition, p. 1.

[16] Henneberger, M., "Italy Plans to Have Private Sector Run Museums." *New York Times*, December 3, 2001, internet edition, p. 1.

[17] Kearns, R., "Finding Profit in At-Risk Kids," *Children's Voice*, 8, *1*, Fall, 1998, pp. 44-5, 14-15.

[18] Clark, R. E., R. A. Dorwart and S. S. Epstein, "Managing Competition in Public and Private Mental Health Agencies: Implications for Services and Policy," *The Milbank Quarterly*, 72, *4*, 11994, pp. 653-674.

[19] Wilhelmsson, T., and S. Hurri (Eds.), *From Dissonance to Sense: Welfare State Expectations, Privatisation and Private Law.* Dartmouth: Ashgate, 1999.

[20] Pring, R., "Privatization in Education," *Education Policy*, 2, *4*, 1987, pp. 289-299.

[21] Goodin, R. E., *Reasons for Welfare: The Political Theory of the Welfare State.* Princeton: Princeton University Press, 1988.

[22] Stoesz, D., " A New Paradigm for Social Welfare," *Journal of Sociology & Social Welfare*, 16, *2*, 1989, pp. 127-150.

[23] Carrier, J., and I. Kendall, *Health and the National Health Service.* London: Athlone, 1998, p. 291 (Italics in original).

[24] Reich, R., *Ethics, Public Service and Income Inequality.* Paper delivered on May 28, 2000, Laromme Hotel, Jerusalem, Israel, sponsored by Mishkenot Sha'ananim.

[25] Macarov, D., and U. Yanay, *Images of the Poor and Poverty in Jerusalem.* Jerusalem: Paul Baerwald School of Social Work, The Hebrew University, 1975, pp. 1-69.

[26] Pirie, *op cit.,* see endnote 1.

[27] Jennings, J. 'Persistent Poverty in the United States," in L. Kushnik and J. Jennings (Eds.), *A New Introduction to Poverty: The Role of Race, Power and Politics.* New York: New York University Press. 1999. p. 20.

[28] *Ibid.*

[29] Margalit, A., *The Decent Society*, Cambridge: Harvard University Press, 1996, p. 214.

[30] *Exodus*, 18, *18-21.*

[31] Weber, M., "Bureaucracy," in Gerth, H. H., and C. W. Mills (Eds.), *From Max Weber: Essays in Sociology.* London: Routledge and Kegan Paul, 1948.

[32] Pirie, *op cit.,* see endnote 1.

[33] Demone, *op cit.,* see endnote 10.

[34] Murphy, D. E., "Bloomberg Stresses Private Business as Key to Revival," *New York Times*, November 2, 2001, internet edition, p. 1.

[35] Kramer, *et al, op cit.,* see endnote 4.

[36] Barnett and Barnett, *op cit.,* see endnote 5.

[37] Pirie, *op cit.,* p. 9, see endnote 1.

[38] Pirie, *op cit.*, p. 11, see endnote 1.

[39] There is, of course, room for some altruism in company policies, but as Jenck points out, altruism diminishes as its costs expand. Jencks, C., "Introduction," Edin, K., and L. Lein, *Making Ends Meet: How Single Mothers Survive Welfare and Low-Wage Work.* New York: Russell Sage, 1997, p. xvi.

[40] Luttwak, E., *Turbo-Capitalism; Winners and Losers in the Global Economy.* New York: Harper Collins, 1999.

[41] Moss, M., and A. Appel, "Company's Silence Countered Safety Fears About Asbestos." *New York Times*, September 7, 2001, p. 1, internet edition

[42] Tuchman, B. W., *The March of Folly: From Troy to Vietnam.* London: Abacus, 1994, p. 3.

[43] Brown, A., "The Invisible Fist," *The Futurist, 33*, 9, November 1999, p. 26-28.

[44] See, Boyle, F. A., *The Criminality of Nuclear Deterrence.* Atlanta: Clarity, 2002.

[45] Birdsall, N., "Why Inequality Matters; Some Economic Issues." *Ethics and International Affairs*, 15, 2, 2001, pp. 3-28.

[46] Kelly, G. M., "Employment and Concepts of Work in the New Global Economy." *International Labour Review*, 139, 1, 2001, pp. 5-32.

[47] See, for one example, Dwyer, P., and D. Seddon, *The New Wave? A Global Perspective on Popular Protest.* Paper presented at the 8th International Conference on Alternative Futures and Popular Protest, Manchester, UK, April, 2002.

[48] Macarov, D., *Social Welfare: Structure and Practice.* Thousand Oaks: Sage, 1995, especially Chapter 12.

[49] Pirie, *op cit.*, see endnote 1.

[50] Schlesinger, A.M., *The Crisis of the Old Order: 1919-1933.* Boston: Houghton Mifflin 1957, p. 21.

[51] Jones, B. G., *The Growth of Inequality: The Structural Determination of Need in the Era of Globalisation.* Paper presented at the Conference on Globalisation, Growth and (In)Equality. Coventry: Warwick University, 2002.

[52] Killick, T., "Responding to Inequality." *Briefing Paper No. 3.* Oxford: UK Department for International Development, March, 2002, p. 3.

[53] Herman, R. D. and D. O. Renz, "Theses on Nonprofit Organizational Effectiveness," *Nonprofit and Voluntary Sector Quarterly, 28*, 2, (June, 1999) 107-125.

[54] Kramer, *et al, op cit.*, see endnote 4.

[55] O'Connell, D., "So Now It's Back to a Nationalised Railway." *Sunday Times*, June 30, 2002, p. 20.

[56] "Britain's Railways 'Are Worst in World'," *Metro*, March 12, 2002, p. 1.

[57] "Railtrack Tumbles on Blair Decision." *International Herald Tribune*, June 7, 2001, p. 18.

[58] "Government Bails Out Nuclear Energy Giant." *The Guardian*, September 9, 2002, internet edition.

[59] Fisher, J., "As Poland Endures Hard Times, Capitalism Comes Under Attack." *New York Times,* June 12, 2002, p.1, internet edition.

[60] *Ibid.*

[61] Smith, S. R. *Changing Government-Nonprofit Relations in Social Policy.* Arnulf M. Pins Memorial Lecture, Paul Baerwald School of Social Work, The Hebrew University, Jerusalem, Israel, 1999, pp. 38-39.

[62] Qadeer, I., in "A North-South Dialogue on the Prospects for a Socially Progressive Globalization." *Global Social Policy*, 1, 2, August, 2001, pp. 147-162.

[63] Scarpaci, J. L., "The Theory and Practice of Health Services Privatization," in Scarpacia, J. L. (Ed.), *Health Services Privatization in Industrial Societies.* London: Jessica Kinglsey, 1991, pp. 1-23.

[64] Dwyer and. Seddon, *op cit.*, see endnote 47.

[65] *Ibid.*

[66] In August, 2000, the National Labor Relations Board made it possible for some temporary workers to join labor unions. "Unions Win in Ruling on Temporary Workers," *New York Times*, August 31, 2000, internet edition, p. 1.

[67] *Ibid.*

[68] Coren, O., and H. Bior, "Histadrut Signs Deal for Temporary Workers." *Ha'Aretz*, December 17, 2001, p. 1 (Hebrew).

[69] Shostak, A., Philadelphia: Drexel University, August 24, 2002 (personal communication).

[70] *Statistical Abstract of the United States.* Washington: U. S. Department of Commerce, various dates.

[71] Levitan, A, G. L. Magnum and S. L. Magnum, *Programs in Aid of the Poor.* Baltimore: Johns Hopkins, 1998, p. 28 (seventh edition).

[72] Mead, L. M., "Raising Work Levels Among the Poor," in Darby, M. R. (Ed.), *Reducing Poverty in America: Views and Approaches.* Thousand Oaks: Sage, 1996, pp. 251-282.

[73] Quinlan, M., C. Mayhew and P. Bohle. "The Global Expansion of Precarious Employment, Work Disorganization, and Consequences for Occupational Health: Placing the Debate in a Comparative Historical Context." *International Journal of Health Services, 31, 3,* 2001, pp. 507-536.

[74] Ferriss, S., "Sugar Symbolizes a Bitter Failure," *Atlanta Journal-Constitution*, September 7, 2001, p. B-1.

[75] Andrews, E. L., "Controller Sent Jets Into Crash, Flight Data Show." *New York Times,* July 9, 2002, p. 1, internet edition.

[76] "Politics and Society," *Leta Daily Press Review*, September 27, 2000, p. 1.

[77] *Building Institutions for Markets. World Development Report 2002.* Washington: World Bank, 2002, p. III.

[78] Walford, *op cit.*, p. 64, see endnote 7.

[79] Walford, *ibid.*

[80] Barnett and Barnett, *op cit.*, see endnote 5.

[81] Feder, J., and W. T. Scanlon, "Problems and Prospects in Financing Long-Term Care," in McLennan, K., and J. A. Meyer (Eds.), *Care and Costs: Current Issues in Health Care Policy.* Boulder: Westview, 1989, pp. 67-85.

[82] Smart, T., "An Idea Coming of Age?" *AARP Bulletin, 42, 11,* December, 2001, p. 6.

[83] Estes, C. E., Swan, J. H., & Associates, *The Long-term Care Crisis: Elders Trapped in the No Care Zone.* Newbury Park: Sage, 1993.

[84] Estes, C. L., and L. Close, "Public Policy and Long-Term Care," in Abeles, R. P., H. C. Gift, and M. G. Ory, (Eds.), *Aging and Quality of Life.* New York: Spring, 1994, pp. 319-366.

[85] Binstock, R. H., "The Financing and Organization of Long-Term Care," in Walker, L. C., E. H. Bradley and T. Wetle, (Eds,), *Public and Private Responsibilities in Long Term Care: Finding the Balance.* Baltimore: Johns Hopkins, 1998.

[86] Davidson, H., E. Hickey, L. Camberg, M. B. Davidson, D. C. Kern and J. R. Kelly, "Homemaker and Home Health Aide Services in Veteran Affairs: Purchase of Care in a Federal System," in Gibelman, M., and H. W. Demone, Jr. (Eds), *The Privatization of Human Services, Volume Two.* New York: Springer, 1998, pp. 165-182.

[87] Feder and Scanlon, *op cit.,* see endnote 81.

[88] *Ibid.*

[89] *Ibid.*

[90] Greider, L., "Care Managers Emerge as New Force in Helping." *AARP Bulletin, 42, 11,* December, 2001, p. 9.

[91] Dukakis, M., "Personal Reflections on Purchase of Service: A View from a State Capitol," in Gibelman and Demone, *op cit.,* see endnote 10.

[92] Barnett and Barnett, *op cit.,* see endnote 5.

[93] Kronenfeld, J.J. and M.L. Whicker. *Captive Populations: Caring for the Youth, the Sick, the Imprisoned, and the Elderly.* New York: Praeger, 1990.

[94] Robinson, S., "Scarred," *Time Magazine,* 160, August 3, 2002, pp. 23-25.

[95] Newbrander, W., and P. Moser, "Private Health Sector Growth in Asia: An Introduction," in W. Newbrander (Ed.), *Private Health Sector Growth in Asia: Issues and Implications.* Toronto: Wiley, 1997, pp. 3-10.

[96] Dung, P. H., "The Political Process to Increase the Private Health Sector's Role in Vietnam," in Newbrander, *op cit.,* see endnote 95.

[97] Yang, B. M., The Role of Health Insurance in the Growth of the Private Health Sector in Korea," in Newbrander, *op cit.*, pp. 61-81, see endnote 95.

[98] Kronenfeld, J. J. and M. L. Whicker, *Captive Populations: Caring for the Young, the Sick, the Imprisoned, and the Elderly.* New York: Praeger, 1990.

[99] Baer, E. D., C. M. Fagin and S. Gordon, (Eds.), *Abandonment of the Patient: The Impact of Profit-Driven Health Care on the Public.* New York: Springer, 1996.

[100] *Ibid.*

[101] Gorton, E., "Cash-for-Beds Scandal in National Health Service," *World Socialist Web Site*, January 17, 2002.

[102] Belluck, P., "Doctors' New Practices Offer Deluxe Service for Deluxe Fee," *New York Times*, January 14, 2002, internet edition, p. 1.

[103] Shadmi, H., "Attorney General Outlaws Private Hospital Medical Services," *HaAretz*, February 18, 2002, internet edition, p. 1.

[104] "Hospital Continues Private Services After They Were Outlawed," *HaAretz*, October 7, 2002.

[105] Pear, R., "Lobbyists Seek Special Spin on Federal Bioterrorism Bill." *New York Times*, December 11, 2001, internet edition, p. 1.

[106] Stolberg, S. G., "A Drug Plan is Great, But Who Sets Prices?" *New York Times*, July 9, 2000, p. 1 internet edition, p. 1.

[107] Barry, P., "Drug Profits vs. Research," *AARP Bulletin*, 43, 6. June, 2002, pp. 8-10.

[108] McNeil, D. G., Jr., "As Devastating Epidemics Increase, Nations Take On Drug Companies," *New York Times*, July 9, 2000, internet edition, p. 1.

[109] Meier, B., "Hospital Products Get Seal of Approval at a Price." *New York Times*, April 23, 2002, internet edition, p. 1.

[110] *Ibid.*

[111] Freudenheim, M., "Many H.M.O.'s for the Elderly Make Deep Cuts in Drug Aid." *New York Times*, January 25, 2002, internet edition, p. 1.

[112] Shadmi, H., "Dollars and Sense: How Economics Shape Medical Care." *HaAretz*, January 23, 2002, internet edition, p. 1.

[113] Andres, M., "Birth Control is Changing, and Its Price is Rising." *New York Times*, April 22, 2002, internet edition, p. 1.

[114] Hessel, R. M., and E. P. Steinberg, "Medical Research and Teaching in a Market-Driven Health Care System," in McLennan, K., and J. A. Meyer, (Eds.), *Care and Costs: Current Issues in Health Care Policy.* Boulder: Westview, 1989, pp. 133-145.

[115] Kronenfeld and Whicker, *op cit.*, see endnote 93

[116] Judge, K., and M. Knapp, "Efficiency in the Production of Welfare: The Public and Private Sectors Compared," in Klein, R., and M. O'Higgins, (Eds) *The Future of Welfare*. Oxford: Basil Blackwell, 1985.

[117] Harrington, C., S. Woolhandler, J. Mullan, and D. U. Himmelstein, "Does Investor Ownership of Nursing Homes Compromise the Quality of Care?" *American Journal of Public Health*, 91, 9, September, 2001, pp. 1452-1455.

[118] Barnett and Barnett, *op cit.*, see endnote 5.

[119] Hamilton, V., "The Impact of Ownership Form and Regulatory Measures on Firm Behavior: A Study of Hospices." *Nonprofit Management & Leadership,* 4, 4, Summer, 1994, pp. 415-430.

[120] Clark, R. E., R. A. Dorwat and S. S. Epstein, " Managing Competition in Public and Private Mental Health Agencies: Implications for Services and Policy," *Milbank Quarterly*, 72, 4, 1994, pp. 653-675.

[121] Dumont, M. P., "Privatization of Mental Health Services: The Invisible Hand at Our Throats," *American Journal of Orthopsychiatry,* 3, 62, July, 1992, pp. 328-329

[122] Winerip, M., "The Never-Promised Rose Garden and the Snake Pit," *New York Times*, May 5, 2002, internet edition, p. 1.

[123] Clark, Dowart and Epstein, *op cit.,* see endnote 119.

[124] Macarov, D., "Management in the Social Work Curriculum." *Administration in Social Work.* 1, 2, 1977, pp. 135-148; and Kazmerski, K. J., and D. Macarov, *Administration in the Social Work Curriculum: Report of a Survey.* New York: Council on Social Work Education, 1976.

[125] Smith, *op cit.*, p. 39, see endnote 61.

[126] Winter, G., "U. S. Loan Program Squeezes Doctors Sent to Treat the Poor." *New York Times*, July 30, 2000, internet edition, p. 1.

[127] Chan, C-K, in "A North-South Dialogue on the Prospects for a Socially Progressive Globalization," *Global Social Policy*, 1, *2*, August, 2001, pp. 147-162.

[128] Fagin, M. F., and S. Gordon, "Conclusion: What Can We Do to Protect Quality Care?" in Baer, E. D., C. M Fagin and S. Gordon (Eds.), *Abandonment of the Patient: The Impact of Profit-Driven Health Care on the Public.* New York: Springer, 1996, pp. 101-113.

[129] Belluck, P., "Small Vote for Universal Care is Seen as Carrying a Lot of Weight," *New York Times*, November 16, 2001, internet edition, p. 1.

[130] Margonis, F., and L. Parker, "Choice, Privatization, and Unspoken Strategies of Containment." *al Policy*, 9, *4*, 1995, pp. 375-403

[131] Walford, *op cit.,* p. 80, see endnote 7.

[132] Tilak, J. B. G., "The Privatization of Higher Education," *Prospects*, 21, *2*, 1991, pp. 227-238

[133] *Ibid.*

[134] *Ibid.*

[135] Molnar, A., *Vouchers, Class Size Reduction, and Student Achievement.* Bloomington: Phi Beta Kappa, 2000.

[136] Canter, A., "Purchasing School Psychological Services," in Gibelman and Demone, *op cit.*, pp. 123-150, see endnote 10.

[137] *Ibid.*

[138] Kallaway, P., "Privatization as an Aspect of the Educational Policies of the New Right: Critical Signposts for Understanding Shifts in Educational Policy in South Africa during the Eighties," *British Journal of Educational Studies*, 37, *3*, August, 1989, pp. 253-276.

[139] Walford, *op cit.,* p. 71, see endnote 7.

[140] Ascher,. C., N. Fruchter and R. Berne, *Hard Lessons: Public Schools and Privatization.* New York: Twentieth Century Fund Press, 1996, pp. 23-42.

[141] Schemo, D. J., "School Defies the Odds and Offers a Lesson." *New York Times*, December 17, 2001, internet edition, p. 1.

[142] Kronenfeld and Whicker, *op cit.,* see endnote 93.

[143] Ascher, Fruchter and Berne, *op cit.,* see endnote 139.

[144] Wyatt, E., "New York City to Privatize Worst Schools," *New York Times*, July 27, 2000, internet edition, p. 1.

[145] Ascher, Fruchter and Berne, *op cit.*, see endnote 139.

[146] Steinberg, J., "Forty-two Schools in Philadelphia to Be Privatized." *New York Times*, April 18, 2002, internet edition, p. 1.

[147] Ascher, Fruchter and Berne, *op cit.,* see endnote 139.

[148] Bishop, T., "Pennsylvania Prepares Privatization of Philadelphia Public Schools," *World Socialist Web Site*, November 15, 2001, pp. 1-5; Steinberg, J., "Fight in Philadelphia Over Schools Takeover," *New York Times*, November 15, 2001, internet edition, p. 1.

[148] Weiner, R. S., "AOL Gets Its Name in Front of Students with New Service," *New York Times*, May 24, 2000.

[150] Tilak, *op cit.,* see endnote 131.

[151] *Ibid.*

[152] *Ibid.*

[153] Walford, *op cit.*, p. 80, see endnote 7.

[154] Gewirtz, S., *The Managerial School.* London: Routledge, 2001.

[155] Kallaway, *op cit.,* see endnote137.

[156] Buchen, I. H., "A Radical Vision for Education," *The Futurist*, 34, *3*, May-June, 2000, pp. 30-34.

[157] Margonis and Parker, *op cit.,* see endnote 129.

[158] Coyle, A. (Ed.), *Capitalist Punishment: Prison Privatization & Human Rights.* Atlanta: Clarity, 2002.

[159] Macarov, D. (Ed.), *Persisting Unemployment: Can It Be Overcome?* Special edition of *The International Journal of Sociology and Social Policy.* 11, *1/2/3*, 1991.

[160] Aulette, J., "The Privatization of Housing in a Declining Economy: the Case of Stepping Stone Housing," *Journal of Sociology and Social Welfare*, 18, *1*, 1991, pp. 149-163.

[161] Forrest, R., and A. Murie, *Selling the Welfare State: The Privatisation of Public Housing*. London: Routledge, 1991.

[162] *Ibid*.

[163] Petr, C. G., and I. C. Johnson, "Privatization of Foster Care in Kansas: A Cautionary Tale." *Social Work*, 44, *3*, May 1999, pp. 263-267.

[164] *Private Fostering: Development of Policy and Practice in Three English Local Authorities*. London: Save The Children, 1997.

[165] M. Knapp, "Searching for Efficiency in Long-Term Care: De-Institutionalization And Privatisation," *British Journal of Social Work*, 18, Supplement, 1987, pp. 149-171.

[166] *Who is Caring for the Children? An Exploratory Survey conducted in Hungary, Poland, Bulgaria and Romania*. The Consultative Group on Early Childhood Care and Development. Geneva: UNICEF, 2000.

[167] Hicks, N., "Child Welfare Privatization Opposed," *Omaha World Herald*, January 3, 2000.

[168] O'Connor, P., "Privatisation and Welfare Services," *Australian Journal of Social Issues*, 25, *1*, February 1990, pp. 27-39.

[169] Park, H.H. and N. Gilbert, "Social Security and the Incremental Privatisation of Retirement Income." *Journal of Sociology and Social Welfare*, 26, 2, June 1999, pp. 187-202.

[170] Kearns, *op cit.*, see endnote 17.

[171] *Ibid*.

[172] *Ibid*.

[173] Etzioni, A., *Next: The Road to the Good Society*. New York: Basic, 2001, p. 49.

[174] Dunlap. E., quoted by Kearn, *op cit.*, see endnote 17.

[175] Macarov, D., "Management in the Social Work Curriculum," *op. cit.*, see endnote 123.

[176] See Harris, J., *The Social Work Business*. London: Routledge, 2002.

[177] Elliott, D., "Social Work and Social Development: Towards an Integrative Model for Social Work Practice," *International Social Work*, 36, 1993, pp. 21-36.

[178] *Ibid*.

[179] Pear. R., "Panel Says Social Security Needs Are Underestimated," *New York Times*, December 7, 1999, internet edition, p. 1.

[180] Kingson, E. R., & J. B. Williamson, "Understanding the Debate Over the Privatization of Social Security." *Journal of Sociology and Social Welfare*, 25, *3*, 1998, pp. 47-61.

[181] Park and Gilbert, *op cit.*, pp. 187-202, see endnote 168.

[182] Moynihan, D. P., "Building Wealth for Everyone," *New York Times*, May 30, 2000, internet edition, p. 1.

[183] Park and Gilbert, *op. cit.*, see endnote 168.

[184] Wilson, T. M., "The Galveston Plan and Social Security: A Comparative Analysis of Two Systems." *Social Security Bulletin*, Vol. 62, No. 1, 1999, pp. 47-64.

[185] Hakim, D., "401(k) Accounts Are Losing Money for the First Time." *New York Times*, July 9, 2001, internet edition, p. 1.

[186] Uchitelle, L., "Do You Plan to Retire? Think Again." *New York Times*, March 31, 2002, internet edition, p. 1.

[187] Brady, R. "Privatizing Social Security." *New York Times*, September 2, 2001, p. 14BU.

[188] "No Single Plan from Social Security Panel." *AARP Bulletin*, 42, *11*, December, 2001, p. 4.

[189] Oppel, R. A.. Jr., "Employees' Retirement Plan is a Victim as Enron Tumbles," *New York Times*, November 22, 2001, internet edition, pp. 1-4.

[190] Shaoul, J., "Britain: Shock for Millions of Workers Who Rely on Private Pensions." *World Socialist Web Site*, 26 March 2002.

[191] Kallawy, P., "Privatization as an Aspect of the Educational Politics of the New Right: Critical Signposts for Understanding Shifts in Educational Policy in South Africa during the Eighties." *British Journal of Educational Studies*, 37, *3*, August, 1989, pp. 253-276.

CHAPTER 5

Globalizing Poverty

"Nothing is illegal if one hundred businessmen decide to do it."
Andrew Young

DEFINITIONS AND SCOPE

One of the ways by which the rich get richer (and the poor are made poorer) is through increased globalization. Globalization has been defined as the collapse of time and space,[1] but more detailed explanations distinguish between "interdependence of markets and production in different countries;" "(perception of) living and working in a world-wide context;" and a "process that affects every aspect in the life of a person, community or nation."[2] A distinction has been made between internationalization, in which a national unit engages in international trade; international agreements such as GATT; and globalization, in which the national unit ceases to exist and becomes a global enterprise.[3] There are also sources that use "modernization" as a synonym for globalization, and it is sometimes subsumed under "liberalization," "neoliberalism," and "post-modernism." Indeed, a whole insider-language has grown up around globalization, with such terms as "transparency," "conditionality," "commodification," "convergence," "microenterprises," "global public spaces," "deregulation," "deterritorialization," and similar phrases used by aid agency personnel and other policy-makers and researchers who in turn have been termed "a priesthood of economic thinkers."[4]

Globalization may be seen as a structure, a process, an ideology, or a combination of these. Proponents of globalization see it as, "A force which is beneficial to all, individuals and states, in all parts of the world,"[5] or as, "Flows of capital and goods (that) should encourage 'economic convergence'—raising living standards in developing countries toward those of the industrial North,"[6] or as a massive process of evolutionary changes—economic, political, cultural, and biological—that have been going on over the entire course of human evolution and have accelerated in recent decades. "We can no more reverse or undo them than we can unscramble an egg."[7]

Opponents of globalization see it "as of benefit to the upper groups in society, to the multinational companies and the affluent world; and as detrimental to the satisfaction of public needs,"[8] and as a "force for the perpetuation and accentuation of inequalities within and between groups of countries for the benefit of multinationals and the upper classes. Its constant emphasis on increased competitiveness involves a race to the bottom,"[9] with special emphasis on the social welfare bottom.[10]

A very specific issue concerns whether globalization limits the social policy choices of countries.[11] Dunham speaks of exploitative societies, and his description of them suits globalization efforts as a whole: "[societies] in which one class appropriates, without full compensation, economic values created by another."[12] In this sense, globalization is not an entirely new phenomenon—empires such as the Roman and the British established overseas colonies in order to exploit them.[13] Regardless of the term used, it is argued that globalization will, among other things, speed up the eradication of poverty. This view ignores the large pockets of poverty that continue and—on a relative basis—are growing in the North, and the evidence that globalization for many countries seems to be associated less with convergence than with divergence.[14]

A number of factors have led to the process called "globalization." As large corporations began diversifying their products and services by buying up smaller enterprises—usually for stock-market, income tax or other financial benefits—they became conglomerates. By then merging with similar—often overseas—conglomerates, they became huge international entities known as MNCs (Multinational Corporations). The economic breakdown of the Soviet Union gave further impetus to globalization as many foreign firms hurried to establish units in so-called economies in transition. Free trade agreements of various kinds further supported this process. MNCs now account for between a quarter and a third of the world's output, 70 percent of world trade and 80 percent of direct international investment.[15]

Perhaps more importantly, international financial institutions, including aid agencies, put conditions on their aid or loans. The World Bank, for example, plays its part by demanding open trade channels as a condition for financial help. Even the partial integration of Europe and the introduction of the Euro made business across former boundaries easier, and consequently, "MNCs are increasingly organizing production and service provisions on an international basis."[16]

As Naess points out, it has been obvious for some time now that transnational corporations rival the nation-states as governing institutions:

> The phrase 'new world order' has ceased to have much meaning...but a new international system of governance is being created...(by) formal international organizations and regimes, the multinational businesses, nongovernmental organizations of all kinds, networks such as the international currency markets, the global news and entertainment media, and the great world-encircling noosphere of bio-information networks.[17]

The International Monetary Fund strongly advocates less or no government intervention in the economy, but its preconditions for loans have grown from about a dozen to over eighty, thus dictating the economic policies of countries vulnerable to its restrictions.[18] It might be salutary to quote the former head of the World Bank: "Founded on the belief that markets often worked badly, it (the IMF) now champions market supremacy with ideological fervor...today the IMF typically provides funds only if countries engage in policies like cutting deficits, raising taxes, or raising interest rates that lead to a *contraction* of the economy."[19]

Contracting economies invariably react by cutting spending in the social sector, thereby exacerbating the condition of the poor. The paradox here is that when countries think they are doing well economically, they believe this is enough to lighten the burden on the lower-income classes; and when they are in a recession, they obviously don't have the money to spend helping the same classes. This has been reduced to an ironic formula concerning social welfare: "When we can afford it, we don't need it. When we need it, we can't afford it."

The activities of international banks and aid programs like the IMF, the World Trade Organization and World Bank are not without immediate consequences for working people, and particularly for the poor. The role and activities of some of these organizations are worth quoting:

> The World Trade Organization was designed as a meeting place where willing nations could sit in equality and negotiate rules of trade for their mutual advantage, in the service of sustainable international development. Instead, it has become an unbalanced institution, largely controlled by the United States and the nations of Europe, and especially the agribusiness, pharmaceutical and financial-services industries in these countries. At WTO meetings, important deals are hammered out in negotiations attended by the trade ministers of a couple dozen powerful nations, while those of poor countries wait in the bar outside for news.
>
> The International Monetary Fund was created to prevent future Great Depressions in part by lending countries in recession money and pressing them to adopt expansionary policies...Over time...it has become a long-term manager of the economies of developing countries, blindly committed to the bitter medicine of contraction no matter what the illness.[20]

The North American Free Trade Agreement (NAFTA) caused seventy-five thousand American workers to lose jobs, and displaced a million and a half Mexican workers.[21] Further, "economic liberalization has done little to close the huge divide between the privileged few and the poor, and left the middle class worse off than before...some 10 percent of Mexicans at the top of the income pyramid controlled close to 40 percent of the nation's wealth."[22] The International Monetary Fund (IMF) offered a seven million dollar loan to Turkey, but on condition that the government speed up privatization of Turk Telecom and Turkish Airlines.[23] As a result of such conditions, more part time workers without benefits are hired, overtime pay is cut and union shops are gutted.[24]

When it comes to their own workers and prices, the large countries that control the international efforts are not so rigid. While President Bush was pressing other countries to cut out subsidies, remove trade barriers and expand open markets, he agreed to an 80 percent increase in American farm subsidies, which will flood the world market with inexpensive corn, wheat, rice and soybeans, sold at half what it costs to produce the grain, thereby ruining millions of farmers in other, poorer, countries.[25]

There is a symbiotic relationship between privatization and globalization. They go hand-in-hand because they both have the same ultimate goal: profits—profits at all costs and regardless of consequences. Corruption, ecological disaster, fraudulent practices, poverty, human degradation and a score of other ills stem from the oft-expressed (although usually cynical) ideology that in the long run, the market-driven society improves the lot of everyone. Indeed, as Mishra points out, globalization is not simply a market-driven phenomenon; it has an ideological and political base.[26] That base holds that anything that increases profits is not only desirable and even moral, but absolutely imperative. This drive for profits enables and causes multinational corporations to exploit the cheapest labor, methods and materials they can find. There is no need to explicate here the many cases of child labor, prison labor, slave labor and starvation labor to which this ideology leads, which has been documented in numerous places.[27] However, it might put the situation in perspective to recall what has been said in one specific case:

> There is no doubt that Nike has wrung billions and billions of dollars from the toil and the sweat and in some cases the physical abuse of impoverished workers—mostly women—in places like China and Vietnam and Indonesia. In the wretched sport of global sweatshop exploitation, Nike...is an absolute champion. It has no peer.[28]

In a very few cases public exposure of such practices has led to a professed change of heart on the part of a MNC, but the very essence of globalization requires that it be continued, even if in other places and under different guises, since to do otherwise would be to 'fall victim' to competitive labor costs and risk business failure.

Another, more peripheral, aspect of globalization is the manner in which it sometimes ignores and/or breaks local methods and traditions. Hiring women for industrial enterprises when their traditional role has been housekeepers and homemakers can be seen as desirable or undesirable, but that it is at variance with traditions in many areas is indisputable. Insensitivity to local conditions is epitomized in the limitation of the choice of books made available by the World Bank to Nigeria, which includes *The History of the Czech Church in the 13th Century*.[29] Similarly, there are areas in which nepotism is not only prevalent, but seen as a positive phenomenon, *i.e.*, "If I can't trust my brother in the job, how can I trust someone else?" And, of course, there are places where bribery is the accepted way of getting things done. Even local corruption has been defended as having positive implications for development.[30] Similarly, traditional methods of taking care of the poor such as donations, in-kind gifts, cooperative enterprises, and religious organs may be challenged by globalized entities that propose unemployment insurance, social security, and company housing—which they may or may not actually provide. Findlay puts this succinctly: "Presenting development by modernisation as essentially beneficial for the majority of communities" ignores the fact that profound fractures may be driven across traditional bonds of socialization.[31]

It should not be assumed that globalization arises from discontent with the local labor force, or even from lack of profitability. Even Japan, which for years was constantly cited as the acme of perfection in the loyalty and productivity of its work force, and which is far from a poor country, is seeking to take advantage of lower labor and other costs by locating its industries in East Asia or Latin America.[32]

The boundaries of globalization (if any) are set at meetings of international financial organizations, such as the World Bank, the World Trade Organization, the International Monetary Fund, and others. Even when these are established and governed on an internationally representative basis, the poorer countries are almost always underrepresented. One reason for this, according to some sources, is that accommodations and salaries at such meetings must be paid for in hard currency, which developing countries either do not have or cannot afford.[33]

RESULTS OF GLOBALIZATION

Lack of Accountability

One consequence of globalization under current conditions is that MNCs exist in a legal and regulatory vacuum. There is no international body with the authority and the ability to regulate and investigate rules of conduct of global bodies, and certainly not to enforce them.[34] As Murray points out: "Globalization is a process, not a thing...it is beyond the control of any single component of worldly power or leadership."[35] That is why the International Confederation of Free Trade Unions has held that "Global markets need global rules."[36] It has also been characterized as: "An arrangement that serves particular interest groups and seeks to justify the expropriation of wealth, power, and humanity from others by portraying the process as inexorable and tied to objectified 'market forces.' In essence, the explanation is and must be ideology recast as science."[37]

Corporations seek to present themselves as, and have made every effort to become, stateless, at least in a legal sense and consequently "national governments can no longer regulate or control these global corporations. The international economic system becomes autonomous and can be regulated only at the international level,"[38] a level which—so far—is not in view.[39] Only seven countries in the world govern direct investment and only five countries govern the world-wide trade of industrial goods.[40] Those barriers to this lack of accountability that do exist will be eliminated if the Multilateral Agreement on Investments (MAI) is adopted, since this gives MNCs unrestricted access to do business in other countries with virtually no accountability to or restrictions by national governments.[41] There is even less accountability (if such be possible) as regards dealings with developing countries. The recent conference in Johannesburg is explicit in this regard: "The conference decided not to include multilateral accountability rules for corporations operating in underdeveloped countries. Such rules had been sharply opposed by businesses in the US and Europe."[42]

Indeed, so great is the power of MNCs that political governance is being replaced by what is called "corporate governance."[43] Increasingly, a greater range of management decisions affecting the interests of non-managerial employees are being taken beyond the scope of national jurisdictions.[44] Coller and Marginson studied a multinational food company and found that "employment policy is no longer primarily a purely local management matter"[45]—although it may impinge upon local tradition and custom.

This means that while MNCs may be sued or charged by the individual countries in which they operate, insofar as they operate in tens of countries, with immense resources, and the power to withdraw both personnel and assets at will, they are almost invulnerable to local laws. Take, as one example, the tobacco industry. Heavily fined for mendacity and creating health risks in the United States, they have blithely paid the fines (by raising their prices) and continued these practices in other parts of the world. Teen-agers give out free samples (often to other teen-agers), honey is added to appeal to sweet-tooths and children are invited to parties where cigarettes are free.[46] In Papua-New Guinea, for example, almost the only billboards on the roads—including narrow, unpaved country roads—are those of foreign cigarette companies. Throughout Europe, the umbrellas that deck the much-vaunted sidewalk cafes are almost invariably decorated with ads for tobacco companies. Indeed, tobacco corporations have publicly declared that their next areas of exploitation are in Europe and in Africa where (presumably) anti-tobacco legislation lags far behind.

Even within the United States the existence of fifty individual states has been exploited by large companies. In 1998 American tobacco companies settled suits brought by several states by signing agreements not to advertise cigarettes in papers or magazines with significant numbers of young readers. With one exception, they have violated their written pledge, mendaciously arguing that they agreed to "guidelines," and not "procedures." As the attorney general of California says, "They kill their customers every year and they need to recruit new ones."[47] Although California won a $15 million judgment against the Reynolds tobacco company for handing out more than $100,000 worth of cigarettes at public events where children were present, (a blatant violation of the previous settlement agreement)[48] companies can rely on the internal "globalization" of the industry, spread over fifty states, which makes it unlikely that they will be charged more than a few times.

Incidentally, it should be recognized that globalization is not confined to industry. There is a growing trend for services, including human services, to become internationalized. This is particularly true of health services, including long-term care services.[49] Imported carers for the elderly and sick, the movement of migrant workers, and medical advice on the internet are all examples of non-industrial globalization. Some of the abuses that accompany the globalization of services have been pointed out by Daenzer, using immigrant non-white "Nannies" in Canada as an example. These include unpaid overtime work; sexual harassment; alienation/isolation; and poor quality of room and board.[50] As another example, take the American Association of Retired Persons—the largest voluntary organization in the world—which now has members all over the world eligible for some of its services, including discounts on things ranging from prescription drugs and life insurance to motor vehicles and cruises.

Nor is all globalization in licit areas. The drug-trade, so-called white slavery (of which much is no longer "white"), the illegal movement of migrants and the surreptitious inter-country adoption of infants pre-dated legal globalization by decades, if not centuries.

It can be and has been argued that globalization offers end result benefits to the populations of the world by providing cheaper goods and services than would be possible if operations were confined to one country—though this can and has undercut domestic production in developing countries, even in such necessary areas as agriculture, where cheaper imported U.S. wheat threatens the commercial viability of local African production, resulting not only in loss of domestic industry, but also socio-cultural losses and destruction. This is explicit in the claims of the Director-General of the World Trade Organization: "Future jobs, development, improvements in social welfare, education, health and environmental protection depend on it (globalization)."[51]

Additionally, as global firms move their operations to wherever costs are lower, they may raise the economic level of that area by providing jobs and other amenities. Thus, the advent of a branch of any global industry or service is usually welcomed by the inhabitants of the region being entered, even if they recognize that the salaries to be paid will be minimal (and usually below the minimum), that the government will use their taxes to subsidize the organization, and that land may even by confiscated to make room for the necessary buildings.

There are a number of international organizations that push globalization, and its required behavior, at all costs. The aforementioned World Trade Organization (WTO) is dedicated to an international economy based on neoliberal rules. The North American Free Trade Agreement (NAFTA) enforces neoliberalism in its area, as does the World Bank as a condition for financial help. Then there is the International Monetary Fund (IMF), and even the International Labour Organization (ILO). Regionally, there are MERCOSUR, ASEAN, SADC, among others. This has been referred to as the globalization of policy-making through negotiations,[52] and/or international Non-Governmental Organizations (NGOs) being substituted for government.[53]

The rationale for most globalization relates to the interest of developed countries, and more explicitly, major transnational corporations, in the acquisition of cheaper labor in both the service and the industrial areas. Whether this is seen as exploitative or beneficial may rest on the circumstances, but the decision to move or to stay is based purely upon the expected bottom line. That globalization increases unemployment in developed countries[54] while driving down wages and salaries all over has been recognized by international organizations, but efforts to alleviate the situation have not succeeded. World Trade officials have pushed developing countries to raise pay and improve working conditions, but "the results have been negligible."[55] Part of the reason seems to be that managers and middle-class consumers—"all with their eyes on the lowest possible cost"— make it difficult to achieve even basic standards, and even harder to maintain them.[56] As regards countries in transition from communism, a newspaper headline says it all: "Workers' Rights Suffering as China Goes Capitalist."[57] In China, inequality is growing fast. A factory worker may acquire $36 a month but only by working ten hour days.[58]

Not only have wages been depressed by privatization and globalization, but the rights of workers in terms of unionization, social protection, and other areas have also been eroded, *viz:* "Liberalized trading regimes for the countries of Latin American have so far been associated with the reduction of workers' rights and the concentration of wealth."[59]

These decisions, driven by stockholders' demands for profits, do not take into account any humanistic, altruistic, ecological or other considerations. Movement out of a region or area may be consummated with no discussion, no concern for the unemployment thus created or the problems caused and, frequently, left behind. "The basic problem is that jobs and capital can move fast these days."[60] When TWA sold out to American Airlines, it suddenly stranded 260 passengers in Israel—passengers who had paid for their tickets and were waiting to board. American Airlines did not fulfill the commitments to passengers of its newly-acquired TWA, for fear that creditors would seize American Airline planes in Israel. The plight of the passengers played no part in the decision to suspend flights to Israel. As an Israeli paper commented: "With the Americans there is no sentiment—they operate according to company interests and no one else."[61]

Not only is there no sentiment in the world of big business but, as Vogl points out, "In the tug and pull of hostile takeovers, do ethics have a place? No."[62] The operations of big business can be likened to a machine that performs according to certain set rules, particularly since "In a machine, nothing is holy."[63] If, as Justice Brandeis once remarked, "Corporations have no souls," MNCs have no consciences. In their pursuit of profits, they may and do adopt H. W. Vanderbilt's famous dictum: "The public be damned." As a result of MNCs' lack of consideration for social concerns, Vanderbilt's dictum can now be revised: "And the poor be doubly damned."

Paradoxically, one effect of globalization has been the growth of the informal economy, including non-regulated enterprises like street-hawking, shoe-shining, door-to-door repairmen and such. Just as no international body can control globalizing enterprises, so there is no legal or structural control over the informal economy. Regulations are devised socially, rather than by legislation, and usually do not include unionization, social security, taxation, or any of the aspects of the formal economy. It is the latter aspect that the International Labour Organization is trying to amend.[64]

Wage depression

One result of the privatization and globalization of industry and services has been a depreciation of salaries and wages. In 1997 a review of its future effects held that globalization would lead to downward pressures on labor standards,[65] but at that time median wages for full-time workers were already nearly 3 percent less than they had been in 1979.[66] In fact, whereas 23.5 percent of all American workers received only poverty level wages in 1973, this had risen to 28.6 percent by 1997.[67] Looked at another way, real wages for relatively low-paid workers fell by 22 percent between 1973 and 1995, and 10 percent for middle-range workers.[68] Low-paid jobs grew by 22 percent in New York City between 1993 and 2000—four times as fast as jobs paying at least $25,000.[69] From 1979 to 1995, 80 percent of jobs created were low-wage and/or part-time.[70] Among men who had less than twelve years of education in 1968, the average weekly wage level was $488 for those who worked full-time year-round. By 1994, this had fallen to $400 (adjusted for inflation).[71] In 1993 high school dropouts earned 22 percent less than they had in 1979, and high school graduates earned 12 percent less.[72] Not incidentally, wages of women not only dropped proportionately as did those of men, but were almost always much lower. As compared to the $400 per week for men mentioned previously, women earned only $287.[73] It is also revealing that in 1995 almost 11 percent of all poor people worked full time, but were under the poverty line nevertheless.[74]

Since both privatization and globalization unceasingly seek the lowest possible costs—of which salaries are an important part—it is certainly clear that this must have an effect on wages generally. Nor should it be assumed that these lowered wages hurt production. Nowhere has it been shown that more satisfied workers work harder and produce more, despite the popular mythology that this is so.[75]

Corruption

> *"We have passed from feudalism to capitalism.*
> *Our current stage is corruption."*
> Jules Feiffer

Lack of accountability, combined with profitability as the only goal, often leads to other anti-social activities by MNCs, such as use of child labor, ignoring minimum wage laws, and bribery of local officials. For example, global corporations that proudly proclaim they are equal opportunity employers in the United States appear on other nations' and international lists of discriminators.[76] Vogl speaks of countries where globalization has brought enormous (usually illegal) gains to ruling individuals or parties, while the population remains untouched. To stay in power, these dictators have used their corrupt gains to bribe their colleagues, notably in the military, who in turn have felt bound to bribe their own colleagues in order to sustain their powerful positions. So corruption among ruling elites became widespread and all at the expense of the ordinary citizens who have been robbed of the opportunity to have a decent education, effective healthcare, basic housing and sanitation. The grand corruption has only been possible because investing MNCs used bribery as a standard policy. [77]

That "ethical multinational corporations" is a pure oxymoron has been pointed out by many observers.[78] As mentioned above, the poverty of large masses of individuals has a strong negative impact on the environment. In the case of globalization, however, the poverty of entire countries is exploited for ecological rape.

For example, in order to safeguard the dense natural forest and the resulting food chain, people in Papua-New Guinea are only allowed to cut down the trees on their own homestead. To evade this restriction, Malaysian MNCs (among others) buy up vast tracts of forest, legally divide them into thousands of individual homesteads, and proceed to deforest the island. Why doesn't the Papuan government put a stop to this practice? Because in its own poverty it needs the income—plus widely believed corruption on the part of some politicians, such as the eighteen-room house built by a member of Parliament at a cost of hundreds of times his annual salary. Unfortunately, there is no international recourse directed toward crimes against the environment,[79] even if they involve corruption.

Corruption is not just a moral issue. Kaufmann quotes a survey that shows African government officials and high-level representatives of civil society feel that the cost of corruption is increasing poverty and reducing access by the poor to public services. "This is a major change. Corruption is no longer seen primarily in moral or ethical terms but in terms of its impact on poverty...We cannot alleviate poverty in a sustainable way without combating corruption."[80] And, unfortunately, the incidence of corruption seems to be on the rise.[81]

It is probably incidental to mention that the amounts of money funneled to well-connected individuals through corruption could, if properly used, considerably ease the fate of the poor—given that their primary effect on the economic well being of their countries is the systemic gearing of domestic laws, regulations and the economy to facilitate domestic exploitation by MNCs.

The Growth of Inequality

Before discussing that which is usually called inequality, it might be in order to explicate the distinction between equality and equity (or inequality and inequity), since much of the literature treats these as synonymous, or—more often—simply says "inequality" and "inequity" indiscriminately. Equality usually refers to everyone being equal in various ways; such as getting the same as everyone else in the same situation. For example, seventy-four countries have child-benefit programs, and everyone with the same number of children receives the same amount,[82] which constitutes equality. Equity, however, means that people receive what they deserve for their efforts, or what they need in order to become equal to others—for example, retirement pay based on length of employment and amount earned.

In the case of veterans' bonuses after World War I, every veteran received four hundred dollars. In Alaska, every resident receives an equal share of the income from oil sales.[83] In Bolivia, each citizen gets a flat pension.[84] Thus, in such instances, equality. If one takes expenses rather than income as an example, sales taxes take the same rate from every purchaser—they are not affected by ability to pay, need, personality, connections or policy. Again—equality.

On the other hand, equity takes individual cases into consideration—one gets what one deserves. One definition of equity is that one takes out what one puts in. Social Security payments are based on this principle. Those who have worked the longest periods at the highest incomes get the best returns. Those who have worked only sporadically, at low-wage jobs, have paid in the least, and therefore get the least (although there are some humane adjustments in place). Sales taxes, although equal in rates for everyone, take a much bigger proportionate bite out of the income of the poor than of the non-poor, thus being inequitable.

Another variant of equity is that one gets enough to reach the level of others—that is, inequity until equality is reached. This was the basis of affirmative action programs—not that everyone should get equal educational opportunities, but that some needed and deserved more help to reach the norm. This is why most social welfare grant programs base payments on individual situations, rather than giving all clients the same amount.[85] In welfare policy, this distinction is sometimes referred to as the "trap of equality."[86] Corbett points out that the search for a rough sense of equality sacrifices any true equity, by not taking into account the real differences between families.[87] The distinction between equality and equity is summed up in Anatole France's famous quip: "The law, in its majesty, makes no distinction between the rich and the poor—both are forbidden to sleep under the bridges of Paris." Because of the lack of clarity between inequality and inequity that runs throughout the research and the literature, and the number of quotations cited in this book which make no distinction, we have used the words synonymously, too.

Further, there is an implicit inference in this book that both equality and equity are Good Things, but they have not always been universally so regarded, nor are they today. Certainly during the period of the Divine Right of Kings no one was equal to the king; the social divisions during the feudal period denied equality; the caste system in India did the same; and much social stratification today is evidence of continuing inequality which is not only tolerated, but in some cases encouraged. Even in terms of political theory, it has been said that a democracy "*needs* a considerable degree of inequality."[88] Some people go even further: "The *production* of inequality, of poverty alongside wealth, is a normal, routine and necessary outcome of capitalist development,"[89] and "The idea that an egalitarian social policy can somehow be pursued in the context of the kind of deregulated capitalism to be found in Britain and the US is simply Utopian."[90] There are those who claim that inequality is good for growth, since it may lead to effort and risk-taking.[91]

Even if equality is not viewed as a moral paradigm, there are pragmatic reasons for equality. The social costs of inequality, as adduced by Wright, include:

1) Unequal distribution generates more human suffering than does generally equal distribution.
2) Unequal distribution generates inequalities in opportunities for future generations.
3) Unequal distribution reduces real freedom—freedom to do things, to make decisions, etc.
4) Unequal distribution undermines democracy by giving some people more resources to influence the political process.

5) Unequal distribution "fractures community, generates envy and resentment, and makes social solidarity more precarious."[92]

There is even the reverse argument—not only does economic growth under present circumstances create inequality, but inequality is said to reduce economic growth as it constrains the poor from participating fully in economic activities.[93]

More and faster globalization has been the theme of many international meetings of organizations such as the World Bank, the World Economic Forum, and other financial movers and doers. The protests with which their policies have been met on the streets have made the names Cancun, Seattle, Davos, Quebec, Genoa and others synonyms for protests against globalization. And well they might protest.

As the participants in such meetings themselves confess, globalization is widening the gap between the rich and the poor, and adding insult to injury when its proponents protest it is good for poor people. The Canadian Prime Minister admits this, albeit in diplomatic language, when he says: "Globalization challenges us to be ever more creative in policy direction."[94] Researchers and outside observers are more explicit: globalization "exponentially widens the gap between rich and poor;"[95] "While globalization had some clear advantages, it has so far not benefited society as a whole."[96] The widening of inequality is beyond doubt, according to many who have studied it. Krugman says: "It has been as firmly established by evidence as the fact that smoking causes cancer."[97] "As the global economic pie grows larger, it may be true that all of the slices are larger, but for those with small slices, it is tempting to believe (and often accurate) that the disparities in size and satisfactions grow even faster."[98] In Sweden, for example, unemployment rose from 1.8 percent in 1990 to 9.5 percent in 1993, and according to some analysts this occurred largely as a result of globalization.[99] Increased trade with China—an absolute desideratum to all globalized enterprises—is likely to worsen income inequality between skilled and unskilled labor in the United States, Japan and Australia,[100] among others.

As an aside, as it were, it should be noted that inequality not only grows as the poor become worse off, but as the wealthy become better off. At issue at the time of writing is a proposal to repeal all estate taxes in the United States—an act that would "benefit the top one-half of one percent of taxpayers...with a ($60 billion annual) tax cut."[101] Adding further insult to such injury is the shocking fact that the poor often pay more taxes, relatively, than do the rich. In Britain, for example, "the tax burden of the top fifth of earners has fallen from 37 percent to 35 percent in the last twenty years. In contrast, the tax burden of the bottom fifth has risen from 31 percent to 38 percent."[102]

Insofar as poor countries are concerned, the net result of globalization is a vast increase in the income of a small minority who take advantage (often unfair advantage) of the situation, with no discernible improvement in the lot of the rest of the population. In 1967 poverty in Hungary was about 10 percent; in 1993, fifty-eight percent of the Hungarian population had an expenditure level below the subsistence minimum.[103] In the year 2001, the Ukraine was listed among the world's poorest countries after the yearly per capita income dropped below $750. Seventy-six percent of the unemployed were poor, and average salaries in the year 2000 dropped from $43 to $42 per month.[104] At the same time, the number of millionaires in local currency rose from less than a dozen in 1997 to 1,221 in 2000.[105]

Although current privatization and globalization operate to exacerbate the condition of the poor, inequality in society is not a new phenomenon. Even between 1950 and 1964 the share of the world's income received by the poorest 20 percent dropped from 3.5 percent to 2.9 percent. The share of the next 20 percent decreased from 4.2 percent to 3.5 percent, while that of the third decreased from 5.5 percent to 4.7 percent [106]

The inequality that exists in any one country pales in comparison to the inequality between countries. As Lockwood comments, the inequality between countries is so great that if the same amount of inequality were to exist in any one country, it would be completely unacceptable.[107] Insofar as the gap between countries is concerned, the Gini index, which measures inequality, indicates that there was a considerable growth between 1988 and 1993.[108] In a study using eight different measures of world inequality, seven showed increasing inequality, and the eighth, no improvement.[109] In the year 2000 the per capita gross income in Luxembourg was more than ninety times that in Sierra Leone,[110] although the former has almost no natural resources, manufacturing, or agriculture. It does, however, encourage offshore corporation registrations, hidden banking services, and other inducements to globalizing corporations.

As the former director of the UN Research Institute for Social Development (UNRISD)—Dharam Ghai—summarizes: "In recent years a growing number of institutions and individuals have become convinced that globalization has not delivered on its promises. In particular, income inequalities have intensified everywhere and hundreds of millions remain mired in poverty and misery."[111] In the United States a study of ninety-one urban communities found that expectations of the global marketplace outweigh its actual benefits.[112]

That globalization ruins the livelihood and lives of many people is of little interest to those who plan it. The founder of the World Economic Forum makes this unusually clear when he insists that the central concern of the WEF is the needs of the business community.[113] As one observer at Davos commented, the industrialists who fuel globalization are so busy chasing profits that they don't even spare the time to meet with those who question the desirability of globalization, or, at best, want a new "Global Compact."[114]

One might ask why consumers don't require companies to be societally responsible. In a few cases, this has paid off, but—as Miller points out—"Many huge global corporations easily shrug off public controversy because they don't sell directly to the public."[115] This is true of arms manufacturers, grain traders, energy conglomerates selling to big industries, invisible subcontractors and hidden owners. One might also ask why the stockholders in international corporations don't make their voices heard in the call for more societal accountability. The answer is, for one thing, that given sentiment versus profits, the latter wins almost every time.[116] More importantly, the great bulk of stocks and bonds are not held by individuals, but by pension funds, banks, investment houses, and so forth, who have as few souls or consciences as do corporations. In Germany, the share of the population that owns shares and mutual funds was less than 20 percent last year.[117] In the United States, the top 1 percent of stock owners held almost half of all stocks, while the bottom 80 percent owned about 4 percent.[118] In any case, "any state that at best questions and at worst appears to deviate too far from the principles of globalization will be punished by currency markets and bondholders and could be cast out into the darkness."[119]

It would be a mistake to think of globalization as extending only to industries. Services, also are now being restructured as international commodities. For-profit managed care services are one of the newest exports at this writing. Seventy percent of all American managed care organizations are now for-profit, and the developing countries have become the newest target. The rhetoric that accompanies this move is familiar: efficiency, economy, ease of access, and so forth. However, the evidence is very slim that such reforms actually achieve their goals. The danger to developing countries is even greater: "As public systems are dismantled and privatized under the auspices of managed care, multinational corporations predictably will enter the field, reap vast profits, and exit within several years. Then developing countries will face the awesome prospect of reconstructing their public systems."[120]

The evils of globalization have not gone unnoticed, as the demonstrations at various meetings of the World Trade Organization and similar groups will attest. There is also an anti-globalization movement (ATTAC) with over thirty thousand dues-paying members in France alone, and twenty-six branches worldwide.[121]

Consequently, the future will probably see much movement and instability, as lower cost conditions are exploited in one place, and corporations then move to another when costs begin to rise, or another location proves cheaper. Further, in order to entice companies to stay in their area, local governments—even, increasingly, in developed countries—offer inducements that include use of non-union labor, tax benefits, subsidies, lowered minimum wages, non-enforcement of ecological regulations, and other legal and semi-legal methods of cutting corners. Ecological damage will continue, and may grow greater, as this "fundamentally neo-liberal hegemony (globalization)…has been demonstrably incapable of dealing with environmental decline or the inequities attached to it.[122]

The inevitable results of the free market were foreseen long ago, by the very progenitor of laissez-faire economics—Adam Smith: "The oppression of the poor must establish the monopoly of the rich, who, by engrossing the whole trade to themselves, will be able to make very large profits."[123]

Goodwin has summarized the results of privatization and globalization thus:

> "Among a large fraction of the human population…global wealth has not translated into the elimination of health-injuring poverty or soul-numbing drudgery. Indeed, rapid GDP growth is sometimes accompanied by increasing inequality and misery, while the environmental impacts of growth threaten reversals in the future…In rich countries inequalities have recently been widening, and even individuals in the upper end of the consumption pyramid do not seem to be achieving the happiness, self-respect, or serenity that some might cite as the purpose of material progress. Capitalism has emerged as the world's triumphant economic system, but, as success comes tantalizingly in sight, there is an uneasy concern that something has gone wrong."[124]

Commentators from areas as far apart as Brazil and the Philippines are more direct:

> Globalization will have a negative effect on social policies and on the quality of life of the poor not only in the short and medium

term but also in the long run…The neo-liberalism of globalization is the extreme variant of a free market economy. It is a political project guided by an absolute belief in markets and thus is in contempt of the state and its regulatory powers.[125]

Even the most avid proponents of globalization have been forced to admit that as a method of fighting poverty, globalization "has come up short."[126]

By the unremitting search for the lowest possible costs in material and labor, regardless of other considerations, globalization enriches the haves and exploits the have-nots, leading to greater and greater economic disparities in society.

ENDNOTES

[1] Findlay, M., *The Globalisation of Crime.* Cambridge, UK: Cambridge University Press, 1999.

[2] Bonoli, G, V. George, and P. Taylor-Gooby, *European Welfare Futures: Towards a Theory of Retrenchment.* Cambridge, U. K.: Polity, 2000, p. 51.

[3] Mishra, R., "The Logic of Globalization," in Mishra, R., (Ed.),*Globalization and the Welfare State.* Toronto: York University Press, 1999, p. 4. (The description is not followed by any examples.)

[4] Higgott, R., and J. Brassett, *Towards an Ethic of Global Poverty Alleviation.* Paper delivered at the Conference on Globalisation, Growth and (In)Equality. Warwick University, Coventry, UK, March, 2002.

[5] Bonoli, *et al, op cit.,* p.52, see endnote 2.

[6] *Overcoming Human Poverty.* New York: United Nations Development Programme, 1998, p. 48.

[7] Anderson, W. T., "Globalization Isn't What It Used to Be." *The Futurist*, 36, *1*, January/February, 2002.

[8] *Ibid.*

[9] Rinehart, J., "The Ideology of Competitiveness," *Monthly Review*, 45, *5*, 1995, pp. 14-24, quoted by Bonoli, *et al, op cit.*, p. 53, see endnote 2.

[10] Deacon, B., *Prospects for Equitable Social Provision in a Globalising World.* Paper delivered at the Conference on Globalisation, Growth and (In)Equality, Warwick University, Coventry, UK, 2002. (Chapter from Dowler, E., and P. Mosley (Eds.), *Poverty and Social Exclusion in North and South.* London: Routledge, forthcoming).

[11] *Ibid.*

[12] Dunham, B., *Heroes and Heretics: A Social History of Dissent.* New York: Knopf, 1964, p. 43.

[13] Exenberger, A., *Globalisation and (in)Equality: Uniformity and Diversity in Trends.* Paper delivered at the Conference on Globalisation, Growth and (In)Equality, University of Warwick, Coventry, UK, 2002.

[14] Bonoli, *et al, op cit.,* see endnote 2.

[15] Deakin, N., *In Search of Civil Society.* Houndmills: Palgrave, 2001, p. 161.

[16] Coller, X., & P. Marginson, "Transnational Management Influence Over Changing Employment Practice: A Case From the Food Industry," *Industrial Relations Journal*, 29, *1*, 1998, pp. 4-17.

[17] Naess, A., "Deep ," in Anderson, W. T. (Ed.), *Evolution Isn't What It Used to Be.* New York: Freeman, 1996, p. 193.

[18] Kapur, D., "The IMF: A Cure or a Curse?" *Cooperation South*, 1, 1999, pp. 26-39.

[19] Stiglitz, J. E., *Globalization and Its Discontents.* New York: Norton, 2002, pp. 12-13, (emphasis added)..

[20] Rosenberg, T., "The Free-Trade Fix." *New York Times*, August 18, 2002, p. 1., internet edition.

[21] Polakow, V., "The Shredded Net; The End of Welfare as We Knew It," in Kushnick, L. and A. Jennings, (Eds.), *A New Introduction to Poverty: The Role of Race, Power and Politics.* New York: New York University Press, 1999, pp. 167-184.

[22] Thompson, G., "Free-Market Upheaval Grinds Mexico's Middle Class." *New York Times*, September 4, 2002, p. 1, internet edition.

[23] Dwyer, P., and D. Seddon, *The New Wave? A Global Perspective on Popular Protest.* Paper given at the 8th International Conference on Alternative Futures and Popular Protest, April, 2002, Manchester Metropolitan University, Manchester, UK.

[24] Polakow, *op cit.,* see endnote 21.

[25] Becker, E., "Raising Farm Subsidies, U.S. Widens International Rift," *New York Times*, June 15, 2002, p. 1, internet edition.

[26] Mishra, *op cit.,* p. 7, see endnote 3.

[27] Quinlan, M.C. Mayhew and P. Bohle, "The Global Expansion of Precarious Employ- ment, Work Disorganization, and Consequences for Occupational Health: Placing the De- bate in a Comparative Historical Context," *International Journal of Health Services*, 31, 3, 2001.

[28] Herbert, B. "Let Nike Stay in the Game." *New York Times*, 6 May, 2002, internet edition, p. 1.

[29] Heap, S., "In the Bad Books," *The Times Higher*, January 12, 2001.

[30] Henderson, J., "Uneven Crises: Institutional Foundations of East Asian Economic Turmoil." *Economy and Society*, 28, 3, 199, pp. 327-368.

[31] Findlay, M., *The Globalization of Crime.* Cambridge: Cambridge University Press, UK, 1999, p. 60.

[32] Mishra, *op cit.*, p. 87, see endnote 3.

[33] Wade, R. H., "The Rising Inequality of World Income Distribution," *Finance and Development*, December, 2001, p. 3.

[34] Ghosal and Miller, quoting Krueger, discuss the lack of any mechanism with the force of universal law to govern international bankruptcies. Ghosal, S., and M. Miller, *Bail-outs, Bail-ins and Bankruptcy: The Evolution of the Global Financial System.* Paper presented at the Conference on Globalisation and (In)Equality, Warwick University, Coventry, UK, March, 2002.

[35] Murray, R. H., "Globalization: Its Contents and Discontents in a Changing World." *Earth Times*, April, 2001, p. 32.

[36] Breitenfellner, A., "Global Unionism: A Potential Player," *International Labour Review*, 136, 4, 1997, pp. 531-555.

[37] Quinlan, Mayhew and Bohle, *op cit.,* see endnote 27.

[38] Mishra, *op cit.*, p. 4, see endnote 3.

[39] Higgott, and Brassett, *op cit.,* see endnote 4.

[40] Juntunen, E. K., *The Economic Influences of Globalisation on Small Countries and Local Districts.* Paper delivered at the Conference on Social Work and Social Policies. Dubrovnik, Croatia, June 17, 2002.

[41] Mishra, *op cit.*, p. 8, see endnote 3.

[42] Kay, J., "UN Summit Subordinates Environment and Development to Corporate Inter- ests," *WSWS*, 11 September, 2002.

[43] *Ibid.*

[44] Coller and Marginson, *op cit.,* see endnote 16.

[45] *Ibid.*

[46] Winter, G., "Big Tobacco is Accused of Crossing an Age Line." *New York Times*, August 24, 2001, internet edtion, pp. 1-3.

[47] Kuczynski, A., "Tobacco Industry Still Advertises in Magazines Read by Youth." *New York Times*, August 15, 2001, internet edition, p. 1.

[48] Winter, G., "Tobacco Company Reneged on Youth Ads, Judge Rules." *New York Times,* June 7, 2002, p. 1., internet edition.

[49] Holden, C., "The Internationalization of Long Term Care Provision." *Global Social Policy*, 2, 1, April, 2002, pp. 47-67.

[50] Daenzer, P. M., "An Affair Between Nations: International Relations and the Move-

ment of Household Service Workers," in Bakan, A. B., and D. Stasiulis (Eds.), *Not One of the Family: Foreign Domestic Workers in Canada.* Toronto: University of Toronto Press, 1997.

[51] Quoted by Koivusalo, M., *World Trade Organisation and Trade-Creep in Health and Social Policies.* University of Sheffield: GASPP Occasional Paper No. 4/1999.

[52] Kohr, M., *A Perspective on Globalisation and Its Implications for Developing Countries.* Paper presented at the Conference on Globalisation, Growth and (In)Equality. Warwick University, Coventry, UK, 2002.

[53] Deacon, *op cit.,* see endnote 10.

[54] Mishra, *op cit.,* see endnote 3.

[55] Kaufman, L., and D. Gonzalez, "Labor Standards Clash with Global Reality," *New York Times,* April 24, 2001, internet edition, p. 1.

[56] *Ibid.*

[57] Eckholm, E., "Workers' Rights Suffering as China Goes Capitalist," *New York Times,* 22 August 2001, internet edition p. 1.

[58] *Ibid.*

[59] Weeks, J., "Wages, Employment and Workers' Rights in Latin America, 1970-1998," *International Labour Review,* 138, 2, 1999, pp. 151-169.

[60] Kaufman and Gonzalez, *op cit.,* see endnote 55.

[61] Blumenkrantz, A., "Struggling TWA Strands 260 Passengers in Israel." *HaAretz,* March 30, 2001, internet edition, p. 1.

[62] Vogl, F., "Mergers and Ethics Don't Mix Well," *Earth Times,* 8, 20, October, 1999, p. 26.

[63] Fox, M., *The Reinvention of Work: A New Vision of Livelihood for Our Time.* San Francisco: Harper, 1995.

[64] Harriss-White, B., *Globalisation, Informal Economies and (In)Decent Work.* Paper delivered at the Conference on Globalisation, Growth and (In)Equality. Warwick University: Coventry, UK, 2002.

[65] Lee, E., "Globalization and Labour Standards: A Review of Issues." *International Labour Review,* 136, 2, 1997, pp. 173-198.

[66] Sanger, D. E., and S. Lohr, "Searching for Ways to Avoid Layoffs." *New York Times,* March 9, 1996, internet edition, p. 1.

[67] Schorr, *A.L., Welfare Reform, Failure and Remedies.* Westport: Praeger, 2001, p. 153.

[68] *Ibid,* p. 52.

[69] *Ibid.*

[70] Anelauskas, V., *Discovering America As It Is.* Atlanta: Clarity, 1999, p. 314.

[71] Blank, R. M., *It Takes a Nation: A New Agenda for Fighting Poverty.* Princeton: Princeton University Press, 1997, p. 61.

[72] *Ibid.*

[73] *Ibid,* p. 61.

[74] Levitan, A., G.L. Magnum and S.L. Magnum, *Programs in Aid of the Poor.* Baltimore: Johns Hopkins, 1998, p. 28 (seventh edition).

[75] Macarov, D., *Worker Productivity: Myths and Reality.* Beverly Hills: Sage, 1982; Macarov, D., "Who Works Hard and Why?" *BaKibbutz,* 1975, pp. 64-78 (Hebrew).

[76] Levine, D., "Editorial," *Industrial Relations,* 37, 4, 1998, pp. 121-123.

[77] Vogl, F., "Ethical Multinational Corporations?" *Conference News Daily,* July 28, 2001, p. 21.

[78] *Ibid.*

[79] Findlay, *op cit.,* p. 51, see endnote 1.

[80] Kaufmann, D., "Governance and Anti: New Insights and Challenges," in Feinstein, O.N., and R. Piccotto, (Eds.), *Evaluation and Poverty Reduction.* New Brunswick: Transaction, 2001, pp. 289-300..

[81] Shah, A., "Comments: Governance and Anticorruption: New Insights and Challenges," in Feinstein and Picciotto, *op cit.,* pp.295-298, see endnote 80.

[82] Dixon, J., *Social Security in Global Perspective.* Westport: Praeger, 1999, p. 162.

[83] Verhovek, S. H., "Drill, Say Alaskans, Who Know Their Pockets Are lined With Oil."

New York Times, March 18, 2001, internet edition, p. 1.

[84] Killick, T., "Responding to Inequality." *Inequality Briefing*, UK Department for International Development by the Economists' Resource Centre, 3, March 2002, p. 3.

[85] For more sophisticated conceptualizations of equality and equity, see Schwartz, J., *Fighting Poverty with Virtue: Moral Reform and America's Urban Poor, 1825-2000.* Bloomington: University of Indiana Press, 2000, and Dworkin, R., *Sovereign Virtue: The Theory and Practice of Equality.* Cambridge: Harvard University Press, 2000.

[86] Corbett, T., "The New Face of Welfare: From Income Transfers to Social Assistance." *Focus*, 22, *1*, Special Issue, 2002, pp. 1-10.

[87] *Ibid.*

[88] Templeton J. M., "A Worldwide Rise in Living Standards." *The Futurist.* 33. *1*, January, 1999, pp. 17-22 (emphasis in original).

[89] Jones, B. G., *The Growth of Inequality: The Structural Determination of Need in the Era of Globalisation.* Paper presented at the Conference on Globalisation, Growth and (In)Equality. Warwick University, Coventry, UK, 2002.

[90] Callinicos, A., *Equality.* Cambridge, UK: Polity, 2000, p. 113.

[91] Wade, R. H., "Making the World Development Report 2000: Attacking Poverty." *World Development,* 29, *8*, 2001. (This is not necessarily Wade's own view).

[92] Wright, E. O., "Reducing Income and Wealth Inequality: Real Utopian Proposals." *Contemporary Sociology*, 29, *1*, January, 2000, pp. 143-156.

[93] Naschold, F., "Why Inequality Matters for Poverty." *Inequality Briefing,* 2, March, 2002, p. 2.

[94] "Summit in Quebec Kicks Off New Riots," *New York Times*, April 22, 2001, internet edition, p. 1.

[95] Sohn, F. A., "Social Development for the New Millennium: Visions and Strategies for Global Transformation," *Social Development Issues*, 22, *1*, 2000, pp. 4-8.

[96] Hahn, T., "It Seems Impossible to Get Organized," *Earth Times,* April, 2000, p. 15.

[97] Krugman, P., "The Wealth Gap is Real and It's Growing," *New York Times*, August 21, 1995, p. A15, quoted by Anelauskas, *op cit.*, p. 39, see endnote 37.

[98] Murray, *op cit.,* see endnote 35.

[99] Mishra, *op cit.*, p. 75, see endnote 3..

[100] Cheung, K., and C. Fan, "Does Trade Lead to Wage Inequality?" *Journal of the Asia Pacific Economy*, 7, *2*, 2002, pp. 147-159.

[101] Hulse, C., "Senate Leader Opens Debate on Estate Tax Repeal," *New York Times*, June 12, 2002, p. 1, internet edition.

[102] "Diary," *Poverty*, 108, Winter 2001, p. 4.

[103] Henderson, *et al, op cit.*, see endnote 30.

[104] Deacon, B., *Profits and Pitfalls in the Measurement of Globalisation.* Paper presented at the Conference on Globalisation, Growth and (In)Equality, University of Warwick, Coventry, UK, 2002.

[105] "What Are We Spending Our Money On?" *The Ukrainian*, 2, 2001, p. 46.

[106] Macarov, D., and G. Fradkin, *The Short Course in Development Training.* Ramat Gan: Massada, 1973, p. 14.

[107] Lockwood, B., *Problems and Pitfalls in the Measurement of Globalisation,* paper delivered at the fifth Annual Conference on Globalisation, Growth and (In)Equality. Coventry: University of Warwick, 2002.

[108] Milanovic, B., "True World Income Distribution, 1998 and 1993: First Calculation Based on Household Surveys Alone." *The Economic Journal*, 112, *476*, January, 2002, pp. 51-92.

[109] Wade, R. H., "The Rising Inequality of World Income Distribution," *Finance and Development,* December, 2001, p. 1.

[110] McKay, A., "Defining and Measuring Inequality," *Inequality Briefing*, 1., March, 2002.

[111] Ghai, D., "At Issue: How to Deal with the Social Impact of Globalization." *Earth Times*, August, 2000, p. 23.

[112] Eisinger, P., and C. Smith, "Globalization and Metropolitan Well-Being in the United States," *Social Science Quarterly*, 2, *81*, June, 2000, pp. 634-644.

[113] Freeman, J., "Annual Meeting 2001 in Davos Promises Fresh Focus on Bridging the 'Social Divide'." *Forum News Daily*, January 23, 2001, p. 3.

[114] Vogl, R., "For Davos Pilgrims, Some Gloomy Realities." *Forum News Daily*, January 23, 2001, p. 27.

[115] Miller, K. L., "The Teflon Shield," *Newsweek*, 137, *11*, March 12, 2001, pp. 26-30.

[116] For an entertaining look at this dilemma, see the movie, *Other People's Money.*

[117] Wallace, C. P., "In the Line of Fire," *Time Magazine*, 157, *18*, May 7, 2001, pp. 42-45.

[118] Lobe, J., *Despite the US Economic "Boom," Inequality Continues to Widen.* New York: InterPress Service, September 4, 2000.

[119] Sonn, *op cit.*, see endnote 95.

[120] Waitzkin, H., and C. Iriart, "How the United States Exports Managed Care to Developing Countries," *International Journal of Health Services*, 31, *3*, 2001, pp. 495-505.

[121] Le Wuessne, N., "Antiglobalization Guerrilla," *Time Magazine*, 158, *20*, November 12, 2001, p. 65.

[122] Elliott, L., *Global Environmental (In)Equity and the Cosmopolitan Project.* Paper presented at the Conference on Globalisation, Growth and (In)Equality. Warwick University, Coventry, UK, 2002. (Parentheses added).

[123] Smith, A., *An Inquiry into the Nature and Causes of the Wealth of Nations.* 1776.

[124] Goodwin, N. R., "Volume Introduction," in Ackerman, R., D. Kiron, N. R. Goodwin, J. M. Harris and K. Gallagher (Eds.), *Human Well-Being and Economic Goals.* Washington: Island, 1997, pp. xxv-xxxii.

[125] "Global Social Policy Forum," *Global Social Policy*, 1, *3*, December, 3001, p. 269.

[126] Kahn, J., "Globalization Proves Disappointing," *New York Times*, March 21, 2002, internet edition, p. 1.

CHAPTER 6

Efforts to Overcome Poverty

"We are faced with insurmountable opportunities."
Pogo

The inability of modern societies to eliminate poverty, or even to reduce it in any meaningful degree, is not from lack of theories, proposals or attempts. Many international and government agencies, non-governmental organizations, think tanks and theorists have published proposals—and less often, programs— for reducing poverty; or more often, principles, ideas or strategies that would presumably be effective if implemented.[1] Some publications even indicate how these programs have been put in place in specific times and places, but almost never accompany these instances with objective evaluations of how much poverty was actually eliminated as a result.

For example, a United Nations Development Program (UNDP) publication cites (favorably) a "poverty initiative" in Honduras; a "Social Strategy Steering Committee" in Kazakhstan; a "National Poverty Eradication Strategy and Plan of Action" in Morocco; a "Poverty Eradication Action Plan" in Uganda; and a "Joint Poverty Alleviation Project" in the Philippines. But there is not one word as to how these or previous such programs have actually reduced poverty.[2] One is led to the suspicion that countries—particularly Third World countries—agree to cooperate with the UNDP and establish such national programs because of the grants that then become available from the UNDP. Indeed, over 50 percent of UNDP allocations are for poverty eradication, and over 80 percent of that money goes to less-developed and low-income countries.[3] But citations of specific poverty reductions are hard to find. (If one were a cynic, one would agree that some poverty is probably reduced—that of the administrators within such programs).

The continuing growth of poverty throughout the world is an indication of the futility of such discussions and the failure of their implementation. In 1996 the United Nations Conference on Social Development set 2015 as the target date for halving the number of people who had been living on one dollar a day in 1993[4] —namely, "more than one billion people.[5] In the year 2001—close to halfway to the target date—the number of people living on one dollar a day had risen to 1.2 billion.[6] In 2002, the largest international meeting ever held, encompassing over 65,000 delegates, took place in Johannesburg. The subject of the conference was sustainable development. Two hundred countries were represented (as were seven hundred companies). The mountain labored, and produced a mouse— or, in more elegant terms, "a final document even more vague and toothless than that which emerged from Rio".[7]

Many of these proposals, programs and panaceas can be summed up as wishful thinking based on the assumptions and operations of the market-driven society, to wit: "If everybody pulls their weight and complies with the agenda, the establishment, (and) the status quo, then there should be no social ills, no hunger, no destitution, (and) no want."[8]

Of the myriad proposals, beliefs and assumptions concerning poverty alleviation, none have, as yet, eradicated poverty in even one country. An examination of the most prominent of these will indicate why.

INCREASED GDP-BASED PROSPERITY AS IRRELEVANT

> *"Never before has our nation enjoyed...*
> *so much prosperity and social progress."*
> President Clinton, A. D. *2000*

> *"In all abundance there is a lack."*
> Hippocrates, cir. 400 B. C.

The most widely-proposed and sincerely believed antidote for poverty is a healthy and growing economy. There is a firm and unquestioned assumption among many policy-makers and economists that GDP-based prosperity benefits everyone. All their policies and theories proceed from this mind-set. For example, a report for the World Bank says flatly: "Growth is the single most important factor in poverty reduction."[9] Glenn and Gordon say: "Without economic growth, all else fails."[10] This is also expressed more popularly in a number of ways, *viz,* "You can't distribute poverty," or "What is good for General Motors is good for the country," or—more recently—"A rising tide raises all the boats." However, experience indicates that the rising tide contains a vicious undertow that pulls many people under—especially those without boats. In actual fact, a prosperous capitalist economy is based upon exploiting poor people—not helping them.

The theory that prosperity helps everyone is grounded in the "trickle down" assumption—that increases at the top and/or in the middle of the income distribution, will automatically and inevitably benefit the lowest level. As Freeman says: "All governments...have operated on the assumption that the benefits of economic growth would not only further enrich the rich and powerful, but would somehow 'trickle down' to improve the lives of the poor as well."[11] According to the United Nations Development Program, economic growth tends to explain only part of poverty reduction and a large share remains unexplained by mere economic growth.[12] This provides scope for public policies that can be used to ensure that economic growth will have positive human development impacts.

This is a very logical position, augmented by commonsense and seasoned with hope. However, it does not distinguish between the condition that researchers call "necessary" and that termed "sufficient." Even if prosperity is necessary for improvement in the position of the poor (which is doubtful), it is not sufficient. There must be active efforts to use the prosperity for the benefit of the poor, which usually do not take place. Economic growth reduces poverty only when the real wages of lower-paid and less-skilled workers increase,[13] and social welfare benefits are increased at least proportionately. Since much growth—particularly as regards privatization and globalization efforts—is based upon exploiting the lowest wages possible—and the wage depression attendant upon both of these phenomena has been detailed previously—economic growth and good wages seem to be in an antagonistic posture.

To expect business as such to devote itself to social concerns is patently unrealistic. Brown optimistically calls on business to address the problems of food and health and sustainable livelihoods by adopting new models, new technologies, new partnerships, and new means of delivery.[14] But business is in business to make money and unless these novelties do so, they have no chance of being adopted. All such problems are left to the government—unless, of course, the government gets in the way of making profits.

In discussing the incidence and dynamics of poverty, one cannot ignore the various surveys, articles and books that indicate a decrease in poverty; or, the success of one or another antipoverty programs. However, it would be well to study the source of such studies, since many of them are self-serving reports of the organization conducting the research. Schorr, for one, recommends "considerable skepticism" in dealing with the literature of welfare reform, since the funding of the reporting organization may arise from national or local governmental sources.[15]

Sometimes the thrust of the report is self-evident. The World Bank's Development Report for 2002 is sub-titled "Building Institutions for Markets"—not institutions for poor people, and not even for people in general, but for commerce.[16] Even when the title is not so direct, the nuances of such reports need scrutiny. Wade, for example, has indicated in great detail how the World Bank's flagship publication—*World Development Report*—is carefully doctored to give the desired impression. The facts are not at issue, but the arguments as to how the Report is to be presented –- which statements to be made first and which last, and how many words in each— have been so heated, and seen as so important, that they have led to the resignation of staff-members.[17] The salt-cellar should be kept handy in reading such organizational-sponsored research.

The Growing Income Gap

Inequity between populations, both within and between countries, has grown worse during the last twenty years despite economic growth.[18] Specifically, for the last thirty years the gap between the richest Americans and everyone else has been growing so much that the level of inequality in the U.S. is higher than in any other industrial nation. Between 1979 and 1994 household incomes in the United States grew about 10 percent. Ninety-seven percent of those gains went to the richest 20 percent of households.[19] Adjusted for inflation, the income of families in the middle of the U.S. income distribution rose from $41,400 in 1979 to $45,100 in 1997, a nine percent increase. Meanwhile the income of families in the top one percent rose from $420,200 to over a million dollars, or 140 percent. That is, the income of families in the top one percent was ten times that of typical families in 1979, but twenty-three times more (and rising) in 1997.[20]

The Census Bureau compared household incomes during three peak economic periods, ten years apart, and found that the gap between the rich and poor narrowed only in Alaska (which, not incidentally, gives money directly to residents). Otherwise, gains in the top 20 percent of the income distribution outstripped any improvement among the bottom 20 percent in forty-four states. In five states the income of the bottom stratum fell while that of the upper stratum grew. To summarize the finding, in New York State alone the upper level made eight times more than the lower level in the 1970s, and that increased to thirteen times more in the 1990s.[21] Thus, there is compelling evidence that prosperity depends upon the continuation, or even deepening, of poverty. In short, prosperity actually "bubbles up" from the less wealthy to the more wealthy, rather than trickling down.

This may be a good point to note that most discussions of the income gap compare the richest to the poorest, as though the middle class was unaffected. However, when proposals to try to overcome poverty are mooted, the reaction is— on the one hand—that these measures will hurt the (larger) middle class and— on the other—that the middle class must be assuaged some way to gain their support for the program. Thus, it might be salutary to realize that:

> If we divide the world population into three groups: the rich (those with incomes greater than Italy's mean income), the poor (those with less than Western countries' poverty line), and the middle class, we find that 11 percent of people are 'world middle class,' 78 percent are poor, and 11 percent are rich.[22]

The assumption that prosperity trickles down to the poor is belied by a whole world of experience, research and statistics. Freeman says:

> Macroeconomic performance, good or bad, does not well predict the magnitude of changes in poverty. Taken together, the three decades from 1970 to 2000 give a depressing picture of the ability of economic growth to reduce poverty: Gross domestic product (GNP) per capita rose by 73 percent, while the rate of poverty among families barely fell, from 9.7 percent in 1969 to 9.3 percent in 1999.[23]

Another few examples: In the 1980s, for every person in the United States who joined the middle class, two joined the group of the poor.[24] For every seventy dollar increase in income among the richest 20 percent in the United States between 1979 and 1989, the poorest 20 percent *lost* a dollar.[25] In the United Kingdom during the same period, for every five thousand pounds sterling increase among the upper 20 percent, the lowest 10 percent *lost* two hundred pounds. From 1978 to 1987 the income of the top fifth of the population in the United States increased by 13 percent, while that of the bottom fifth *declined* by 8 percent.[26] In 1997 the average after-tax income of households in the top 1 percent in the United States was $414,000(!!) higher than in 1979. For the middle fifth of families, the increase was $3,400, but for the bottom fifth, the average *fell* by $100.[27] The economy in Israel grew by 6 percent and salary levels climbed in the year 2000, but the percentage of the poor remained virtually the same.[28]

What conclusion can be drawn from these figures? As one careful researcher put it, "An expanding economy no longer guarantees a decline in poverty."[29] Even during one of the most prosperous recent periods—the booming nineties—analysis indicates that, "The poor got a little poorer, the rich got a lot richer and the large group in the middle emerged slightly worse off than when the decade began."[30]

On a global basis, whereas in 1960 the richest 20 percent of the world population had incomes thirty times greater than the poorest 20 percent, by 1990 this had grown to 60 percent greater, when measured between countries. When the gap is measured within countries, the income of the richest 20 percent is one hundred fifty times greater than that of the poorest.[31] The ten richest people in Britain have wealth that is equivalent to that of a total of twenty-three Third World countries holding 174 million people.[32] The amount spent on jewelry in the United States in 1991 was equivalent to the GDP of twenty poor countries.[33]

Increase in international trade volume, usually thought of as an indication of economic strength, has also been found to have little relationship to changes in the income share of the poorest or to changes in income inequality.[34] The disparity among nations is not static, but is growing because, among other things, "The net flow of resources is from the poor nations to the rich. The cost of debt repayments exceeds the income that poor countries receive from wealthy neighbors. It is no wonder that the rich nations get richer while the poor get poorer."[35]

For example: "Even when average incomes rose in the economic expansion of these decades (1980-1990), the share of income received by low-income households stagnated or declined. In the twenty years after 1978, poverty climbed from 11.4 percent to 12.7 percent of the population."[36] In short, "It is no longer possible to assume that economic growth alone will be beneficial for health and human welfare, however, it may be further argued that economic growth linked to increasing social inequity can be hazardous to social well-being, health and environmental sustainability."[37]

Even the tax system supports the "bubble up" theory: "Britain's tax system now takes more from the poor than it does from the rich...the tax burden of the top fifth of earners has fallen from 37 percent to 35 percent in the last 20 years...the tax burden of the bottom fifth has risen from 31 percent to 38 percent."[38] Similarly, President Bush proposed a tax bill that would increase the income of the highest 1 percent of the population by 6 percent-7 percent; for the middle fifth, 2 percent; and for the bottom fifth, less than 1 percent. As the *New York Times* said: "This is an administration and Congress that galloped to the rescue of the rich."[39]

Not content with these tax cuts, still another was proposed. The primary author of the bill piously proclaimed that the tax cut would benefit, "The hardware store, the diner down the street, the gas station on the corner." These small local industries that were to be helped turned out to be IBM, which saved $1.4 billion in taxes; General Motors, over $800 million; and General Electric, $670 million, none of whom, by the way, deal with hardware, food or gasoline.[40]

As mentioned in Chapter III, the United States Congress is now in the process of canceling all estate taxes. Were they to maintain only those worth over $5 million, the government would collect $20 billion each year and the 3300 unfortunate families affected would be left with an average of only $10 million each.[41] On the other hand, it does not take much imagination to envision how many of the poor people would benefit from having their estate taxes cut.

The logic of the tax cut is clear, at least to economists. By cutting taxes, industrialists and financiers will undertake activities that will bolster the economy. This sanguine presumption is countered by the inescapable reality that fewer tax receipts means less money for government use, which will invariably result in cuts in human services—health, education, and social welfare. As usual, the poor will pay the price, and any bolstering of the economy that results will not redound to their benefit. Take, for example, the rise in worker productivity in the third quarter of 2001—a raise occasioned by cutting workers and hours—hailed as a sign of increasing prosperity. This was called "defending the bottom line in ways we've never seen before,"[42] but "it also means ...worse news for the employment situation and consumers."[43]

The results of "bubble up" are clear. The wealthiest 1 percent of households in the United States now control about 38 percent of the national wealth, while the bottom 80 percent control only 17 percent.[44] In 1998, the one-fifth of families with the lowest incomes received 4.2 percent of total income.

Families in the highest one-fifth received 47.3 percent of all incomes.[45] In 1990 family income in Israel in the top decile was 9.1 percent greater than that in the bottom decile. In 2000 it had grown to 11.9 time higher.[46]

Friedman points out that, seen internationally, the fifth of the world's population in the highest-income countries has 86 percent of the world's gross domestic product; 82 percent of world export markets; 68 percent of foreign direct investments and 74 percent of world telephone lines. The bottom fifth, in the poorest countries, has about 1 percent in each of these sectors. The wealthiest fifth consume 45 percent of all meat and fish while the poorest fifth consume less than 5 percent.[47]

There is little question but that the gap is widening. In 1960 the 20 percent of the world's people who live in the richest countries had thirty times the income of the poorest 20 percent, and by 1995 the richest had 82 percent. In Brazil, the poorest 50 percent of the population received 18 percent of the national income in 1960, and by 1995 they received only 11.6 percent. In Russia, the richest 20 percent now takes home eleven times more of the national income than the lowest 20 percent.

Robert Reich, former Secretary of Labor, says: "The top one percent is doing magnificently, the top five percent is faring better than ever before, the top 20 percent is living quite comfortably. But each rung on the ladder is spaced more widely apart than before...The middle has not progressed, and those on the rungs below them are relatively worse off."[48] At the moment of writing, "The gap between the rich and poor continues to widen...Income inequality is the highest since 1990."[49] In short, not only is the income gap growing throughout the world, but the "trickle down" theory must, in all honesty, give way to the "bubble up" theory of economics.

In summary, stated in almost Marxist terms, the rich get richer by making the poor poorer. Depending upon increased economic prosperity to solve the problem of poverty is like expecting King-Kong to become a pet monkey.

EMPLOYMENT AS A SPURIOUS ANTIDOTE

> *"I've been working hard all my life,*
> *But somehow it seems longer."*
> Seen on a T-shirt

The second most widely spread and deeply believed myth about poverty (after blind faith in prosperity) is that employment is an effective method of alleviating poverty. It does not seem to matter how, or how often, the fact that only a minority of the poor are unemployed, or even in the labor force, is articulated— "Get 'em back to work," is the solution of the man (and woman) in the street, the media, economists, and policy makers. The fact that work is not an option for the children, the aged, the incapacitated, and the single mother of (several) small children who make up the bulk of the poverty population simply does not seem to penetrate. Nor does the fact that close to 60 percent of the adults in poor families in 1999 were unlikely to be able to benefit much from the labor market make any impact. Even if we consider only those aged 18-64, about half of poor adults are subject to problems that limit the benefits they could derive from full employment,[50] and obviously, could benefit even less from the part-time and temporary employment that would probably be their lot if they could work and/or find employment. A study in Israel found that 86 percent of the poor people could not be aided through employment opportunities. They were either already employed, self-employed, over age sixty-five, handicapped, chronically ill, mentally ill, or in prison.[51]

The Working Poor

In discussing employment as a solution to poverty it might be well to take a closer look at the plight of the working poor. These are the people who work, usually not full-time or year round, and remain poor. As corporations privatize and globalize, they hire more and more of their employees on a temporary basis. This not only relieves them of paying salaries during slack times, but also helps them avoid paying the employers' portion of various social security taxes, retirement funds, health programs, etc. Consequently, the number of temporary workers has tripled in the last ten years[52]—on an average day, there are 2.2 million temporary workers in the United States.[53] Of 41,000 jobs that were created in April, 2002, *every one* of them was temporary.[54]

Not only do such people work sporadically, they are paid only about 70 percent of what comparable permanent jobs pay.[55] A full 44 percent of *new* jobs are part-time service-sector jobs that pay less than $7,400 per year.[56] Since the poverty line for a single person is over $8,000, such part-time jobs not only do not reduce the poverty-stricken population, but—insofar as people are forced to move from full-time to part-time employment—they increase it.

Nor, as has been emphasized regarding the working poor, do the long-term unemployed predominate in the poverty-stricken group. Between 41 percent[57] and 63 percent[58] of those under the poverty line worked some time during the year. Further, those who see employment as the solution to poverty often quote the wage rate as being higher than the welfare payment both as an incentive to work, and as a source of income higher than the poverty line. However, they (and the official definition) ignore the significant costs associated with getting to work and paying for childcare when all adults in a household are employed.[59] This often substantially reduces the net effect of the salary. Nor are wages always higher than welfare rates, as will be discussed in the section on welfare reform.

Most of the working poor would remain poor even if they worked at their present salaries forty hours a week fifty-two weeks of the year. As it is, the *average* working poor puts in over thirty-five hours a week but works only two thirds of a year.[60] If earnings are the only source of income available to a family, few less-skilled single mothers earn enough to escape poverty; about three-quarters of less-skilled married men make enough to raise their families out of poverty; and less than two-thirds of single persons earn enough to avoid poverty.[61] And there remain those who are disabled, elderly, or unable to find full-time year-round employment. Only between 19 percent and 28 percent of the poor could conceivably climb out of poverty working full-time year-round, if they were lucky enough to find such jobs (which they can't).[62] The earnings of most of the poor families who left welfare in the 1990s are still well below the poverty line.[63] The "get 'em back to work" attitude also blithely glides over the lack of jobs that characterizes all the countries in the world.

Subsidies

One method of attempting to induce employers to hire the unemployed is to offer them a subsidy for initial costs and training programs. In Massachusetts, employers receive $3.50 an hour for nine months, and $2.50 an hour for the next three months for employees in training programs.[64] Since the minimum wage is $5.15 an hour, this becomes a source of very cheap labor for the employers. And there is no guarantee that the trainee will be retained after the first year. In Israel, as another example, employers of certain new immigrants receive complete subsidies for the first year's salary, on the assumption that the immigrant will then become a permanent worker. There is no enforceable requirement for the latter, however, and experience indicates that many employers exist and profit by the annual turnover of new immigrants hired. These are but two examples of how policies designed to help workers become guarantees of more profits for employers.

In this connection it might be salutary to mention the oft-quoted Speenhamland experience of 1795. The justices in that area of England decided to alleviate the poverty that existed in spite of employment, and to subsidize the difference between the low wages being paid and the high cost of a food basket (actually, the cost of bread). Employers promptly dropped wages, and the workers ended up being paid in great part by the county, while the employers saw their profits increase due to substantially lower labor costs.[65] This established the pattern that still obtains— subsidies generally profit the subsidized and no one else.

Along these same lines, there are many subsidies to industries and services to allow (read: induce) them to create jobs. In the United States this took the form of establishing "enterprise zones," into which businesses would presumably move to take advantage of tax relief, subsidies, and other goodies. "There is very little evidence that new businesses were attracted into these areas. In fact, each new job created in these zones cost (the government) from $4,500 to $13,000 *annually*."[66] Given the fact that the poverty line for a single person was $8,240, there were people who could have been raised out of poverty if given these amounts, without the necessity of enterprise zones, administration, supervision, evaluation or any of the other entangling requirements associated with these unsuccessful programs.

Indeed, many training, subsidy and loan programs that trumpet their successes in putting people to work do not compare their success rate with that of people who were not given such opportunities—and the latter often outweigh the former.[67]

Make-work

Occasionally there surface proposals for some sort of make-work program for the unemployed, and the poor among them, or even just for the poor. Variously termed "community service," "service corps," "works program," and so forth, these are proposed as methods of teaching "work habits," preparing people for jobs, or receiving some return for welfare payments. The largest and longest lasting of such programs took place during the Great Depression, and was termed the Works Progress Administration (WPA). The costs and results of this experiment have been discussed elsewhere,[68] but because of the differences in the social and economic climate today are of limited relevance now. However, a later make-work program, called the Civilian Conservation Corps contains some interesting data: Of those who served a six-month period with the CCC, 77 percent were still unemployed at the end, as were 58 percent of those who stayed for a year. More important, the estimated value of the work done by each enrollee was $664, with per capita costs of $1,004.[69] Viewing more current make-work projects, particularly in the developing countries, Lipton points out that public works do not enable permanent escape from poverty.[70]

Even those who favor public service programs view the current efforts as useless and degrading. These programs "demean participants and displace public employees, who might find themselves doing their old jobs for workfare instead of wages."[71] They do not lead to skill-improvement nor to experience helpful in finding real jobs. At most, they are of some temporary help, on a minimum level, to some of the minority of the poor who can work.

Minimum Wages

In discussing the working poor, the subject of minimum wages must be addressed. Large-scale debates swirl around the determination of a minimum wage. The traditional stance of employers, and those who support them, is that raising the minimum wage will make the work of some people unprofitable, thus causing employers to fire people, thereby increasing the number of the unemployed/needy. Or, alternatively, that raising labor costs will raise prices, thereby increasing the economic difficulties of poor people. The opposing argument is that by raising the minimum wage not only will welfare costs be reduced, but people will have more money to spend on goods and services, thereby helping the economy (read: employers). In any case, rarely are the presumed higher costs of goods and services that the poverty-stricken would have to pay weighed against the real increase in income that they would enjoy.

One wide-scale study undertook to determine if raising minimum wages would, indeed, hurt the poor. The finding: "Our results provide evidence that increase in minimum wages in the 1990s *have* served to reduce poverty."[72] A study in Britain looked at the effect of a minimum wage on unemployment—in eighteen months there had been no job losses.[73] Even when minimum wages seem to reduce employment opportunities, this dissipates through time.[74]

If raising the minimum wage would harm the economy, then perhaps logically it should be completely abolished in order to improve the economy. Employers could surely be depended upon to see to it that nobody suffered. Or could they? At one time the British abolished wages councils, which had regulated wages in certain sectors. Two years later half the jobs were paying less than the council minimum rates.[75]

As it is, minimum wages tend to be so low that they have little impact on the poor as such. For example, the minimum wage in New York is $5.15 an hour. This contrasts with the $14.17 average hourly pay for production workers.[76] Someone working forty hours a week would net $824 a month. Working full-time year round—with no vacation—would give him or her slightly under $10,000, which would leave them well under the poverty line if they were supporting a spouse and/or children. Of the 140,000 new jobs that were projected in 1996 to be available by 2005, one half would not pay enough to cover a minimal budget for an adult with two children.[77]

Along the same lines, note that of the 63 percent of poor families who had a member working, as noted above, the income was so low that welfare benefits continued to be needed. In fact, most adult welfare clients have worked at some time, but low wages, part-time employment, and temporary jobs have kept them in poverty.[78] Two-fifths of welfare mothers are employed but unable to make enough money to leave welfare.[79] The erosion of the purchasing power of minimum wages over time is demonstrated by the fact that in the 1960s, a family of three with a full-time worker making the minimum wage would have been raised above the poverty line, but in 1990 that same family would have been $2000 below the poverty line.[80] Further, violation of minimum wage laws is probably one of the most widespread of so-called white-collar crimes. Most authorities show little interest in enforcing such laws, nor do they have the resources or the personnel to do so. Poignant cases continue to be publicized by enterprising journalists, especially concerning new immigrants, illegal immigrants, and migrant workers. The decline in membership and power of labor unions has also been both the cause and the result of low-paid, exploitative, temporary and part-time work.

In summary, the small proportion of the poor who are unemployed; the slim chances of their finding jobs in face of the real unemployment numbers; the temporary, part-time, low-paying jobs they would fill; and the need of the economic sector for a reservoir of unemployed workers, all mitigate against employment as being a solution of any real dimensions to the problem of poverty.

Young has recapitulated the employment experience thus: "Capitalism has some virtues, but after three hundred years it should be clear that one of them is not employing all able-bodied people at decent wages."[81]

In short, even (so-called) prosperity and (so-called) full employment have not cut the American poverty rate substantially or brought it to a level close to that of other advanced democracies.[82] A study of the effect of employment on poverty says: "A surprising finding is the weak effect of employment growth. Since policymakers often view policies that induce employment growth as a method of reducing income inequality, this study suggests that such policies may not reduce inequality."[83] As Stricker explains it: "No system of organising production has ever been able to provide a productive job for every man and woman who wanted to work."[84]

Insofar as employment is considered an antidote for poverty (which it isn't, but is usually considered so), the fact that the present system cannot, and never could (except during wartime) provide paid employment for everyone who was ready, able and willing to work is an important indictment of the system—and especially its effect on poverty.

The reason why this is so is well stated by the Secretary-General of the UN Conference on Trade and Development: "Markets never lift the lowest fifth of incomes, because employer interests depend on unemployment to restrain wages; short of a big war, there will much unemployment or many low-wage workers, or both…(poverty arises) not from 'the foibles of the poor' but (from) the limits of market capitalism."[85] Part of these limits is the view of employers that the existence of an unemployed stratum is an implied threat—and thus a prod—to workers. Conversely, full employment is a threat to themselves, as higher wages may be necessary in order to acquire workers.

Despite the research and the experience accumulated over the years that indicate that employment—even full employment—cannot solve the problem of poverty within a free market economy, work continues to be cited as a solution to poverty, not only by experts, but by the great majority of the population. This need to blame lack of working for poverty seems to arise from deep-seated feelings about work itself.

The Mystique of Work

The concept of work underlies and overarches every aspect of modern life. If one were to search for a single paradigm that defines, shapes, directs, and bounds modern society, work is almost the only item that fits the description. On an individual basis, people are judged not only by the work they do, but also the manner in which they perform it. Work is seen as spiritually uplifting, morally desirable, and psychologically fulfilling. People who do not work, or cannot work, are seen as outside the mainstream of life. "Hard worker" is invariably an accolade, and to be branded as lazy is to wear a scarlet L for life.

Work structures time, determines attitudes, shapes self- and other-images, and permeates every aspect of human existence. The concept of work even outranks religion as a belief system, since there are organized groups of agnostics and atheists who speak out against religion, but almost nobody dares question the desirability and value of work.

From an institutional point of view, work permeates the educational system, as schools and universities are evaluated in terms of the jobs found and held by graduates. Family functioning is influenced by job status, job location, work hours and income, among other things. Economists recommend unemployment as an antidote to inflation; therapists use work as both treatment and goal; prisons use it for both punishment and rehabilitation; gerontologists urge their patients to try to keep working, and training and retraining programs (as noted) almost invariably try to prepare participants for work—never to become a better parent, a better citizen, a better neighbor, or a happier person.

Consequently, it is possible to pose the basic paradigm of modern society in one sentence: *Society needs the labor of everyone capable of working, and everyone in society needs and wants to work.*

Increasingly, however, neither of these is true. The widespread belief that societies need all the work that everyone is capable of doing, and/or that more people working harder will inevitably lead to increasing prosperity, needs to be revised as a result of continually improving technology. As it is, society cannot find a use for all the human labor available. In almost every country in the world today governments are seized with the problem of maintaining employment—or, conversely, of containing unemployment. All governmental policies are based on the need to reach full employment, even if this means definitional deceit, numerical nonsense, and statistical subterfuge. For example, Jansen and van Koppen mention how the Dutch government manipulates definitions and counting in order to reduce the perception of unemployment.[86] In order to reduce unemployment figures, unnecessary jobs are created, existing jobs are divided and the time required to do the job is stretched.

Reduction in the need for human labor is also evidenced by the continuing reduction of the workweek. In 1900 the average workweek in the United States was 53 hours, in 1979 it was 35.6 hours, in 1987 it was 34.8 hours; and in 1990 it was 34.4 hours.[87] One study found that the average employee spends three hours a week surfing the net for non-business reasons,[88] and such time wasted at work grows at the rate of about 1 percent a year.[89]

In addition, there are more holidays and longer vacations. People also enter the labor force later and leave it sooner. Indeed, increase in the length of compulsory education is seen by some as deliberate manipulation to keep people out of the labor force so as to reduce unemployment figures.[90] Recently there has been a rise in hourly working figures, but most of this comes from people who hold multiple jobs in order to get by.

Diminution in the need for human labor is squarely based on the growth of technology, in both its low and high forms. The reduction of agricultural workers in developed countries from over 80 percent to less than 5 percent is a direct effect of technology. The shift from 80 percent of workers from industry to services is a continuation of that trend, and the current reduction in the number of service workers, at least in certain sectors, also stems from the entrance of technology into the service sector.

As compared with machines, human labor is very inefficient. Changes in types or amounts of human labor are responsible for only 10 percent to 25 percent of increases in productivity, while changes in methods, materials and machines can increase productivity from 75 percent to 90 percent.[91] In one study, people were found to use only 44 percent of their potential effort at work, while machines can be geared as high as necessary.[92] In another study, not one correspondent said they used all of their possible effort at work.[93] Another study holds that in 1850 people used 13 percent of their total energy at work, and today they use less than 1 percent[94] —a direct result of labor-saving technology.

Those countries that emphasize a labor-intensive economy almost invariably experience lower living standards for their people. Thus, the ability to attain more and better products is a function of better technology, rather than harder or better human labor. There is almost nothing in demand today that is in short supply because of lack of human labor. Rather, production is deliberately limited to expected consumer demand. It is probably wise that this is done, because the Great Depression of the Thirties was—from a business point of view —a result of oversupply and lack of purchasing power, not shortage of goods.[95]

Yet, society maintains the facade that everyone's work is needed, which leads to absurd situations of make-work, feather-bedding, and gold-bricking. In short, we do not need and cannot use all the labor of everyone capable of working, and the need for human labor is being constantly reduced.

Although the almost-workless world is seen by some as utopia and by others as dystopia, many researchers assume that this will come about sooner or later as technology continues to replace workers.[96] The result will require massive re-adjustments in ideology, education and the economy, since the present system by which income is determined almost entirely by work done will not be able to maintain itself under those circumstances.

The presumed need for massive human labor is an artifact that is rapidly becoming a fossil. As has been said:

> Full employment could prove to be a nightmare. It could amount to a return to the conditions of the nineteenth century. It could mean that workers become so impoverished that they are obliged to accept work which is exhausting, soul-destroying or unsafe. It could mean the direction of labour and the loss of personal freedom.[97]

The other half of the equation—that people need and want to work—is equally untrue. Although socialized from nursery school through the university, abetted by the family, the media, the church, and every other instrument of indoctrination to see work—or to say they see work—as necessary for a healthy, happy life, people behave differently. The only constant, reliable, generalizable incentive to work is money, and even that loses its spur over time, or at a certain level.[98]

The fact that people would elect not to work if given sufficient other income is the very basis for the "wage stop"—explained below—in every welfare program. Further, every offer of early retirement with decent income is overwhelmed with responses. In the United States, where men can retire on full pensions at age 65, over 90 percent of current retirees elect to give up three year's salary and 20 percent of their pensions for life in order to retire at age 62.[99]

Nor does lack of work necessarily have deleterious consequences. Retirees who have enough money on which to live decently report themselves as happy in their retirement, glad they retired, and sorry they hadn't retired earlier. Men who retire close to their retirement ages do not report themselves as less happy than those who continue working.[100] Although 10 percent of blue-collar employees polled indicated that their health had declined after retirement, 25 percent reported health improvement.[101] Occupational stress plays an important role in 75 percent of heart disease cases and job dissatisfaction is associated with many other psychological problems.[102] Evidently there is a pragmatic basis for the popular expressions, "Blue Monday," and "Thank God It's Friday." Even the myth that not working leads to interpersonal tensions at home is confounded by the research finding that there is a positive correlation between leisure time and better marital cohesion.[103] In short, as Rudyard Kipling said, long ago, "More men [sic] are killed by overwork than the importance of the world justifies."[104]

Thus, the world does not need the labor of everyone capable of working, nor do people have any innate or psychological need to work, despite the socialization process that tries to convince them otherwise. Why, then, this continual pounding on the subject of work as needed and desirable?

One basic and understandable reason is that the present system of economics and the ideology of work operate hand-in-hand to keep the powerful, rich and greedy in place. Belief that work is necessary and desirable for both society and individuals is surely promoted by and/or derived from the interests of the corporate elites. Whole schools of business teach how to get more work from workers, and the welfare system is skewed to keep the choice of "to work or not to work" in the hands of the employing classes, who are more free to lay workers off than the employees are to quit. Were most people to realize that they benefit from only a portion of the work performed in the world, demands for change might threaten the existing structure.

It is also possible that continual emphasis on the necessity and desirability of work has lead to a widespread manifestation of the Freudian phenomenon of projection. When one has feelings of which he or she is ashamed, or are at variance with what society demands (such as not liking work, not wanting to work, and/or getting no satisfaction from work), these feelings can be repressed in the individual, and exorcised by projecting them onto others, thus making it possible to punish them instead of oneself. In short, this is a collective laying the sins of the people on the scapegoat and sending it into the desert to die. That the poor are scapegoated by the rest of society in innumerable ways is manifest throughout the entire fabric of modern society.

This may be the reason that the actual working ability of most of the poor is ignored, and why "get 'em back to work" is so vociferously espoused as an answer to poverty. But depending on employment to solve the problem of poverty is like prescribing a placebo instead of carrying out an operation.

EDUCATION AS A COP-OUT

One proposal regarding overcoming poverty is to invest more in, and make more effort toward, improved education. Although this is often put forward as a general solution to poverty, education—like many other proposals—is irrelevant to the great majority of the poor, who are the aged, the incapacitated, and (single) mothers of small children. Indeed, education is usually proposed as an antidote to unemployment, rather than poverty, on the mistaken assumption that most of the poor are unemployed, and that improved education will enhance their employment prospects.

In any case, the image of education as the panacea for either unemployment or poverty simply sidesteps the basic question discussed in the previous section on the privatization of education—to what extent education should be used to shape well-rounded, responsible, mature individuals, and to what extent to produce efficient and effective members of the economic order. Most proponents of educating the poor opt for the latter. They envision education as improving literacy, giving some basic mathematical (or, more likely, arithmetical) abilities, instilling good work habits (read: work discipline) and teaching some vocational skills. As a British expert puts it: "The overarching aim is now to provide individuals with the skills needed to participate in the labour market."[105] Rarely, if ever, do they think in terms of philosophy, history, psychology, the arts, or any other area of the humanities. In short, education for the non-poor is to broaden their horizons, to prepare them for effective citizenship and—not coincidentally—to give them a base for further education resulting in professional, academic and even business achievements. Education for the poor is to make them (better) workers.

This has not always been the case. The single most widespread educational effort ever undertaken by the American government was the GI Bill of Rights (technically, the Servicemen's Readjustment Act of 1944) that offered veterans— among other things—free university tuition and financial support while studying. The program was not limited to acquisition of basic or technical skills, or to any certain areas of study, and two-and-a-quarter million veterans took advantage of the program. It supplied America with a reservoir of engineers, teachers, scientists, doctor and dentists, as well as many other professionals and technicians.[106] It offered many of them job and career opportunities that they would not otherwise have enjoyed, and certainly kept them from joining the ranks of the poor. Current demands for educational improvements to overcome poverty have neither this vision nor these possibilities.

A good example of the manpower approach to education was the School-to-Work-Opportunities Act of 1994:

> The classroom experience was to be restructured so that students could learn how their academic subjects related to the world of work. Teachers were to work with employers to develop broad-based curriculums to help students understand the skills needed in the workplace. Teachers and students were to work in interdisciplinary teams to design projects capable of teaching both the academic subjects and their workplace relevance. Employers were to provide workplace learning opportunities in which the real-life relevance of academic subject matter could be tested, broad transferable skills could be learned, problem solving experience could be gained, and *workplace discipline* could be experienced.[107]

It is clear that the goal of the program was to make "academic" subjects relevant to the world of work. There is no evidence of a desire to use the work experience to illuminate broader areas, such as equality/inequality, democracy, citizenship or independent thinking. This was basically a proposal for vocational training in its most narrow sense, clothed with an academic veneer.

From one whose advocacy of children has been steadfast, it is surprising to hear the executive director of UNICEF, also speak of the need for "kids" to be educated to be "consumers and workers."[108] It is equally surprising to find an article in the journal of the Child Welfare League of America calling for increased funding for child-care in order to create a stable workforce.[109] It is even more surprising to realize that due to conditions imposed by the 1996 welfare reform act, many people attending university had to drop out—twenty thousand in New York City alone.[110] Evidently lawmakers don't believe their own credo that education overcomes poverty.

Speaking of vocational training, it is worth looking at the record of training and retraining courses. The failure of training courses to reduce poverty in any substantial amount is very clear. First, even proponents of training courses know that there will be no jobs for all the graduates—they are training for non-existing jobs. The jobs that do exist for the untrained require few skills, and thus fewer training courses. It requires only a few hours of instruction to hand out hamburgers at McDonalds, to guard art in a museum, to sell jeans in a mall, and for similar tasks. However, establishing such courses allows the participants to be listed as students getting subsidies instead of the unemployed drawing compensation, thus reducing the published unemployment figures.

TRAINING AS STONEWALLING

The record of training courses in training people for employment is dismal. Most published articles about this phenomenon speak about the plans, projections, methods, strategies and evaluation procedures, but few of them report the concrete results. One of the few reported results is typical of the others: In Kansas, a government program called Job Opportunities and Basic Skills (JOBS) attracted 8500 participants. Only 18.1 percent completed the course. Only 12.8 percent found full-time employment and 8.6 percent part-time work.[111] And this was during a period when unemployment was falling to record lows. From such experiences, a rule of thumb has been developed, as follows:

> Most people who begin such courses don't finish.
> Most people who finish such courses don't get jobs.
> Most people who finish such courses and get jobs don't work in the area they studied.
> Most people who get jobs in the area they studied make less money and suffer worse conditions than in the job they had before the course.[112]

As one example of the failure of training courses, it has been noted that actually working results in more skill development than do training courses in terms of short-run gains.[113] In 1984, to cite another instance, 1.2 million workers received basic trade readjustment benefits to train themselves for new jobs. Only seventy thousand of these undertook such training, and only twenty-eight thousand finished the training. Of these, less than forty-five hundred found jobs using their new skills.[114]   A study of a Federal job training program called the Job Training Partnership Act found that those who had enrolled in the program earned 8 percent *less* than those given no training.[115] The program was labeled a "dud" by those who studied it.[116]   Training programs in general have been found to be "no easy solution for the poverty program."[117] Despite all the hoopla about retraining unemployed workers, the failure of training programs to reduce unemployment seems to be recognized by those in charge, since in January, 2002, the government's support for training programs was cut drastically although unemployment was rising.[118]

In any case, not only is education as a solution to poverty highly questionable, but attempts to raise educational levels as an antidote to poverty are more like pious hopes than practical attainments. For example, in an attempt to improve the school attendance of children from poor families, Wisconsin instituted "Learnfare," a program that financially penalized welfare families for their children's truancy. (Notice that non-welfare families were not penalized). Similarly, Ohio instituted the LEAP program that offered payments for good school attendance and fines for truancy (also only for welfare recipients). The programs increased attendance only marginally, but "a significant number of all mothers in the study reported diminished spending on essentials for their families, especially clothing and food."[119]   In other words, the program increased poverty.

In Britain, efforts to establish targets for schools in terms of grades has been attacked on the basis that "schools would be forced to concentrate their efforts on the more able pupils, at the expense of low-achievers."[120]

In fact, efforts to decrease poverty by increasing educational attainments are clear examples of putting the cart before the horse. It is not that lack of education causes poverty—it is poverty that leads to lack of education. Children raised in an atmosphere of hard-scrabbling to stay fed, tension caused by uncertainty, denial of extra-curricular activities, and lack of successful role models would be paragons indeed if they overcame these problems through devotion to their studies. Turkey, for example, attributes the poverty of its people to lack of education, although it is more true that lack of education comes from poverty. Turkey spends $200 a year per student, whereas industrial countries spend an average of $3,850.[121] Is it any wonder that the level of education in Turkey is low? Consequently, it is no surprise that research has found, "a general underlying factor, related to poverty, that contributes substantially to differences in school performance."[122]

Distance-learning, long-distance-learning and the globalization of education[123] (to use almost synonymous terms) is being viewed in some quarters as the rising star of social development, as top-level teachers, interesting material and new methods of instruction become available through communications technology. There is little doubt that this trend offers enormous potential for the spread of certain areas of education. It can even be envisioned as making traditional methods and structures (including the physical structure of schoolhouses and universities) unnecessary.

However, just as every solution creates a problem, so there is a downside to this globalization of education. If it were to really take off throughout the educational systems of the world, unemployment among teachers would become a problem, as would the production of educational materials—books, desks, blackboards, etc.

More importantly, insofar as taking advantage of this movement means having access to communications technology, the poor—as usual—are left out. People living on a hundred dollars a year, or a dollar a day, or at or under the poverty line of most countries, are far from being able to access such educational opportunities. They will, in fact, slip further behind those who have the necessary resources to exploit distance education.

There is also the fact that distance learning lends itself to profit-motivated dishonesty. Insofar as higher education is concerned, there has lately developed—

–as mentioned previously—a booming business in correspondence, overseas, internet and limited-attendance courses, thick with MBAs and replete with Ph.D.s. Some of these are extended through well-respected universities of long standing, but the great bulk seem to be offered by little known institutions and—it is feared— by so-called universities established for just this purpose, leading to what has been described as "diploma inflation."

Many magazines with overseas subscribers are replete with offers of such easily-acquired college degrees. "Branches" of several overseas universities were established in Israel, and "graduates," who had often spent considerable sums for their so-called studies, were chagrined to find that their "degrees" were not recognized by academic accrediting bodies, and therefore not by potential employers, or by employers who pay bonuses or higher salaries to workers with scholastic degrees. In fact, the flood of such offers brought about a requirement that such advertisers specify "not accredited" in their ads. In the meantime, a spate of criminal investigations is turning up top-level administrators—among others—who did not write their own required papers and tests, and even did not pay their own tuition in exchange for touting a particular distant university.

The primary appeal of such educational businesses is to overseas students, often from countries in which higher education is difficult to attain due to scholastic or financial constraints. Entrance into the modern business world requires accreditation, and market forces are quicker to respond to such demands than is the academic world. Mason makes the same point in speaking of courses offered in countries around the Pacific Rim:

Some are outright cons; others are just poor quality; many are 'sold' for high prices which are then used to defray the deficit incurred by students taught face-to-face in the home institution.[124]

Not incidentally, it should be noted that the move toward globalization of education is not fueled by concerns about ignorance, illiteracy, or disadvantages. As Mason points out, "The most critical factor forcing administrators and policy makers to look to global markets (is) as a way of making up for falling government revenues and falling numbers of traditional learners."[125]

Although income from employment tends to rise with increased education, this is of little help to most of the poor who are in the labor market. Since a sizeable portion of the poverty-stricken population consists of women and minorities, who face discrimination barriers to advancement, increased basic education would be of little avail for these groups; the jobs they would acquire would in all likelihood still be entry-level (read: poorly paid) temporary and part-time work. As indicated in the above section on the working poor, the extent that such jobs would lift them above the poverty threshold—especially if they have dependents—is very slim. A large survey of the results of training programs finds that "even the most recently conceived education and training programs, and especially those targeted at young teen-age mothers, have simply not been effective in raising their earnings capacity, reducing fertility, or reducing the welfare caseloads."[126]

One expert holds that acquisition of a high school education would improve an income about 30 percent.[127] That sounds impressive, but if the full-time year-round worker mentioned above, who makes $826 per month, were to increase his or her earnings by 30 percent, they would still be beneath the poverty line if he or she were the breadwinner for a spouse and two children.

Even those who attain higher education are not necessarily better off. Egypt has made tremendous efforts to improve the educational system, and every year twenty thousand new lawyers are graduated—only to join the pool of what has been called "the educated poor."[128] Similarly, it has been reported that "The state of Kerala (in India) is threatened with an ever-increasing rate of educated unemployment."[129] Finally, it has been pointed out that,"The United States has a higher proportion of its population receiving tertiary education than almost any other country, yet has the highest levels of labor market inequalities among the developed economies."[130]

Given the ideological, economic and structural factors outlined in this book, increased education for the poverty-stricken populations would, at best, lead to a better educated group of poor people, perhaps with more resentment concerning their lot than previously. Positing education as a solution to poverty is as useless as aspirin in place of heart surgery.

SOCIAL WELFARE: MORE HOLES THAN NET

Every solution creates a problem.
Anonymous

The single, most meaningful and far-reaching measure to ensure the welfare of the American population, and particularly vulnerable people within it, was the Social Security Act of 1935. This act established a pension plan for the elderly; compensation to various groups of the incapacitated, including the blind; aid to dependent children; compensation for the unemployed and some supplementary programs. At a later date medical services for the aged were added.

There were three major motivations for the original Social Security Act. One was purely political. Dr. Francis E. Townsend, in California, had put forward a plan to pay all people over sixty years old two hundred dollars a month, provided they spent it within the month. This plan attracted such widespread support, especially among the elderly—an estimated ten million voters—that not only did its supporters become a formidable political force, but they elected a number of Congressmen pledged to the plan. Other politicians, like Huey Long in Louisiana, with his "every man a king" platform, were seen as similar political threats, and Social Security was—in part—a preemptive political tactic of Franklin D. Roosevelt to undermine the opposition.[131]

There was another motive, which was economic. In the throes of the Great Depression with incomes down, consumer spending very weak, and unemployment growing, governments viewed putting money into hands that would presumably spend it rather than invest it—the unemployed and the elderly—as one means to slow, if not stop, the downward spiral.

Finally, there was a genuine humanitarian motive to Social Security—to safeguard the elderly from plunging into penury when they retired (or were retired) from the workforce, and to tide workers over from one job to another. However, it is doubtful whether altruism alone would have created social security without the other elements, since most welfare provisions arise from considerations that have little to do with humanitarianism. For example, the Food-Stamp program in the United States was not instituted to reduce hunger, but to reduce surplus stockpiles of agricultural products that were depressing farmers' incomes.[132] In fact, the original Act begins, "An Act to strengthen the agricultural economy..."[133] In Israel, unemployment insurance was introduced as an anti-inflationary measure—that is, to soak up income from working people.[134] Vocational training and retraining programs, as mentioned above, are used to re-classify the unemployed as students getting stipends, thus reducing the unemployment rate, and public works programs and public service programs are often used to keep the unemployed quiet and out of sight.[135]

There had been previous insurance-type social security programs, notably in Austria in 1854 and in Germany in 1882,[136] and by the mid-nineties the number had grown to include 178 countries, 78 percent of then-extant countries and territories.[137] The Social Security program had far-reaching ramifications in the United States. In 1999 Social Security provided more than half the total income for a majority of its beneficiaries and the lowest income quintile gets 82 percent of its income from Social Security.[138] Nevertheless, 9 percent of beneficiaries remain poor with their Social Security support, and this figure rises to 23 percent among Americans of African descent beneficiaries.[139] Even the Supplementary Security Income program, which adds to the income of the elderly and disabled, reaches only about half of those who are eligible.[140] Given the fact that some social insurance programs are well over a century old, and that American Social Security is over sixty-five years old, why does any poverty, especially among those who were to be protected, still exist?

Coverage

The major reason why social security programs throughout the world have not been able to wipe out poverty—even among the groups they were designed to assist—has both ideological and economic roots, and can be summed up as the work-welfare link.[141] In the vast majority of countries and in the bulk of social insurance programs, coverage is restricted to people who have worked, are working, or have paid premiums into the program (which almost always means having worked). Of the 172 existing social insurance programs throughout the world, 87 percent of the old age programs are only for workers; 91 percent of cash sickness and maternity benefits have specified work requirements; as do 65 percent of family and children's allowances programs. Obviously, 100 percent of unemployment and workers' disability programs are for workers only. Many of these programs specify "employees," "workers," "wage earners," or some such phrase, as the exclusive beneficiaries of the program.

However, not even all of those who are working or have worked are included in the programs. Many programs specifically exclude farm workers, transient workers, household workers, illegal immigrants and part-time workers.[142] The linkage of social security programs to work is almost immutable. The figures given above are virtually unchanged since those reported in 1977.[143]

As a consequence of these provisions -- programs only for workers, vestedness requirements, and premium payments—people who have never worked for pay, do not work, or are not working regularly, are left out of the program's covered population. This usually penalizes housewives, those unable to work due to a physical or mental handicap, those unable to find work despite their own best efforts either due to personal deficiencies (illiteracy), social inequalities (race) or economic factors (no available work), mothers (often single) of small children, and those taking care of the ill and incapacitated.[144]

Social security is also of no help to people working at salaries too low to support them. In Britain, the number of people working for substandard wages has increased from 8 million to 9.4 million since 1979.

Vestedness

It is not enough, however, to be a worker. One must also have worked long enough in a job covered by the programs, and in some cases to have earned enough, to be eligible for payments. The qualifying period of work for old-age programs, for example, varies throughout the world from 5 years to 45 years, averaging around 15 years.[145]

Insofar as health insurance is concerned, generally a recipient must be gainfully employed at the time when he or she becomes ill, in addition to having a record of sufficiently long employment.

As a consequence of such restrictions, many people who have worked only sporadically, involuntarily ceased working due to illness or lack of employment opportunities, performed mostly part-time work, or who are not working at the time of application gain little or no benefits from social security programs. In this respect, social insurance programs are highly regressive: those who have worked regularly throughout their prime years, especially those who were well-rewarded for their work, tend to receive larger payments for longer periods than those who have had difficulty working all their lives and, as a consequence, may be in greater need.

Administrative Regulations

There are also administrative regulations that are linked to the world of work. In Israel, as noted previously, an unemployed laborer must report in person to the employment office three times a week to remain eligible for compensation. In Burundi, allowances are reduced by half if recipients work less than four hours a day. Many countries have waiting periods before payments begin—periods during which there often is no compensation at all. Generally, these periods are intended to ascertain that the person is really not working and to discourage repeated applications, even if they are legitimate. There are also countries that limit the amount of time one may draw compensation—after that time the person is declared "unemployable," and thus thrust out of the labor force (and unemployment figures). In the United States unemployment benefits generally cease after a 26 week period, although due to the recession, efforts have been made to increase this by 13 more weeks.[146]

Not only are payments linked to work, but in some countries one is not even considered unemployed until a period of time without work has passed. And then, if one remains unemployed beyond a given period, one is no longer eligible for payment, being declared "unfit for employment," or "out of the labor market." It has been humorously suggested that by lengthening the waiting time and shortening the time until people are declared out of the labor market until the two meet, unemployment as a statistic could be completely wiped out.[147]

"Wage Stop"

The impact of these limitations on social security programs is great, but even so they pale beside the effect of the so-called "wage stop." This regulation makes it certain that almost no one can receive from social security programs what he or she could presumably earn if they were working. The assumption, of course, is that people will not work if they can get the same amount of money by not working that they could by work. Thus, throughout the world, benefit payments are generally determined as a percentage, often a very small percentage, of wages: average, median, past, going, sectoral or minimum wages. And, due to the various restrictions attached to eligibility, only 40 percent of unemployed Americans receive compensation today—this compares with 55 percent in the 1950s.[148]

Throughout the world, unemployment benefits pay only 40 percent to 75 percent of the average wage.[149] In the United States, unemployment benefits are 35.3 percent of the weekly average wage (down from 37 percent at the start of the 90s)[150] and the average old-age pension paid to single persons is less than the legal minimum wage.[151] The same situation of "wage stop" applies to the majority of programs in most countries.

The widespread assumption that higher welfare payments lead to less work effort is belied, in the case of unemployment benefits, by the fact that the relative generosity of benefits within the European Union and the prevailing unemployment rates in 1993 shows no correlation between the two. There are countries with generous benefit systems that have both high and low rates of unemployment. Vice versa, countries with modest benefit systems can have high and low rates of unemployment.[152]

Social insurance programs, which are presumed to protect populations against some of the most common exigencies of life, provide at best minimum care for most people and no care at all for large groups—children, those who have never worked, and many part-time and temporary workers. Furthermore, the widespread assumption that social insurance programs adequately protect the total population leads to neglecting reforms of these programs and militates against creating additional ones.

It is not surprising, therefore, that poverty in most of the western industrialized countries varies between 10 percent and 15 percent of the population, according to their own definitions, and has done so since the advent of widespread social insurance programs. In some countries—notably developing countries moving from an agricultural-based to an industrial-based economy—the percentage of the population in poverty can be much higher. In the United States, despite a widespread social security program, poor people were no better off in the 1980s than they were in the 1960s and 1970s (Littman, 1989). In the year 2001, income support as compared to average earnings was at the lowest level in twenty years in Great Britain.[153] In the United States the safety net for families with children in which the adults were unable to work provided less than it has for decades.[154] In both countries, the economy was not only not in a recession, but said to be booming.

Although Social Security is one of the largest social welfare programs, it is, in essence, an insurance type program. There are many other programs that are so-called grant programs. They undoubtedly help many of the people for whom they are targeted, but usually do little to actually raise them out of poverty. For example, child support raises only 6 percent of poor families above the poverty line; social security accounts for another 4 percent, and welfare another 6 percent.[155]

Part of the reason for this situation is the Catch-22 of social welfare. When countries are prosperous, there is a widespread feeling that anyone who wants a job can get one, and that if people remain poor under such conditions it is because they are not really trying to change their condition—and therefore they shouldn't be pampered. When the economy weakens, budget cuts and falling tax revenue offer excuses as to why more can't be done on the welfare front and why—in fact—there must be cuts in the costs. To repeat, when we need it we can't afford it and when we can afford it, we don't need it.

An outstanding example of Catch 22 took place in the state of Georgia in 2002. In 1999,

The Legislature suspended the unemployment insurance tax

for thousands of businesses (due to robust employment figures) with few effects on the needy. But today, with tens of thousands of unemployed Georgians making do with $230 in average weekly jobless benefits and two-thirds of the state's 170,000 unemployed people not even qualifying for benefit, legislators may have to choose between restoring the tax and making the benefits even smaller.[156]

Another reason that social welfare programs do not eliminate poverty arises from the fact that in order to get a program accepted, many voters who are not poor need to be appeased to get their political support.[157] Benefits may therefore be extended to the non-poor as well. It has been estimated that from 64 percent to 88 percent of social welfare programs go to the non-poor—a phenomenon now referred to as "leakage", [158] though initially such universality had served to dispel the possibility of being shamed as a benefit recipient. In many countries, for each unit of currency disbursed to a poor person by a social assistance program, seven units go to the non-poor.[159]

Retirement Programs

Turning to retirement programs under various social security plans, the problem facing all such programs—governmental, fraternal or private—is how to maintain payments to growing groups of recipients for longer than anticipated periods of time. This will probably become more difficult, since no life insurance or pension program in the world was or is actuarially based on the anticipation of people living to age eighty or more, and the fastest growing group of the aged are those over eighty-five. The average retiree already collects benefits for about a third of his or her life.[160] There has already been a 5 percent reduction in the value of old age pensions for new retirees in Japan.[161] In the United States, smaller and smaller proportions of payments are going to the oldest and poorest recipients, due to the increase in single heads of households who do not qualify for spousal and survivors benefits, and due to the fact that people are living longer and retiring earlier.[162] Apropos, a Polish journalist wrote, albeit jocularly, that the average Pole does his last duty to the state by dying soon after going into retirement.[163]

The simplest solution for the economic problem of retirement programs would be to raise the retirement age considerably, or to eliminate it entirely. However, this proposal runs head-on into one of the major and most intractable problems facing modern governments—that of unemployment. If older persons remain at work, job opportunities for younger people are proportionately limited. It is for this reason that the United States government—which for some time has been seized of the problem of the liquidity of Social Security in the future—has responded by gradually lengthening the age at which pensions will be paid—but by only two years, and that long in the future.

As Gal points out, changes in social security systems will probably take the form of new non-means tested and non-contributory benefits for new groups of beneficiaries, the introduction of more stringent eligibility conditions for existing programs and a greater dependence upon private markets.[164] Means-testing may be introduced for the elderly, especially for those at higher income levels.

It is more likely that pension payments will be reduced, as that is the easiest method of dealing with the problem, despite its political ramifications.

Such reductions may not come under the guise of cuts in payments, but in reductions in cost-of-living allowances, payments made later, and more stringent requirements for payment. As it is today, almost 90 percent of social security programs for the elderly throughout the world are only for workers.[165] The failure of social welfare programs to eliminate poverty is not new, of course. A study of the effect of public welfare over time concluded that:

> "Most programs and services benefited the middle and upper classes and corporations. Analysis of private welfare also illustrates that program services and benefits are targeted at the non-poor population."[166]

As regards social security as it exists, the rise in absolute and relative poverty from 1994 to 2000 noted in Sri Lanka is directly related to decreases in government transfer payments.[167]

For all of the reasons mentioned above, Social Security can be seen as a great help to many people who have reasonable work records throughout their lives, and of some help to those with spotty work records, but given its limitations and regulations, it operates in great measure to guarantee that hosts of people will be poor in their older years. Certainly, as a panacea for poverty it has been weighed in the balance and found wanting.

Welfare Reform as Persecuting the Poor

Beginning with the Reagan administration in the United States and the Thatcher regime in Britain, there have been determined efforts on national, regional and municipal levels to "reform" the welfare system. This obviously does not mean increasing grants to the poor, advising people of the programs available to them, reaching-out to those who are not taking full advantage of benefits, improving physical or personnel conditions in welfare offices, or finding full-time well-paying permanent jobs for the unemployed. Indeed, rather than adding to individuals' welfare, Catastrophic Health Insurance was repealed in 1989—the only retraction of a social insurance program in American history.

Basically the efforts for so-called welfare reform consisted of putting a time limit on the periods during which social welfare payments would be made, in order to get recipients to move into employment. If no "real" employment was available, the authorities were to make work for recipients to do. The results of this move were forecast by every unbiased scientist who looked at both the composition of the poverty population and the requirements of the job market. A typical projection said: "The transformation of welfare into work is likely to be the transformation of welfare into unemployment and cause earnings so low as once to have been thought unacceptable for fellow citizens."[168]

Demonstration projects along the Welfare to Work lines were conducted in the 1980s by the Manpower Demonstration Research Corporation. They found that the largest increase in earnings for successful participants averaged $415 per year. When the loss of cash benefits was figured in, the *largest* increase in net income was, as they put it, "a negligible $263," or about 3 percent of the poverty line for a three person family at that time.[169] Another study of women leaving welfare for work found that less than a third of them had higher incomes than they did on welfare.[170]

The payment periods began to end in early 2002, and scattered results are already in. There is no question but that welfare rolls have been cut—estimates vary from 50 percent to over 60 percent. However, from 1996 through 2000 the poverty rate has been reduced by only 14 percent.[171] If the basis for welfare reform is correct, it seems that the poverty rate should have decreased by 50 percent to 60 percent, but this is not what happened. In fact, "the proportion of Americans living in poverty rose significantly" in 2001.[172]

What has happened to the people thus denied welfare payments is not encouraging. Between 20 percent and 30 percent of those who left welfare needed to return to the program, and a third of all former recipients had poor physical or mental health. Of those who are working, the median hourly wages in 1999 dollars are slightly above seven dollars. Taking all sources of income into account, including Earned Income Tax Credits, the median in 1999 dollars is $1,151. This is almost exactly the poverty line for a family of three. Thus, one half of the families who left welfare for work were still below the line, and one half above (but how much above the median doesn't indicate).[173] Seen differently: During the prosperous times that followed the 1996 beginning of the welfare reform program, "the average income of all single parents and of welfare clients in particular declined. After welfare reform, the poorest 20 percent of single-parent families, typically families who had left welfare, *lost* an average of $577 a year."[174]

Applications for public assistance in New York rose from 15,000 in June, 2002, to 19,000 in July. Average monthly applications for 2002 are also up by about 800 people over the monthly average in 2001. In 2001, 26 states had rising caseloads. The use of food stamps in ten major urban areas studied rose from June, 2001, to June, 2002, in every area except New York. Anecdotal evidence is also contained in the fact of "swelling lines at food pantries and housing shelters."[175]

One result is that policies which were intended to help people in times of distress have become punitive programs that punish them for not bowing to the dictates of the economy (read: job market). The effect of "workfare" (welfare reform's mask) on people has been clearly outlined by Krinsky:

> "Workfare workers are caught in the middle between welfare and work...Welfare workers are not paid a wage, but have their hours set by dividing their total benefits by the minimum wage. This means that the City government—in whose agencies most workfare workers work—does not have to pay unemployment benefits for dismissed workfare workers, does not have to make social security contributions for them, pay payroll taxes for them, and does not have to collectively bargain with their elected representatives (where these exist). Because Workfare workers are cast as *compensating the city* for the benefits they receive, rather than as being compensated by the (considerable) work they do for the city, they are also unable to claim their income as 'earned,' and are ineligible for the Earned Income Tax Credit that has lifted many poor working families above the federal poverty level...the City can send workfare workers where it wants without having to answer to the workers.[176]

Social workers find themselves neglecting personal and relationship problems in order to prepare people for jobs (or so-called training courses); locating possible jobs; and coercing people to work, often for less than their welfare grants would be. "Increasingly, welfare policy is becoming labor market policy,"[177] and social workers, many of whom likely entered the profession with a view to helping people, must now play the role of enforcers of the systemic attacks upon the poorest.

A typical example: Of 9,509 people sent to clean up subways and subway platforms in New York in 1999, 4,400 showed up. The program was designed to move the workfare recipients into real jobs as they gained experience, and as employers realized that they needed these jobs done. Of the four thousand plus who worked in the New York subways, only 301 were eventually hired, and of these, only 122 by the subway system. This was said to compare favorably with other workfare sites in the city. [178] If so, the four-part record of training programs, listed above, could equally well apply to workfare efforts. Stoesz sums up by saying that welfare reform has "offered most of the welfare poor little more than an opportunity to join the ranks of the working poor."[179] Schorr says that welfare reform simply shifts people from "parsimonious government support to parsimonious employer wages."[180]

It is, incidentally, worth noting that the kinds of jobs designated for welfare recipients who cannot find real employment—that is, cleaning subways, streets, parks, etc.—are the same kinds of jobs that criminals sentenced to community service perform. The similarity between criminals and welfare recipients is present, if not purposive.

The new welfare arrangements attempt to go beyond overcoming income poverty—they also involve trying to change family structure as regards marriage and child-bearing, and personal habits. For example, unwed mothers younger than eighteen must live with an adult relative, or attend school, or have a high school diploma, in order to receive aid.[181] Welfare reform is said to contain "a sermon about premarital sex" and an attempt to "push unwed mothers into marriage."[182] It is therefore undoubtedly discouraging for the welfare reformers to learn that replacing welfare with work in Iowa and Connecticut has been found to discourage marriage significantly. If this is true of the entire country, then about a quarter-million women would not be getting married in any one year.[183]

On a general basis, one of the efforts of welfare reform is to move from universal programs, such as social security, to "targeted" programs designed for special groups of clients. As those most in need are targeted, they must prove by their behavior, personal attributes and compliance that they are worthy of help. This is a return to the old English Poor Law which distinguished between the deserving and the undeserving poor.[184]

Even those portions of social welfare that are not being "reformed" act to perpetuate the situation of the poor. Take, for example, Medicaid, which is intended to provide medical care for those who cannot afford it themselves. Although the program covers prescription drugs in every state, one-fourth of patients in the program could not afford the drugs prescribed—a figure that approximates the proportion of persons with no health insurance.[185]

Has welfare reform decreased poverty? In 1999, three years after the beginnings of welfare reform, the poverty rate was 11.8 percent. In 1979, twenty years earlier, it was 11.7 percent. Further, while from 1992 to date welfare rolls dropped almost 50 percent, poverty numbers dropped only 22 percent.[186]

Few of the jobs found by welfare leavers pay decent salaries, and few of them provide benefits. Only 23 percent receive employer-sponsored health insurance, and fewer of those who are eligible participate in Medicaid, food stamps, or child care assistance. One-third of welfare leavers report "having to cut meal size or skip meals, and nearly 40 percent report problems paying rent, mortgage or utility bills."[187]   This is reform?

Earned Income Tax Credit (EITC)

As part of efforts to "reform" welfare, a program called Earned Income Tax Credit (EITC) was instituted. Under this program, anyone whose employment income falls below a designated level is entitled to supplemental income from the government. The results were predictable: For American children under age eighteen the EITC netted only 1.2 percent increase in disposable income, and a modest reduction (15 percent) in child poverty. One reason for this disappointing result is the extremely limiting aspects of EITC, which is available only to working parents. A person at home with children and not working is not entitled to benefits. This excludes many children whose parents are unemployed or doing minimal work. Indeed, two-thirds of children in extreme poverty (below 50 percent of the poverty line) are not helped by EITC at all.[188]   Bird says flatly: "EITC is an inefficient security program. Dollar for dollar it provides less security than traditional means-tested transfers."[189]   In May, 2001, the child tax credit was doubled—from $500 to $1000 *per year*. And even this niggardly amount is refundable only for families making more than $10,000.[190]   As can be seen, such programs are based on the usual misapprehension that most of the poor are in the work force (which they aren't), and on a desire to encourage work efforts. In England, too, working families tax credits are—obviously—only for workers, but in this case they do not get additional cash from the government, but have the credit deducted from their taxes.[191]   Clearly, if they don't make enough to pay taxes, the program has no meaning for them.

Leaving EITC and returning to the record of welfare reform as a whole, figures are available for both Wisconsin and California. In the former, three years after leaving welfare most of the families were still earning significantly below the poverty line, despite the "extremely strong Wisconsin economy."[192]   In California, after six years, average earnings were still far below the poverty line, despite the "strong California economy."[193]   Even taking into consideration other family income, five years after leaving welfare 40.5 percent of the women had incomes below the poverty line.[194]   In summary, it is clear that the earnings of people leaving welfare for work frequently do not emerge from poverty even after several years of such work—and these data are from periods and locales when and where the economy was very strong.

The entire welfare reform movement was instituted during a period when economic strength was great and unemployment was at record lows. Suddenly, the economy became depressed and unemployment began rising inexorably. Has the welfare reform movement been reversed, or even slowed? In no way. The only solutions offered have been to extend the period of unemployment benefits somewhat (but not welfare payments), and to wait for the economy to recover (which for the poor would only put things back on the terrible basis that they had been before the recession).

In addition to actually creating poverty, welfare reform offered the government a more active role in controlling the lives of the poor. In February, 2002, President Bush announced a plan to try to promote marriage (among the poor).[195]   Given that the divorce rate in America hovers around 50 percent, one would think that was a problem of at least equal intensity, but divorce costs the government little money, while out-of-wedlock weddings result in non-working mothers.

Welfare reform also contributes to homelessness. Requests for emergency shelter for families rose 5 percent in the year 2000, a period of high prosperity.[196]

The basic problem has been that getting people into employment does not necessarily mean getting them out of poverty. People leaving welfare for work generally get wages that pay between $6 and $8 an hour, which is below the income needed to bring a family of three out of poverty. Even those who remain employed for as long as three years experience no significant gain in wages.[197]

In short, success in welfare reform means people working "in jobs without public assistance and with incomes above the poverty line," which as been described as "impossible."[198]

ENTREPRENEURSHIP: STARTING UP AND SHUTTING DOWN

> *"It's so American to start one's own business."*
> Anne McDonnell Ford

One proposed solution to the problem of poverty that keeps surfacing from time to time may be called entrepreneurship. Under this rubric it is proposed that the poor overcome their problem by starting businesses, engaging in producing and selling handicrafts, or providing services to their neighbors for pay. Indeed, it is often argued that income from such self-employment would be even more profitable than the wages the poor could command as workers. However, research has indicated that the latter is not true. Not only does census income data overstate the incomes of the self-employed, but careful statistical studies have "demolished the assumption that self-employment was always superior to wage employment in respect to income."[199] Nor is self-employment even for lower incomes a very successful endeavor.

For example, in the late nineteen seventies, the lower end of Columbus Avenue in Manhattan underwent a short-lived gentrification. Close to the wealthy area around Lincoln Center, it suddenly blossomed with sidewalk cafes, beauty salons, pet shops, florist shops, fruit and vegetable stores, souvenir stores and specialty shops (usually "shoppes"). Most of these ventures were Mom-and-Pop (Joan and Darby, in the British parlance) operations, started with little capital in low-rent premises. This phenomenon was welcomed and glorified by the media and by some politicians and social planners as the solution to the problem of poverty. It spoke of initiative, enterprise, risk-taking—all of the elements of successful capitalism. Unfortunately, within five years over 50 percent of the stores were out of business, usually through bankruptcy, often due to rising rents. Such enterprises, with little capital and often requiring large loans, are very susceptible to economic changes. As Bernstein says, "When the economy sneezes, these people catch pneumonia."[200] Others have found, not surprisingly, that this kind of entrepreneurial effort is helped by—if not dependent upon—coming from a background of some wealth,[201] and consequently is of little comfort or help to the poor. A survey of a broad array of microcredit programs (almost always designed to encourage entrepreneurship) in California found that the number of clients served by the programs is very limited and none of the programs are close to attaining financial sustainability.[202] Another study found that it required an average of nine years before business earnings were enough to bring such entrepreneurs off welfare.[203]

Almost all research on micro enterprise programs report results in terms of pride, empowerment, sense of achievement, and even self-actualization. One large-scale study at a California resource center for women (Mi Casa Resource Center) found that these results were achievable. However, "the stated aim of micro enterprise development is almost always…economic independence, increased income, (and) economic freedom. In this sense, the …program at Mi Casa has serious problems."[204]

A rather general observation arising from accounts of entrepreneurship in developing countries indicates that this is almost entirely within the informal sector, not only as street-corner or door-to-door selling of local products and/or handiworks, but often as barter. To expect such efforts to raise large numbers of people out of poverty is entirely unrealistic.

Microloans

Such anecdotal evidence deters neither theories nor proposals for so-called bootstrap efforts. A recent example of such thinking is exhibited by Stoesz, who reports positively on the success of microloans in developing countries as helping people leave the rolls of the poor.[205] One might have some question about who really benefits from these enterprises, since Friedman reports, enthusiastically, that such microloans are extended at 4 percent to 5 percent monthly interest.[206] This, compounded, becomes more than 50 percent a year. Weber also reports 20 percent, 30 percent, and 40 percent interest on microloans.[207] This is not only outright usury—even the Mafia would be pleased to loan money at such rates (and probably does).

There have been successful microloan plans, such as the Grameen Bank in Bangladesh, which deals primarily with rural people. However, even this plan, when tried in Comilla, India, "missed the poorest" and was not replicable.[208] When formal-sector lenders increased their share of the lending market, their loans reached only a small proportion and provided much smaller amounts per person than for the non-poor.[209]

In the final analysis concerning microloans to poor people as an anti-poverty program, there is very little published evidence as to how many of them are actually raised out of poverty, and for how long, by such measures. Most microloan evaluations done in the United States lack comparisons with control groups, and do not include cost-benefit analyses. Almost all of them are based on a few non-random cases and often on anecdotal evidence.[210] One international study found that of two hundred programs, only seven served significant numbers of welfare recipients.[211] In Israel, following ancient traditions, there are numerous free loan funds offered by various religious groups. The best-known and best-funded secular effort is the Israel Free Loan Association. This does not, however, have much impact on poverty, since not only is the ability to repay an *a priori* condition of the loan, but—as the founder of the fund says—"We will not approve a loan to someone who earns less than the minimum wage or who is on welfare."[212]

Many evaluations of microloan programs report on how long the programs themselves lasted, rather than the effect of poor people. In a large-scale survey in California, 27 out of 87 initially identified programs were no longer in existence after a few years.[213]

The microfinance dead-end has been summarized by Cohn as follows:

> Many defenders of microfinance give the impression that it can help the poor climb out of poverty and raise their living standards. Clearly the real world is not so simple…overselling the benefits

of microfinance can raise unrealistic expectations and create disillusionment...Microfinance may help move persons from casual labor to self-employment, but has little effect on alleviating poverty.[214]

Even on a much wider level, the success of local enterprise in reducing poverty is very disappointing. In 1995 Shell set out to prove that it cared for the people who lived in its production areas. It poured more than $150 million dollars into local development schemes. Three years later a report on the project makes depressing reading. Having looked at 82 of the 408 projects on Shell's books, a commission found that less than a third have been successful.[215] As a method of moving people from the unemployment roles, microloans have severe limitations. A study by the Aspen Institute found that in the United States it costs about $4,000 for every job created.[216] Given the number of American unemployed, the total sum that would be necessary to reduce that number appreciably would be formidable.

In short, as a solution to the ubiquitous problem of poverty, entrepreneurship would be as effective as the old (and politically incorrect) saw about the women of Ireland managing financially by taking in each other's washing. Nevertheless, the seductive myth that microenterprises will eliminate poverty continues to be promulgated, even by serious social planners who should know better.[217]

NATIONAL AND INTERNATIONAL EFFORTS AS SHAMS

"If a free society cannot help the many who are poor,
it cannot save the few who are rich."
John F. Kennedy

What is the record of national and international efforts to wipe out—or to ameliorate—poverty? One study looked at the effectiveness of child support payments, social insurance and welfare among mother-only families in 1995, and found that all of this combined raised less than 6 percent of the mothers over the poverty line.[218] Perhaps even more revealing are the figures from the U.S. Bureau of the Census: In 1996, over thirty-six million Americans were living under the poverty line. In the year 2000, over thirty-one million were still under the poverty line.[219] This means that with all of the anti-poverty programs, including welfare reform that began in 1996, less than 7 percent of the poor had been raised even slightly above the poverty line. Obviously a rate of about 2 percent a year would require over fifty years to wipe out poverty—not an encouraging forecast.

A number of reports from organizations like the World Trade Organization, the International Monetary Fund and the World Bank indicate progress in relieving poverty, although most of these focus on the developing world, where poverty is so deep that even a minor effort can result in some improvement. However, since so many of the reports concerning poverty reduction are written by organizations engaged in the process, one must read the reports with special pleading kept in mind.[220] For example, the outgoing Director-General of the World Trade Organization said that the motivation of the organization was the people it served, but it has been pointed out that in countries like India, where agricultural policy has been geared to being self-sufficient in food, the very same WTO presses for markets to be open, which causes local agriculture to be destroyed by big foreign food producers.[221]

It is also notable that few of the reports of such organizations actually provide financial data on the end results of poverty-reduction efforts. They speak in terms of empowerment, feelings of community, expanding social opportunities, building organizations, grassroots capacity, and so forth. It is assumed that these will reduce poverty, but the assumption is rarely tested.[222]

Would it actually be possible to wipe out poverty, at least in an absolute sense, if governments really wanted to do so and were willing to pay the price? One authority has determined that achieving universal access to basic social services—education, health, nutrition, reproductive health, family planning, safe water and sanitation—although not resolving income poverty—would cost about $40 billion per year. "That is less than what Europeans spend on cigarettes, and one tenth of the world trade in illegal drugs."[223] Similarly, about $84 billion would be needed to eliminate income poverty in the United States. This is about 1 percent of the Gross Domestic Product,[224] and compares with the fact that Americans spend about $60 billion a year on personal beauty products, while in the United Kingdom over a billion pounds sterling is spent each year on pet food.[225]

By comparison, the United States is engaged in a program to spend $56 billion (in 1998 dollars) on submarines, which—according to a reputable research institute—are not needed.[226] One *Seawolf* submarine alone costs $2.4 billion, and as one observer remarks, "The truth of the *Seawolf* matter seems to be that not even the Navy wants it. It's Congress that wants it because it makes jobs. The old name for this was 'boondoggle'."[227] The *Seawolf* project was cancelled after three submarines had been built, in favor of a new version called the New Attack Submarine (NSSN) which cost only $1.5 billion each. It is planned to cut the submarine force to fifty vessels, but expert opinion says that with only twenty-five vessels the US would still have "the best force in the world."[228]

Similarly, the United States has contracted to buy three thousand fighter jets for $200 billion dollars.[229] Part of the argument that gave Lockheed this contract was that it would provide nine thousand jobs, mostly in Texas (which is the home state of the President). If only two thousand jets were built, then conceivably only six thousand jobs would be provided, leaving three thousand Texans unemployed. However, the savings from building only two thousand new jets could eliminate all income poverty in the United States, including the unfortunate Texans. Further, the combined Navy and Air Force programs on new air weapons could cost more than $400 billion[230]—over four times the cost of wiping out poverty. Could not the armed services of the United State possibly do with only $300 billions worth of air power so that all Americans could live with dignity? Evidently not.

Finally, Congress has agreed to provide $180 billion dollars in subsidies to American farmers over the next ten years.[231] Regrettably, however, these subsidies are primarily directed at the agrobusiness folks, many of whom are in Texas. Not much is reaching the small American farmer. If this money, and other subsidies like it, were diverted to direct aid to the poor, not only would this go a good way to alleviating the lot of many poor people who are not farmers, it would also be in line with present government policy of *not* getting involved in the workings of the free market.

Finally, in this connection, the $20 billion that the government would receive if estate taxes were only cut below the $5 million dollar limit, instead of totally—as mentioned above—could be used to wipe out almost a quarter of income poverty if it were earmarked for this purpose.

Is it conceivably possible for a society to operate on other than economic principles? There have been examples, including ancient Greece and modern *kibbutzim*, as mentioned previously. Communist Russia, in its early days and pure state, was basically motivated by a desire for equality. There have also been periods, such as during the two World Wars, in which every effort was geared toward military victory rather than a profitable economy (although many individual fortunes were made then). And there were societies, like Taliban Afghanistan, in which economic decisions were subordinated to the maintenance of religious practices. There are also socioeconomic structures that temper the need for profit with a great deal of humane safeguards and practices, such as the Scandinavian countries. In short, even economies can be based upon goals other than only profit.

Why, then, do most governments invariably make decisions that are based upon the market-driven society, with all the misery and discontent that ensues? Barbara Tuchman asks this question in a broader context:

> A phenomenon noticeable throughout history…is the pursuit by governments of policies contrary to their own interests…Why do holders of high office so often act contrary to (the) way reason points and enlightened self-interest suggests?[232]

One obvious answer is that those who make political, social and economic decisions are at a level where the market-driven society not only upholds their present position, but offers them promise of upward-mobility (read: more money, position and power) in the future. Accordingly, they may well view their self-interest not only as *not* tied to the advancement of public well-being in general or that of the poor in particular, but even, in actuality, as frequently in conflict with it.

In any case, an international meeting on the results of new global policies held that:

> The pursuit of neo-liberal policies over the past twenty years has produced very poor results—not only in terms of poverty and income distribution, but also as far as economic growth is concerned…Despite such accumulated evidence of failure… there has been very little change in the objectives pursued through macro-economic policy.[233]

Can the negative effects of globalization be controlled, if not reversed? Marien lists the steps necessary to achieve this end, but concludes: "No one has argued against undertaking these global reforms; rather, the many arguments for doing so are simply ignored."[234]

Local Programs

There have been many local attempts to lessen poverty, or to overcome—or at least mitigate—its results. These include efforts to "empower" the poor, to loan them seed-money, to organize them for political power[235]—in fact, to do anything but give them money. Many of these are reported on at social work and social welfare conferences, although almost all of these are presented as plans, not programs that have been carried out. Even in cases where they are successful, they are not large enough to make a dent in the poverty population, [236] nor can they be replicated on a larger scale elsewhere.[237] These include initiating contact with parents who had not sent their children to school, getting a public utility to refrain from cutting off power to some poor families,[238] establishing a youth foundation in rural India,[239] and Structural Adjustment Programs in Zambia.[240] This is not to denigrate those programs that undoubtedly have helped some people[241]—as the Talmud says: "He who saves one person is as though he had saved the world." However, as possible answers to the widespread and devastating poverty that grips millions of people, such local programs have only a minute effect.

It is also very important to realize that, just as the wealthy become so at the expense of the non-wealthy, so efforts to reduce poverty may show some statistical success in the number of people raised above the poverty line, but it may not indicate how much of this was achieved at the expense of even poorer people. For example, it would conceivably be possible to cut the benefits given to the poorest of the poor, and to divert those funds to people just under the poverty line. This would allow for heartening results on the number of people rescued from poverty, but would ignore the even worse conditions of those who remained. That this is not just a fanciful idea is evidenced that the fact the United Nations Development Programme and the World Bank explicitly try to avoid this result in their proposals for reducing poverty.[242]

SOME PROPOSED SOLUTIONS

Tinkering

Many of the people trying to devise methods of alleviating poverty shy away from overall or drastic solutions, preferring either to make what are usually small changes in existing programs, or proposals that might take generations to bear fruit. Much of this bias comes from a belief that drastic and/or immediate changes are not feasible, and would not be accepted by politicians or the electorate, and therefore more palatable—if limited—proposals must be made instead.

On the other hand, some proposals require very deep changes in the socioeconomic system. They sound more like wish-lists, or pre-conditions, than programs. Schorr lists seven prerequisites for overcoming poverty. One of these says: "Social norms and the programs related to them should support a wage for full-time work that would support a family of three with at least minimum adequacy."[243] Another prerequisite: "A single parent or one parent in a family with two adults should have sufficient income to stay home and refrain from outside work."[244] Levitan, *et al*, call for the prevention of premature, out-of-wedlock pregnancies, more Head Start programs, better elementary and secondary education, school to work transition, second-chance programs, programs for out-of-school youth, access to jobs, income maintenance, and making work pay.[245] Who can disagree? And who thinks these things will happen? The World Bank's proposals are more amorphous: "Promoting opportunity...facilitating empower-ment...(and) enhancing security."[246] These are more philosophical musings than programs for the reduction of poverty.

Instead of visionary grandiose programs, it is possible that small changes in existing programs will make a difference. Incrementalism has been defended as a practical, accountable method of making changes, and indeed, it sometimes is. When President Clinton could not get the total overhaul of the medical system that he recommended, he began approaching the same goal through small, less controversial, methods. However, as Bok points out, the drawbacks of incrementalism may outweigh the advantages. "If policy-makers were always free to learn from their mistakes and improve at will on existing policies,"[247] incremental changes might improve the overall situation. However, "small step-by-step changes often create vested interests and changed conditions that limit the options available in future policymaking...piecemeal reform can gradually result in a frozen mix of half-measures and partial programs that not only cause vast inefficiencies but dim the prospects for comprehensive reform."[248]

Giving Money to the Poor

The most obvious, clearest, easiest way to overcome poverty is to give poor people enough money to raise them above the poverty line. The usual objections to this proposal are at least four-fold. First, that giving people money without demanding anything (read: work) in exchange is immoral for society, and would also ruin the morals of the poor. Secondly, it would be a disincentive to work: corporations would be less able to count on workers' fears of unemployment to ensure a pliant work force. Third: It would be no long-term solution as the poor would simply spend the money (on beer and pretzels) instead of investing it in education, health, or the market (as we would). And finally, that it would be too expensive to carry out.

One such proposed method for alleviating, if not eradicating, poverty has been discussed for over fifty years. In essence, it consists of simply giving money—sometimes to everyone and sometimes just to the poor. It has been called, variously, a demogrant, a guaranteed minimum income, and a basic income. First proposed by various people in the 1960s, mostly from the left side of the political/economic spectrum, it gained unexpected strength when it was endorsed by then-Presidential candidate Senator Barry Goldwater, who was the acknowledged leader of the conservative wing of the Republican party.

True, Senator Goldwater was not acting from humane or altruistic sentiments. He expressed his support for the plan as a method of doing away with the entire social welfare system. In his words, it would wipe out the bleeding heart social workers, their administrative structure and personnel, and—presumably—schools of social work with their staffs. Senator Goldwater saw them as similar to the beneficiaries of social welfare—parasitic, non-productive elements in society. All of this apparatus—beneficiaries and employees—would be replaced by direct payments from the Internal Revenue Service.

Many arguments swirled around the guaranteed minimum income proposal, many of which continue until today. Should payments be made to everyone, including the middle-class and the rich, or should it be selective, going only to the poor? The chances of its acceptance would be considerably enhanced if the middle-classes supported it, which meant if they also benefited from it. But this would multiply the costs by a large factor. This argument is countered by discussing "claw-back," that is, how much of the payments the non-poor would return in income tax.[249]

Then there is the ubiquitous question of the effect of unearned money on incentives to work. Despite all the avowals of the importance of work to individual physical, emotional and spiritual aspects, it was and is taken as a given by society as a whole that if people can get as much from not working as they can from working, they will certainly choose the former. This is the basis for the almost universal "wage stop" in social security and welfare programs mentioned previously. From this widespread belief arose the conditions proposed for guaranteed incomes—proposals to diminish payments as work-related income increased, or, conversely, not to reduce payments so as not to punish people for working. Many intricate formulae were devised to find a point at which poverty would be relieved but incentives to work would not suffer.

One experiment that fell between a guaranteed income and an employment study was tried in Milwaukee about ten years ago. Several hundred low-income adults were offered jobs of 30 hours a week, with the guarantee that "you and your family will no longer be poor." Although there were some interesting results, the bottom line was that 73 percent of the group remained poor without additional support from welfare or a second earner.[250]

Despite a great deal of interest in the guaranteed minimum income proposals, the plan failed to get very far in Congress, mostly because the right-wing considered the payments proposed as excessive, while the left-wing thought them inadequate. However, pieces of the plan were adopted under various guises. Social Security began making supplementary payments to those in need; the Earned Income Tax Credit also drew on the guaranteed income idea, although in an altered form; and other countries have variants of the plan, including children's allowances and family allowances. However, no country has a program to give enough money, without conditions, to raise everyone out of poverty.

Despite the rejection of a negative income tax, or a guaranteed minimum income, as discussed in the United States in the sixties, the basic idea has continued to intrigue social planners and reformers elsewhere. Now the major thrust of advocacy for payments to everyone is in Europe. There an organization called the Basic Income European Network has been very active in publicizing and promoting the idea embodied in its name. Very serious discussions have taken place concerning financing possibilities, levels of payment, populations to be included, the effect on labor and on taxes, and other complex questions. Interestingly, most proposals speak of a very minimum payment—at most, enough to bring people out of poverty. This is obviously due to fear of enormous costs, which would defeat the proposals. Only one voice seems to have been raised for a "rich basic income," although details and methods are not mentioned.[251]

The basic income idea has spread beyond Europe, and while there were twelve national groups discussing these proposals in the year 2000, there were fourteen within the next year, and international meetings are held annually. There are members of parliaments in several countries committed to the idea of a basic income, as well as several members of the European Parliament.

Among other proposals there is one for "stakeholder" grants, in which everyone would have a sum (or stocks and/or bonds) put aside at birth, payable at the age of maturity. Another variation is for an unconditional universal basic income payment, and a third is called market socialism, based on a "sustainably egalitarian distribution of stock ownership."[252] Tony Blair is reported to have proposed a "baby bond" of 750 Euros, to be invested until the child reaches age eighteen, whereupon it could be drawn on.[253]

A non-European example of basic income comes from Brazil, where three states have adopted variations of the plan. Interestingly, the basic income in these areas is linked to other socially-desired objectives. Conditions for receiving the payments include enrolling children in school and enforcing their attendance, while adults are required to participate in professional training programs and educational meetings.[254]

There is, of course, the question of paying for the demograms. A number of proposals have been put forward, including Henry George's hoary old land tax proposal; a tax on energy, and, more lately, a tax on financial transactions, and particularly on transnational capital flows. The latter has been pursued—although not in the context of a basic income—by the French Association for the Taxation of Financial Transactions for the Aid of Citizens (ATTAC), which has now spread beyond France.

It would also be possible to eliminate poverty by raising present welfare grants to the point where no family is under the poverty line. Among the factors which prevent this from coming about include the cost. But Nobel prize-winner Herbert A. Simon has pointed out that a flat tax of 70 percent in the United States would support all government programs and allow for an annual payment of $8,000 per person, or about $25,000 for a family of three.[255] This would effectively eliminate poverty in the United States.

This will not be done, of course, because of the omnipresent fear that this would damage incentives to work. Among all the other proofs that this is probably not so, there stands the fact that we cannot provide work for everyone who wants it even today—as witness the constant unemployment problem. But the presumed morality of work overshadows all other considerations.

WHAT WORKS?

With the plethora of theories, experiments, projects and "benign neglect" outlined previously, where do efforts to reduce, if not eliminate, poverty stand? Despite reasonable economic growth in the developing world, the number of poor in those countries was about the same in 1998 as it had been ten years previously.[256] Blank makes the case that none of these programs were even intended to eliminate poverty, or even to raise people above the poverty line, but rather the programs were "designed as a safety net, to give poor families somewhat higher incomes or better access to food and health care than they would otherwise have"[257]—in other words, to ameliorate, but not eradicate, poverty. As regards whether it does so, she is unequivocal: "Cash transfers make people less poor."[258] Lasch explains, in somewhat different terms, that the people who make policy, run organizations, and manage information have less experience with the difficulties that afflict ordinary people. Consequently, they have little incentive to want to change anything, least of all a redistribution of resources.[259] Scholz and Levine summarize beautifully: "If society's goal is the elimination of income poverty, the lack of progress is unsettling...we do not know what works"[260]— although, one might add, we do know what makes things worse.

Why does nothing work when it comes to eliminating poverty, or even lowering the poverty rate substantially? For one thing, most of the sectors of society which are better off never actually *see* the poor. They read about the poor, they hear about them, occasionally they know someone they think is poor, they even pass through poor neighborhoods—if only by frightful accident, as is the theme of many a B-grade Hollywood movie. But all too frequently, town planning has assured that they won't come face-to-face with groups of the poor:

Most poor people are beyond the reach of simple, direct charity and we do not see them. This is not entirely because they and we live separately, as of course we do, but because *we do not see them.* We watch them pay with food stamps in the supermarket or we walk past them where they lie on the street, and we do not see them. We say that they are invisible but it is irritation that blinds us. Therefore, we do not make the *collective* provisions that would greatly ameliorate poverty.[261]

Some writers are unambiguous—America hates the poor[262]—or, even more—despises them[263] and that is why it will do nothing to really help them. Tropman holds that, akin to the psychological phenomenon of projection mentioned above as regards work, so the poor represent one's own fear of becoming poor. One loathes this possibility, and therefore one hates the poor.

Since one hates them, one feels justified in—or seeks justification for—exploiting them. This exploitation will result—through so-called welfare reform—in free and/or cheap work, and the resulting profit will probably benefit the higher classes.[264] Which is why the poor will remain poor.

Since globalization is one of the factors making for increasing inequality, the question arises as to whether globalization itself can be stopped or reversed. Most expert opinion says no. It has taken on its own momentum and, as Ferkiss says, "is no more reversible than evolution itself."[265] Consequently, efforts to combat globalization should probably be centered on discovering which aspects of globalization are natural to the development of communications, technology, international institutions and the spread of commerce, and which seek to exploit and entrench unequal relations, and attempt to address the negative or preventable aspects of the latter.

ENDNOTES

[1] For some examples see: *Poverty Reduction Strategies: A Review.* New York: United Nations, 1998; *World Development Report 1990—Poverty.* Oxford: The World Bank, 1990; *Overcoming Human Poverty.* New York: United Nations Development Programme, 1998; Lipton, M., *Successes in Anti-Poverty.* Geneva: International Labour Organization, 1998

[2] *Overcoming Human Poverty, op cit.,* pp. 26-27, see endnote 1.

[3] *Ibid.,* p. 88.

[4] *Ibid.,* p. 15.

[5] *Poverty.* Washington: World Bank (published by Oxford University Press, Oxford), 1990, p. 1.

[6] *Attacking Poverty.* Washington: World Bank (published by Oxford University Press, Oxford), 2001, p. vi.

[7] Kay, J., "UN Summit Subordinates Environment and Development to Corporate Interests." *World Socialist Website,* September 11, 2002.

[8] Dicks, M., "Down and Out in America: Living in a Death-Oriented Society," *Journal of Poverty,* 5, *2,* 2001, pp. 115-119, (parentheses added).

[9] Klein, M., C. Aaron and B. Hadjimichael, "Foreign Direct Investment and Poverty Reduction," *Working Paper 2613,* June, 2001, Washington: World Bank.

[10] Glenn, J. C., and T. J. Gordon, "State of the Future at the Millenium," *Futurecasts,* 3, 7, July 1, 2001.

[11] Freeman, J., "The Poor, They Shall Always Be With Thee. Why Should This Be The Case?" *Earth Times,* October 16, 2000, p. 28.

[12] *Overcoming Human Poverty, op cit.,* p. 22, see endnote 1.

[13] Freeman, R., "The Rising Tide Lifts...?" *Focus,* 21, *2,* Fall, 2000, pp. 27-31.

[14] Brown, A., "Business Tackles a Hungry World," *International Herald Tribune,* June 7, 2001, p. 12.

[15] Schorr, A. L., personal communication.

[16] *World Development Report 2002: Building Institutions for Markets.* Oxford: Oxford University Press, 2002.

[17] Wade, R. H., "Making the World Development Report: Attacking Poverty," *World Development Report: 2000,* 29, *8,* 2001, pp 1435-1441.

[18] Koivusalo, M., *World Trade Organisation and Trade-Creep in Health and Social Policies.* Sheffield: GASPP Occasional Paper No. 4/1999, 1999.

[19] Sanger, D., and S. Lohr, "Searching for Ways to Avoid Layoffs." *New York Times,* March 9, 1996, internet edition, p. 1.

[20] Krugman, P., "America the Polarized." *New York Times,* Janauary 4, 2002, internet edition, p. 1.

[21] Stevenson, R. W., "Income Gap Widens Between Rich and Poor in 5 States and Narrows in 1." *New York Times,* April 24, 2002, internet edition, p. 1.

[22] Milanovic, B., and S. Yitzhaki, "Decomposing World Income Distribution: Does the World Have a Middle Class?" *Review of Income and Wealth*, 48, *2*, June 2002, pp. 155-204.

[23] *Ibid.*

[24] Roper, R. H., *Persistent Poverty; The American Dream Turned Nightmare.* New York: Plenum, 1991, p. 180.

[25] Townsend, P., *The International Analysis of Poverty.* New York: Harvester Wheatsheaf, 1993, p. 15.

[26] Roper, *op cit*, p. 57, see endnote 24.

[27] "Richer and Richer," *International Herald Tribune*, June 7, 2001, p. 8, (parentheses added).

[28] Sinai, R., "1.16M Israelis Live Below Poverty Line." *HaAretz*, December 11, 2000, p. 1 (Hebrew).

[29] Blank, R. M., *It Takes a Nation: A New Agenda for Fighting Poverty.* Princeton: Princeton University Press, 1997, p. 54.

[30] Scott, J., "Boom of the 1990's Missed Many in Middle Class, Data Suggests." *New York Times*, August 31, 2001, internet edition, p. 1.

[31] *Poverty and the Environment.* New York: United Nations, 1995, pp. 7-10.

[32] Kawewe, S. S. M., and R. A. Dibie, *Hunger, Malnutrition and Public Policy in Third World Nations.* Paper delivered at the 28th International Conference on Social Work, Jerusalem, 1998, p. 10.

[33] *Ibid.*

[34] Dollar, D., and A. Kraay, "Trade, Growth and Poverty." *Working Paper 2615*, June, 2001. Washington: World Bank.

[35] Blackburn, R. M., "Understanding Social Inequality," *International Journal of Sociology and Social Policy.* 19, *9/10/11*, 1999, pp. 10.

[36] Burtless, G., and T. M. Smeeding, "The Level, Trend and Composition of Poverty," *Focus*, 21, *2*, Fall, 2000, p. 4-9.

[37] Koivusalo, *op cit.*, see endnote 18.

[38] "Diary," *Poverty*, 108, Winter 2001, p. 4

[39] "Richer and Richer," *op cit.,* p. 8, see endnote 27.

[40] Herbert, B., "Shame in the House," *New York Times*, October 29, 2001, internet edition, p. 2.

[41] Krugman, P., "Heart of Cheapness," *New York Times*, May 31, 2002, p. 1., internet edition.

[42] Swonk,, D., chief economist at Bank One in Chicago, quoted in, "Worker Productivity Strong as Firms Cut Hours," *New York Times*, November 7, 2001, internet edition, p. 1.

[43] *Ibid.*

[44] Lobe, J., *Despite the US Economic "Boom," Inequality Continues to Widen.* New York: InterPress Service, September 4, 2000.

[45] Burtless and Smeeding, *op cit.,* see endnote 36.

[46] Strasler, N., "The Poverty Trap." *HaAretz*, December 6, 2001, p. 1 (Hebrew).

[47] Friedman, T. L., *The Lexus and the Olive Tree.* New York: Anchor, 2000, pp. 319-320.

[48] Reich, R. B., *The Future of Success.* New York: Knopf, 2000.

[49] "Budget 2000: Winning the War Against Child Poverty?" *Poverty,* 106, Summer, 2000, p. 5.

[50] Freeman, R., *op cit.,* see endnote 11.

[51] Macarov, D., and U. Yanay, *Images of the Poor and Poverty in Jerusalem.* Jerusalem: Paul Baerwald School of Social Work, Hebrew University, 1975.

[52] Greenhouse, S., "Temporary Workers Seeking Code of Conduct for Job Agencies, " *New York Times*, January 31, 2000, internet edition, p. 1.

[53] Zipkin, A., "Temporary Work is Sidestepping a Slowdown," *New York Times*, July 22, 2001, internet edition, p. 1.

[54] Leonhardt, D., "U. S. Jobless Rate Increases to 6 percent, Highest in 8 Years." *New York Times*, May 4, 2002, internet edition, p. 1.

[55] Greenhouse, *op cit.*, see endnote 52.

[56] Stoesz, D., *A Poverty of Imagination*. Madison: University of Wisconsin Press, 2001, p. 165.

[57] Schorr, A. L., *Welfare Reform: Failure and Remedies*. Westport: Praeger, 2001, p. 137.

[58] Stoesz, *op. cit.*, p. 165, see endnote 56.

[59] Burtless and Smeeding, *op cit.*, see endnote 36.

[60] Kim, M., "The Working Poor: Lousy Jobs or Lazy Workers?" in Kushnick, L., and Jennings, A., (Eds.), *A New Introduction to Poverty: The Role of Race, Power, and Politics*. New York: New York University Press, 1999, pp. 307-319.

[61] Blank, *op cit.*, pp. 79-80, see endnote 29.

[62] Kim, *op cit.*, see endnote 60.

[63] Hotz, V. J., C. H. Mullin and J. K. Scholz, "Welfare Reform, Employment, and Advancement," *Focus*, 22, 1, (Special Edition), 2002, pp. 51-55.

[64] Levin-Waldman, M., "Testing the New Welfare: Lessons From a Survey of Small Business." *Policy Sciences*, 33, 4, March, 2000, pp. 55-71.

[65] Macarov, D., *Social Welfare: Structure and Practice*. Thousand Oaks: Sage, 1995, p. 129.

[66] Blank, *op cit.* (parentheses added), see endnote 29.

[67] Pfefferman, B., "The Start of Reform in the Labor Market." *HaAretz*, April 7, 2002, internet edition, p. 1.

[68] Blank, *op cit.*, pp. 191-194, see endnote 60.

[69] Salmond, J. A., *The CCC, 1933-1942: A New Deal Case Study*. Durham, NC: Duke University Press, 1967.

[70] Lipton, M., *Successes in Anti-Poverty*. Geneva: International Labour Organization, 1998, p. 73.

[71] Simmons, L., M. Bok, N. Churchill, and A. Pritchard, "Urban Economic Development: What's Welfare to Work Got to do With It?" *Journal of Poverty*, 5, 2, 2001, pp. 87-114.

[72] Addison, J. T. and L. Blackburn-McKinley, "Minimum Wages and Poverty." *International and Labor Relations Review*, 52, 3, April, 1999, pp. 393-409 (italics in original).

[73] Smith L., "The Case for a Decent Minimum Wage." *Poverty*, 109, Winter, 2001, p. 3.

[74] *Ibid.*

[75] Cook, D., *Poverty, Crime and Punishment*. London: Child Poverty Action Group, 1997, p. 25.

[76] Uchitelle, L., "Job Loss in March Biggest in Nine Years," *New York Times*, April 7, 2001, internet edition, p. 1.

[77] Geoghegan, T., "The State of the Worker," *New York Times,* January 25, 1996, p. 8.

[78] Stoesz, *op cit.*, see endnote 56.

[79] Lens, V., "Welfare Mothers and Welfare Work," *Jewish Social Work Forum*, 33, Winter/Spring, 1998, pp. 15-21.

[80] *Ibid.*

[81] Young, I. M., "Mother, Citizenship and Independence: A Critique of Pure Family Values." *Ethics*, 105, 3, 1995, pp. 535-556.

[82] Bok, D., *The Trouble with Government*. Cambridge: Harvard University Press, 2001, p. 188. (parentheses added).

[83] Levernier, W., "An Analysis of Family Income Inequality in Metropolitan Counties," *Social Service Quarterly*, 80, 1, March, 1999, pp. 154-165.

[84] Stricker, F., "Why American Poverty Rates Stopped Falling in the 70's, and Why a Better Story Was Not Told About It." *Journal of Poverty*, 4, 2001, pp. 1-21.

[85] Ricupero, R., "Putting a Human Face on Development," *International Social Science Journal,* 166, December 2000, pp. 441-446.

[86] Jansen, R. W. J., and P. J. van Koppen, *Armed Robberies and Unemployment*. ISINI Conference paper, 1997, p. 6.

[87] *Yearbook of Labour Statistics, 1989-1990*. Geneva: International Labour Office, (1990); also McCarthy, E., and W. McGaughey, *Nonfinancial Economics: The Case for Shorter Hours of Work*. New York: Praeger, 1990.

[88] Overly, M. R., *E-Policy: How to Develop Computer, E-Mail and Internet Guidelines*

to Protect Your Company and Its Assets. New York: Amacom, 1999.

[89] Kendrick, J. W., "Productivity Trends and the Recent Slowdown," in Fellner, W. E., (Ed.), *Contemporary Economic Problems*. Washington D. C.: American Enterprise Institute, 1979.

[90] Jansen and Koppen, *op cit.*, see endnote 86.

[91] Walfish, B., "Job Satisfaction Declines in Major Aspects of Work, Says Michigan Study." *World of Work Report*, 4, *9*, 1979, p. 2.

[92] Walbank, M., "Effort in Motivated Work Behaviour," in Duncan, K. D., D. Wallis and M. M. Gruneberg, (Eds.), *Changes in Working Life*. Chichester: John Wiley, 1979.

[93] Macarov, D., *Worker Productivity: Myths and Reality*. Beverly Hills: Sage, 1980.

[94] *How to Avoid Heart Disease*. Jerusalem: Government of Israel; Ministry of Health, 1988.

[95] Schlesinger, A. M., *The Crisis of the Old Order—1919-1939*. Boston: Houghton Mifflin, 1957; Bird, C., *The Invisible Scar*. New York: Pocket Books, 1966.

[96] Macarov, D., "Planning for a Probability: The Almost-Workless World," *International Labour Review*, 124, 1985, pp. 629-542: translated into French in *Futuribles*, 104, Novembre, 1986, 15-36, and in "Vers l'an 2000...et après?" *Les Cahiers Francais*, 232, Juillet-Septembre, 1987, p. 30; into Spanish in *Grupcaixa*, 11, Septiembre-Octubre, 1986, 62-68; and into Finnish in *Sosiaalinen Aikakauskirja*, 4,1987, 45-47;

[97] Britton, A., "Full Employment in the Industrialized Countries," *International Labour Review*, 136, *3*, 1997, pp. 293-339.

[98] Macarov, D., *Incentives to Work*. San Francisco: Jossey-Bass, 1970.

[99] *Social Security Bulletin*, 54, *6*, p. 10; Hurwitz, D. S., "Retirement and Pension Plans," in Minihan, A., (Ed.), *Encyclopedia of Social Work*. Silver Spring: National Association of Social Workers, 1991, pp. 507-512.

[100] Beck, S. H., "Adjustment to and Satisfaction with Retirement," *Journal of Gerontology*, 37, 1982, pp. 616-624.

[101] Eisdorfer, C., and D. Cohen, "Health and Retirement: Retirement and Health: Background and Future Directions," in Parnes, H. S., (Ed.), *Policy Issues in Work and Retirement*. Kalamazoo: Upjohn, 1983.

[102] Fraser, T. M., *Human Stress, Work and Job Satisfaction*. Geneva: International Labour Office, 1983; and Rizzo, C., I Reynolds and H. Gallagher, "Job Satisfaction: A Study of Sydney Adults," *Australian Journal of Social Issues*, 16, 1981, pp. 138-148.

[103] Varga, K., "Marital Cohesion as Reflected in Time Budgets," in Szalai, A., (Ed.), *The Use of Time*. The Hague: Mouton, 1972.

[104] Kipling, R., "The Phantom Rickshaw," *The Complete Works of Rudyard Kipling*. London: Allyn and Uwin, 1913.

[105] Callinicos, A., *Equality*. Cambridge, UK: Polity, 2000, p. 99.

[106] Haydock, M. D., "The GI Bill," *American History*, 34, *4*, October, 1999.

[107] Levitan, S. A., G. L. Magnum and S. L. Magnum, *Programs in Aid of the Poor*. Baltimore: Johns Hopkins, 1998, p. 166 (emphasis added).

[108] Crossette, B., "Globalization Tops Agenda for World Leaders at U.N. Summit," *New York Times*, September 3, 2000, internet edition, pp. 1-6.

[109] Campbell, N. D., "Child Care: Is It All That It Can Be?" *Children's Voice*, 10, *1*, January 2001, pp. 16-18.

[110] Schorr, *op cit.* p. 32, see endnote 57.

[111] Silverstein, G., "Measuring Client Success," *Public Welfare*, 52, *4*, 1994, pp. 6-23.

[112] Macarov, D., *Quitting Time: The End of Work*. Patrington: Barmarick Press, 1988.

[113] Hotz, *et al, op cit.*, see endnote 63.

[114] *New York Times*, August 10, 1986, p. A23.

[115] DeParle, J., "Debris of Past Failures Impedes Poverty Program," *New York Times*, November 7, 1993, p. 21E.

[116] *Time Magazine*, October 29, 1993, p. 22.

[117] Hotz, *et al, op cit.* p. 54, see endnote 63.

[118] Herbert, B., "As Bush's Stature Rises...," *New York Times*, January 31, 2002, internet edition, p. 1; Pear, R., "Bush Budget Will Seek Cuts in Programs for Job Training," *Ibid*.

[119] Stoesz, D., *op cit.,* p.99. (parentheses added), see endnote 56.

[120] O'Leary, J., "Primary Schools Set New Targets for Math and English," *The London Times,* March 14, 2002, p. 2.

[121] Frantz, D., "Poverty Forces new Methods for Educating Turkish Youth." *New York Times,* July 1, 2001, p. 1, internet edition.

[122] McCallum, I., and G. Redhead, "Poverty and Educational Performance," *Poverty,* 106, Summer, 2000, pp. 14-17.

[123] Mason, R., "The Globalisation of Education," in *Globalising Education: Trends and Applications.* London: Routledge, 1998, pp. 3-18.

[124] *Ibid,* p 8.

[125] *Ibid,* p. 6.

[126] O'Neill, D. M., and J. E. O'Neill, *Lessons for Welfare Reform.* Kalamazoo: Upjohn, 1997, p. 82.

[127] James Heckman, quoted by Stille, A., "Grounded by an Income Gap." *New York Times,* December 15, 2001, internet edition, p. 1.

[128] "The Despair Beneath the Arab World's Growing Rage," *New York Times,* October 14, 2001, p. 1, internet edition.

[129] Prasad, K. N., and R. Hariprasad, "The Links Between Education, Employment, and Demographic Change—The Paradox of the Kerala Model, Characterized by High Human Development and Low Growth Syndrome." *Social Development Issues,* 23, 3, 2001, pp. 60-71.

[130] Wright, E. O., "Reducing Income and Wealth Inequality: Real Utopian Proposals." *Contemporary Sociology, 29, 1,* January, 2000, pp. 143-156.

[131] Macarov, D., *The Design of Social Welfare.* New York: Holt, Rinehart and Winston, 1978, p. 100; see also Fried, A., *FDR and His Enemies.* New York: St Martin's Press, 1999.

[132] Moynihan, D. P., *The Politics of a Guaranteed Income: The Nixon Administration and the Family Assistance Plan.* New York: Free Press, 1969.

[133] *Who Gets Food Stamps?* Select Committee on Nutrition and Human Need, U. S. Senate. Washington: Government Printing Office, 1975, p. 29.

[134] Macarov, D., "Israel," in Dixon, J., (Ed.), *Social Welfare in the Middle East.* London: Croom Helm, 1987, pp. 32-70.

[135] Macarov, D., "Social Security as Poverty's Guardian," *Policy Studies Review,* 12, 1/ 2, Spring/Summer 1993, pp. 92-101

[136] *Ibid.*

[137] Dixon, J., *Social Security in Global Perspective.* Westport: Praeger, 1999, p. 2.

[138] *Annual Statistical Supplement, 1999.* Washington: Social Security Administration, 2000.

[139] *Ibid.*

[140] Johnson, R. W., *The Redistributional Implications of Reductions in Social Security COLAs."* The Retirement Project, Brief Series no. 5, June, 1999. Washington: Urban Institute, p. 3, quoted by Schorr, *op cit,* p. 85, see endnote 57.

[141] Macarov, D., *Work and Welfare: The Unholy Alliance.* Sage: Beverly HIlls, 1980.

[142] *Social Security Programs Throughout the World 1999.* Washington: Social Security Administration, 1999.

[143] Macarov, D., *Work and Welfare: The Unholy Alliance, op cit.,* pp. 39-40, see endnote 141.

[144] For a fuller discussion of this problem, see Macarov, D., "Social Security as Poverty's Guardian," *Policy Studies Review,* 12, 1/2, 1993, pp. 92-101.

[145] *Social Security Programs Throughout the World, op cit.,* see endnote 142.

[146] Stevenson, R. W., "Little Movement on Stimulus Plan as Lawmakers' Recess Looms." *New York Times,* December 13, 2001, internet edition, p. 1.

[147] Macarov, D., *Quitting Time: The End of Work.* Patrington, Hull: MCB University Press, 1988, p. 30.

[148] Leonhardt, D., "Georgia Finds Itself in Jobless Benefits Bind," *New York Times,* January 16, 2002, internet edition, p. 1.

[149] *Social Security Programs Throughout the World, op cit.,* see endnote 142.

[150] *Ibid.*

[151] *Ibid.*

[152] Bonoli, G., V. George and P. Taylor-Gooby, *European Welfare Futures: Towards a Theory of Retrenchment.* Cambridge, UK: Polity, 2000, p. 111.

[153] "Diary," *Poverty,* 108, Winter 2001, p. 4.

[154] Scholz, J. K., and K. Levine, "The Evolution of Income Support Policy in Recent Years." *Focus,* 21, *2,* Fall, 2000, pp. 9-15.

[155] Meyer, D. R., and M-C, Hu. "A Note on the Antipoverty Effectiveness of Child Support Among Mother-Only Families." *Journal of Human Resources,* XXXIV, *1,* Winter, 1999, pp. 225-235.

[156] Leonhardt, *op cit.,* see endnote 54.

[157] As Bird points out, a real-world antipoverty program must generate enough middle-class support to be acceptable. Bird, E., "Provision and Effect of Welfare Programs." *Journal of Policy Analysis and Management,* 15, *1,* Winter, 1996, pp. 1-31.

[158] Braithwaite, J., C. Grootart and B. Milanovic, *Poverty and Social Assistance in Transitional Countries.* London: Macmillan, 2000, p. 27.

[159] *Ibid.,* p. 165.

[160] Steuerle, C. E., and A. Carasso. *Why the Politics of Social Security Could Improve the Status of the Poor.* New York: Urban Institute, November 15, 2001.

[161] *Time Magazine,* April 10, 2000, p. 16.

[162] Carasso, A., and C. E. Steuerle. *Social Security's Additional Dollars Could Buy Less Poverty.* Washington: Urban League, October 30, 2001.

[163] Synak, *op cit.,* see endnote 161.

[164] Gal, J., *The Changing Relationship between Work and Social Security--Reflections on Future Trends.* Paper delivered at the 28th International Conference on Social Welfare, Jerusalem, Israel, 1998.

[165] *Social Security Programs Throughout the World, 1997.* Washington: U. S. Department of Health and Human Welfare, 1998.

[166] Hoefer, R., and I. C. Coby, "Social Welfare Expenditures: Private," *Encyclopedia of Social Work.* Washington: National Association of Social Workers, 1998, pp. 274-281.

[167] Weerahewa J., *The Contributions of Technology, Trade and Government Transfers to Overall Changes in Poverty in Sri Lanka.* Paper presented at the Conference on Globalisation, Growth and (In)Equality. Warwick University, Coventry, UK, 2002.

[168] Solow, A. M., "Preface to the Lectures," in Gutmann, A., *Work and Welfare.* Princeton: Princeton University Press, 1998, p. 39.

[169] Friedlander, D., and G. Burtless. *Five Years After: The Long-Term Effects of Welfare-to-Work Programs.* New York: Russell Sage Foundation, 1995.

[170] Cancian, M., R. Haveman., D. R. Meyer., and B. Wolfe. *Before and After TANF: The Economic Well-Being of Women Leaving Welfare.* Madison, Wis: Institute for Research on Poverty, University of Wisconsin-Madison, 1999.

[171] *Annual Demographic Survey, March Supplement.* Washington: U. S. Bureau of the Census, 1996-2000,

[172] Pear, R., "Number of People Living in Poverty Increases in U.S." *New York Times,* September 25, 2002, internet edition, p. 1.

[173] Loprest, P., "How Are Families That Left Welfare Doing? A Comparison of Early and Recent Welfare Leavers." *New Federalism,* Series B., No. B-36, April, 2001, pp. 1-7.

[174] Schorr, *op cit.,* p. 27, see endnote 57.

[175] Kaufman, L., "Economy Dips While Welfare Drops in Cities." *New York Times,* August 31, 2002, p. 1., internet edition.

[176] Krinsky, J., "Is *This* Our Strategy? Is This *Our* Strategy? Space, Time, and Narrative Uncertainties in the Struggle Against Workfare in New York City," in Barker, C., and M. Tyldesley, (Eds.), *Conference Papers, Volume 1, 2001, 7th International Conference on Alternative Futures and Popular Protest.* Manchester, UK: Manchester Metropolitan University, 2001, (emphasis and parentheses in original).

[177] Pierson, C., A. Forster and E. Jones, "The Politics of Europe: (Un)employment Ambivalence," in Towers, B., and M. Terry (Eds.), *Industrial Relations Journal: European*

Annual Review 1997. 1998, pp. 5-22.

178 Bernstein, N., "As Welfare Comes to an End, So Do the Jobs." *New York Times*, December 17, 2001, internet edition, p. 1.

179 Stoesz, *op cit.,* see endnote 56.

180 Schorr, *op cit.*, p. 57, see endnote 57.

181 Schorr, *op cit.*, p. 7, see endnote 57.

182 Keller, B., "The Soul of George W. Bush," *New York Times*, March 23, 2002, internet edition, p. 1.

183 Bernstein, N., "Strict Limits on Welfare Benefits Discourage Marriage, Studies Say." *New York Times*, June 3, 2002, p. 1., internet edition.

184 Doron, A., "Targeting Social Protection Benefits," *Benefits*, 31, May/June, 2001

185 Pear, R., "Many on Medicaid Lack Drugs, Study Says," *New York Times*, April 9, 2002, internet edition, p. 1.

186 Kilty, K. M., and E. A. Segal, "Introduction: Examining the Impact of 'Ending Welfare as We Know It'." *Journal of Poverty*, 5, 2, 2001, pp. 1-3.

187 Loprest, P. J., *Families Who Left Welfare: Who Are They and How Are They Doing?* New York: Urban Institute, July 1, 1999.

188 Kim, R. Y., "The Effects of Earned Income Tax Credit on Children's Income and Poverty: Who Fares Better?" *Journal of Poverty*, 5, 1, 2001, pp. 1-22.

189 Bird, *op cit.,* p. 2, see endnote 157.

190 "United States; A Modest Step Towards Refundable Tax Credits," *News Flash #13.* Geneva: Basic Income European Network, January, 2002.

191 McCrae, J., and J. Taylor, "The Working Families Tax Credit." *Poverty*, 100, Summer, 1998, p. 7.

192 Hotz, *et al., op cit.*, p. 52, see endnote 63.

193 *Ibid.*

194 *Ibid.*

195 Toner, R., and R. Pear, "Bush Urges Work and Marriage Programs in Welfare Plan," *New York Times*, February 27, 2002, internet edition, p. 1.

196 Schorr, *op cit.*, p. 42, see endnote 57.

197 Kazis, R., and M. S. Miller, *Low-Wage Workers in the New Economy.* New York: Urban Institute, 2002.

198 Hotz, *et al., op cit.*, p. 54, see endnote 63.

199 Esser, H., T. Jurado, I. Light, C. Petry and G. Pieri, *Towards Emerging Ethnic Classes in Europe*, Volume 1. Weinheim, Germany: Freudenberg Stiftung GmbH, February, 2000, p. 99.

200 Bernstein, J., Economic Policy Institute, quoted in "Nigeria and Shell: Helping, But Not Developing." *The Economist*, May 12-18, 2001, p. 48.

201 Shavit, Y., and Yuchtman-Yaar, E., " Ethnicity, Education, and Other Determinants of Self-Employment in Israel." *International Journal of Sociology*, 31, 1, Spring 2001, pp. 59-91.

202 Painter, G., and S-Y Taang, "The Microcredit Challenge: A Survey of Programs in California," *Journal of Developmental Entrepreneurship*, 5, 1, April, 2001, pp. 1-16.

203 Jurik, N., and J. Cowgill, "Women and Microenterprise: Empowerment or Hegemony," *Conference Proceedings*, Fifth Women's Policy Research Conference. Washington: George Washington University, 1998, pp. 321-324.

204 *Ibid.*

205 Stoesz, *op cit.,* p. 157, see endnote 56.

206 Friedman, T. L., *The Lexus and the Olive Tree.* New York: Anchor, 2000, pp. 210-211.

207 Weber, H., *The Poverty Reduction Strategy Papers and 'New Constitutionalism':* *Global Governance and Development.* Paper delivered at the Conference on Globalisation, Growth and (In)Equality. Warwick University, Coventry, UK, 2002.

208 Kahn, A. H., *Reflections on the Comilla Rural Development Projects.* OLC Paper #3. Washington: Overseas Liaison Committee, American Council on Education, 1974, quoted by Lipton, M., *Successes in Anti-Poverty.* Geneva: International Labour Office, 1998, p. 2.

[209] Lipton, *ibid*, p. 42.

[210] Painter, G., and Tang, S-Y. "The Microcredit Challenge: A Survey of Programs in California." *Journal of Developmental Entrepreneurship.* 6, *1*, 2001, pp. 1-16.

[211] Jurik and Cowgill, *op cit.,* see endnote 203.

[212] Whurgaft, N., "The Little Extra Push," *HaAretz*, March 1, 2002; see also Lichtman, G., "Helping People to Help Themselves," *Jerusalem Post*, March 12, 1999; and Jaffe, E. D., "The Role of Interest Free Loan Associations in Indigenous, Trans-Generational Involvement in Caring Societies," in Schervish, P., V. Hodgkinson, M. Gates and Associates, (Eds.), *Care and Community in Modern Society: Passing On the Tradition of Service to Future Generations.* San Francisco: Jossey-Bass, 1995.

[213] Painter and Tang, *op cit,* see endnote 210.

[214] Cohen, M., "Evaluating Microfinance's Impact: Going Down Market," in Feinstein, O. N., and R. Picciotto, (Eds.), *Evaluation and Poverty Reduction.* New Brunswick: Transaction, 2001, pp. 193-207.

[215] "Nigeria and Shell: Helping but Not Developing," *The Economist,* May12-18, 2001, p. 48.

[216] Roe, K. D., "From Dhaka to Dallas: Applicability of the Grameen Model to Urban Poverty in the United States." *Social Development Issues*, 23, *2*, 2001, pp. 18-26.

[217] Glenn and Gordon, *op cit.,* see endnote 10.

[218] Meyer, D. R., "A Note on the Antipoverty Effectiveness of Child Support Among Mother-Only Families." *Journal of Human Resources*, 34, *1*, Winter, 1999, pp. 225-234.

[219] *Annual Demographic Survey, March Supplement.* Washington: U.S. Bureau of the Census, Table 1, 2002.

[220] Comments made by Barbara Harriss-White at the Conference on Globalisation, Growth and (In)Equality, Unversity of Warwick, Coventry, UK, 2002, discussing her paper, *Globalisation, Informal Economies and (In)Decent Work.*

[221] Paringaux, R-P., *Monde Diplomatique*, September 11, 2002.

[222] See, for one example, "Social Mobilization in Bangladesh," *Overcoming Human Poverty.* New York: UN Development Program, 2000, p.74.

[223] Danker, S., "Global Cohort of Poverty Increases," *Earth Times,* 8, *15,* August 16-31, 1999, pp. 22-23.

[224] Burtless and Smeeding, *op cit.,* see endnote 36.

[225] Ormerod, P., *The Death of Economics.* London: Faber and Faber, 1994, quoted by Riches, G., *First World Hunger: Food Security and Welfare Politics.* London: Macmillan, 1997, p. 8.

[226] Eland, I., "Subtract Unneeded Nuclear Attack Submarines from the Fleet," *Cato Foreign Policy Briefing No. 47,* April 2, 1998: Washington: Cato Institute.

[227] Baker, R., "Seawolf Needs an Enemy." *New York Times*, August 12, 1997, p. FE7.

[228] Eland, *op cit.,* see endnote 226.

[229] Dao, J., and L. M. Holson, "Lockheed Wins $200 Billion Deal for Fighter Jet," *New York Times*, October 27, 2001, internet edition, pp. 1-4.

[230] *Ibid.*

[231] Krugman, P., "True Blue Americans," *New York Times,* May 7, 2002, internet edition, p. 1.

[232] Tuchman, B. W., *The March of Folly: From Troy to Vietnam.* London: Little, Brown and Company, 1994.

[233] "Global Social Policy Forum," *Global Social Policy*, 1, *3,* December, 2001, p. 271.

[234] Marien, M., "A Positive Outcome?" *The Futurist*, 36, *1*, January/February, 2002, p. 22.

[235] See, for example, the Kensington Welfare Rights Union, reported by Honkala, C., W. Baptist, P. Grugan, E. Thul, and R. Goldstein, *The Effects of Globalization on Humankind in the USA.* Paper delivered at the 28th International Conference on Social Welfare, Jerusalem, 1998.

[236] Njobvu, C. A., *Rural Poverty and Poverty Alleviation in Zambia.* Paper delivered at the 28th International Conference on Social Welfare, Jerusalem, 1998.

[237] See, for example, Knowles, G., *Case Studies in Poverty Alleviation Through Community Development*, paper delivered at the 28th International Conference on Social Welfare, Jerusalem, 1998.

[238] Rosenfeld, J. M., "Social Exclusion and Social Justice," in *Proceedings*. 28th International Conference on Social Welfare, Jerusalem, 1998, pp. 143-151

[239] Patil, D S., *Poverty and Inequality in Rural Communities in India*. Paper delivered at the 28th International Conference on Social Welfare, Jerusalem, July 5-8, 1998.

[240] Njobvu, C. A., *Rural Poverty and Poverty Alleviation in Zambia*. Paper delivered at the 28th International Conference on Social Welfare, Jerusalem, July 5-8, 1998.

[241] Such as ATD Fourth World, *ibid*.

[242] *Overcoming Human Poverty*. New York: United Nations Development Programme, 1998, p. 15.

[243] Schorr, *op cit.*, p. 84, see endnote 57.

[244] *Ibid*.

[245] Levitan, A., G. L. Mangum and S. L. Mangum, *Programs in Aid of the Poor*. Baltimore: Johns Hopkins, 1998 (seventh edition), pp. 226-236..

[246] *World Development Report, op cit.,* pp. 6-7, see endnote 1.

[247] Bok, *op cit.*, p. 144, see endnote 82.

[248] *Ibid*.

[249] There is a voluminous literature about the history and provisions of a guaranteed minimum income. See, for examples, Levitan, Mangum and Mangum, *op cit*, pp. 102-105, see endnote 107; Schorr, *op cit.,* pp. 157-159, see endnote 57; Macarov, *Incentives to Work, op cit.*, pp. 1-17, see endnote 98.

[250] DeParle, J., "Project to Rescue Needy Stumbles Against Persistence of Poverty." *New York Times*, May 15, 1999, p. 1, internet edition.

[251] Etzioni, A., *Next: The Road to the Good Society*. New York: Basic Books, 2001, p. 74.

[252] Wright, *op cit.*, pp. 143-156, see endnote 130.

[253] "United Kingdom: Blair Proposes a Modest Basic Endowment for Every Baby." *Basic Income*, 36, July, 2001, p. 7.

[254] Silva e Silva, M. O., *The Basic Income as a Strategy for Increasing Child Education in Brazil*. Paper delivered at the 28th International Conference on Social Welfare, Jerusalem, July 5-8, 1998.

[255] "Death of a Prominent BI Supporter," *Basic Income*, 36, July 2001, p. 2.

[256] Ravallion, M., *Growth, Inequality and Poverty: Looking Beyond Averages*. Washington: World Bank, 2001.

[257] Blank, *op cit.,* see endnote 29.

[258] *Ibid*, p. 136.

[259] Lasch, C., "Politics and Culture," *Salamagundi*, 98-99, 1993, p. 6, quoted in Gagnier, R., *The Insatiability of Human Wants: Economics and Aesthetics in Market Society*. Chicago: University of Chicago Press, 2000, p. 207.

[260] Scholz and Levine, *op cit.,* see endnote 154.

[261] Schorr, *op cit*, p. 82, (emphasis in original), see endnote 57.

[262] Tropman, J. E., *Does America Hate the Poor? The Other American Dilemma*. Westport: Praeger, 1998.

[263] Ritz, J. P. *The Despised Poor*. Boston: Beacon, 1966.

[264] Tropman, *op cit.,* see endnote 262.

[265] Ferkiss, V., "Globalization's Growing Pains," *The Futurist*, 36, 2, March/April, 2002; reviewing Anderson,, W. T., *All Connected Now: Life in the First Global Civilization*. New York: Westview Press, 2001.

CHAPTER 7

What Future for Poverty?

The widespread and deeply-rooted attitudes toward work, welfare, poverty and the poor that have been discussed above have become a dynamic, synergic, tangled web that is deeply entrenched in society, and is sustained by its more powerful members. These attitudes have become a structure that has hardened in place.[1] It reverberates through, determines, and supports the current socioeconomic ethos, which is becoming a seamless global web, increasingly moving towards a dog-eat-dog, unrestrained, laissez faire capitalism, in which the poor are ignored, rejected, patronized, blamed and hated. Motives and actions that do not exist are imputed to the poor, the fears and guilt of others are projected onto them, and they are punished and scapegoated in various ways, not the least of which is exploitation for the gain of others. Many societal institutions are being bifurcated, with one for the well-to-do and another for the poor. None of the overarching so-called remedies for poverty attempted to date has managed to reduce poverty substantially and local programs succeed only on a very small scale in specific localities for a limited amount of time.

The role for which governments were created, such as securing and enlarging citizens' rights to life, liberty and the pursuit of happiness—as enjoined in the American Declaration of Independence—is being constantly eroded under the guise of deregulation, neo-liberalism, free-markets, privatization and globalization. Multinational corporations are overriding governments in establishing their own operating procedures, trade agreements and cartels, including sanctioned corruption, undisclosed illegal practices, and environmental degradation. International financial institutions are demanding as a prerequisite for help—particularly from newly-emerging, underdeveloped, transition countries—the adoption of policies that impinge directly and ruthlessly on their poor. Profit-driven entities are driving out humane, altruistic, people-oriented organizations.

What would be at least theoretically necessary to turn the present headlong dash to inequality into a search for a more humane, just and caring society? There are a number of possible scenarios, even if they do not seem to be presently probable. Each of these interacts with and affects the others.

WHAT COULD HAPPEN

The "Great Man" Scenario

One possibility for a return to humaneness as an important element in society would be the rise of a charismatic personality to whose leadership great numbers of people would be attracted. It is to be hoped that this character would arise in democratic settings, for the record of adored persons in autocratic settings, such as Hitler, Mussolini, Peron, Stalin and others, is not a development to be desired even though some of these came to power through a so-called populist platform. But a Roosevelt, Gandhi, Mandela, Ataturk or Martin Luther King, Jr., dedicated to arriving at a better society by peaceful means, might be able to attract enough adherents to redirect or mitigate the present situation, especially if their rise coincided with other conducive developments.

Unfortunately, even the rise of such a person or persons would probably lead to minimal change in their own country or countries at best, since the very essence of globalization, as its name implies, is that it is supra-national. Consequently, even a towering figure with mobs of adherents in any one country would probably make little impact on events world-wide. It is difficult to conceive of a figure so popular and so powerful that he or she could halt the relentless growth of privatization and globalization. The figure of King Canute intrudes.

Crises

Another possibility might have to do with events, rather than people; or, events and people combined. A major catastrophe, such as an asteroid striking the earth; or a continuing series of Twin Tower disasters in many countries; or a worldwide continuing drought; or a devastating world war; or a global depression; or the collapse of the global financial system under waves of speculation and swift transfers of capital: any of these might bring about governmental measures to take care of people regardless of, or at the expense of, profits to enterprises. Such events have been referred to as "ruptures" in the fabric of society, and might make possible or give rise to the emergence of the type of great man mentioned above. However, history teaches that societal ruptures do not necessarily result in a better world.

New Inventions

One type of rupture is a new and unexpected invention. Historically, the invention of the wheel, the domestication of the horse, the harnessing of water-power, the printing press, the steam engine, and electricity all changed society immeasurably. There are those who hope and/or believe that future developments in instant communication, for example, will bring about profound changes in society, despite the fact that as long as radio and television are commercial activities, profits will determine their content. Nevertheless, even unintended exposure to these media has had measurable effects. The *content* of computer activities, in particular—especially e-mail, chat-programs, and personal web-sites—seems to be almost uncontrollable by for-profit organizations, and there is more reason to believe that it may create profound changes in the structure of society. For example, poor women, mostly in developing countries, are beginning to have fewer children, which has enormous implications for economics, social welfare, and poverty, [2] bearing in mind that large families have served as a social safety net in developing countries. Although the reasons for this change have not been pinpointed, certainly new methods of communication—radio, television, the internet, cell-phones and others—have had an effect by disseminating information, showing alternative methods of living, and so forth And what effects will inventions so far undreamed-of have?

Regional and Global Protest Movements

Modern communications have stimulated material desires on an order that could result in disaster for the increasingly fragile and depleted environment. Popular discontent may rise to the point where socioeconomic structures, as well as governments, are radically changed, either through revolution or by far-reaching compromises. One of the most powerful tools in the hands of the current movers-and-doers is, paradoxically, the powerlessness of the poor. Although there have been some successes registered by movements or parties of the poor,[3] these have been mostly in Third World and/or rural countries, with limited amount or type of change. The existing power structure and the compliance of the middle classes to date has militated against widespread success by this means in the more developed countries though it is difficult to foretell what direction middle class protest might take, were its own well-being to be threatened by the increasing tendency of the global economy to stream the world into rich and poor.

One example of the non-poor blocking help to the poor is evidenced in recent changes in American social welfare: in 2002 the government planned cutbacks in Medicaid, which is purely for the politically irrelevant poor, but not in Medicare, which includes masses of influential middle class members,[4] although Medicare is a much, much more expensive program.

One might see elements of the same mechanism operating in the tumultuous history of Latin America, *e.g.,* Guatemala, Nicaragua, El Salvador, Chile, and Venezuela, where entrenched elites have even sought outside help to remain in power.

It might be well to distinguish between social organizations, social movements, and social protests, although one can find some overlap between them. The Red Cross, Amnesty, UNICEF and similar groups are social organizations—non-profit and with non-economic goals—but with structure, hierarchy and permanent staffs. They may represent an ideological stance, but they are not based on widespread volunteer activity. They rarely engage in overt protest activities, although—like Greenpeace—they may.

Social movements, as distinct from organizations, do not necessarily have structure and staff. They tend to be made up of "believers" rather than activists, or even members. The anti-Vietnam war movement was one example, prohibition and anti-prohibition was another, and women's suffrage was still another. Some such "believers" do sometimes engage in active protests, as testified by members of pro- and anti-abortion movements. Movements may engage in protest activities, and may have some sort of structure, but they are basically ideologically-driven, represent a broader, more diverse social base, and express themselves by a variety of means, rather than through the activities of any particular organization. Over time, movements may evolve (or devolve) into specific organizations. The Green movement has, in some places, become a political party.

Social protest is a much more general term, and has been used to label everything from political parties to consumer organizations. Indeed, almost any proposal or activity toward change can be viewed as a protest against the status quo. However, "social protest" is more often used with regard to mass meetings, parades, demonstrations, sit-ins, physical boycotts, and similar activities. So far, activities against privatization and globalization, and for the poor, are more in the nature of protests than of movements or organizations.

Although social organizations rarely use protest activities and social movements only sometimes do, there are also protests that arise from specific situations, rooted in neither organizations nor movements. Tax revolts and protests against closing a factory or building a highway are cases in point.[5]

Where privatization and globalization are concerned, there are very few *organizations* as such with the declared aim of opposing them, or even ameliorating their effects, although a few have come into being. Interestingly, the anti-capitalist *movement*—so far disparate, to judge by its many names[6]—seems to be beginning once again to coalesce,[7] and is taking on the nature of a movement formed through protests, rather than protests sponsored by movements. Its most significant activity so far has been the organization of demonstrations at international meetings of world-wide financial institutions, such as G-8, the World Bank, the International Monetary Fund and the World Trade Organization, as well as international conferences concerning social protest.[8]

As concerns poverty as such, there is a dearth of anti-poverty organizations, movements against domestic poverty, or even protests specifically naming poverty as the enemy. Israel, as one exception, has an anti-poverty lobby made up of representatives of organizations and individuals (including some of the poor), concentrating almost entirely on pressuring politicians. Most activities of anti-poverty organizations elsewhere are subsumed under general anti-capitalist activities, which may focus on ecology, empowerment, governmental changes, etc.

There is nevertheless some hope for the protest movement in the fact that it does not necessarily need to encompass a majority of the people. As Dunham says, "Small groups of people whose rather limited aim is to live decently with one another may become, under certain circumstances, a great social force."[9] The Black civil rights movement in the United States, the feminist movement, the student movement, the Gay rights movement and the Green movement never contained more than a small majority of citizens, but wrought changes that seem almost irreversible. On the other hand, most protests do not succeed in bringing about change. Almost every day there is a protest of some sort in front of the UN building in New York,[10] with no discernible result. Similarly, the students who protested the privatization of Philadelphia schools—mentioned previously—by chanting, "I am not for sale," were nevertheless "sold."[11]

One of the students and observers of protest movements summarizes this very clearly:

> We should not exaggerate the effects of protest movements. They may develop new ways of thinking and acting...but this does not mean that their innovations will be universally adopted. Corporations and governments have considerable power to resist, and protest movements can rarely force them to change. Even the civil rights movement, one of the most successful protests in American history, after its legal victories in the mid-1900s, has had disappointingly little effect on the lives of poor African Americans. Citizenship movements must change cultural attitudes, not just laws. It is not easy to change either one.[12]

As to changing cultural attitudes, one of the questions is whether the lower economic strata even want a new economic order, or whether they want to use the present situation to rise to the upper strata. As was said of the British worker before World War I, "He [*sic*] was not interested in a new social system...but in having a fairer treatment in this one."[13] If this turns out to be true today, it will have dire implications for the possibilities of real change via social protest.

On the other hand, Dwyer and Seddon speak of the possibilities of a "radical middle class protest" coming about, and point out that popular protest and resistance seem to come in waves.[14] However, not all of those protests are based on economics. Many of them are for changes in government, or government policy, such as the struggles in Mexico and Algeria against their one-party political systems.[15] The struggle in Algeria relates to the FIS having been denied the right to govern that which it won at the polls, and the struggle largely remains to claim that victory, or, as another example, the al-Qaeda network, which is religiously-based. An ambitious attempt to survey the evidence of a "genuine, popular-based anti-globalization international movement," concludes that, "Its greatest achievement has been to put global decision-makers…under the microscope."[16]

Has the popular protest movement been successful in its economic (as distinct from political) efforts? In some cases the answer is certainly yes. The protest against the Third World underpaid, exploited labor used by sport-shoe manufacturers is a case in point as, in another context, was the Save the Whales campaign.

Whether the anti-globalization movement has or will reach a critical mass is a matter of opinion, but the numerical growth of protestors is striking. In 1995 only 25 people protested at the World Bank/IMF meeting in Washington; in April, 2000, it was 30,000; in December, 2000, 100,000 people marched in protest; in Barcelona there was a half-million strong demonstration, and at the 2001 meeting 24 million names were signed to a petition. As has been pointed out, this was more than the number of people who signed the Princess Diana condolence book.[17] The cooperation between labor unions and groups like ecological protestors—colloquially called the Teamster-Turtle alliance[18]—has heartened those who believe the protests will become an influential movement.

There is also some progress toward a transnational protest movement. Churches, labor unions and some other coalitions that take social action seriously are already international, and are being termed TNPMs (Transnational Popular Movements).[19] But whether even a sustained, powerful, international protest movement can or will slow down, stop, or reverse the move toward privatization and globalization is not a given; and even the extent to which it can (or cannot) ameliorate the effects of such powerful trends remains an open question.[20]

Civil Society

The social element presently referred to as civil society is not the opposite of an uncivil society—that is, it does not denote people being polite to each other. It is, rather, the move to organize a third element of society, as distinguished from the political and economic elements. That element would consist of voluntary organizations, volunteers, civic and fraternal organizations, religious groups, interest groups, affinity groups, and other groups referred to as "uncoerced."[21] Many non-governmental organizations (NGOs) exist in the area of civil society—in fact, they can be seen as the mainstay of the movement. The purpose is to provide a buffer between politics and business—a buffer that would also be active in opposing inimical trends in both. The concept came into being during the 1990s, and is sometimes called the "third sector."

Perhaps the clearest outline and exposition of the civil society as such is contained in the literature of communitarianism—a movement founded and promulgated by the sociologist Amitai Etzioni—which emphasizes human responsibilities as well as human rights.[22]

As attractive as civil society sounds, it has its limitations: "Civil society is paramount to overseeing both state and market, and in deterring the agents of each from corrupting the other. However…even civil society is unlikely to provide a level playing-field for the poor."[23] In fact, Edwards and Hulme find no evidence that civil society, as represented by NGOs, provides services cheaper than governments. Specifically, it usually fails to reach the poorest people.[24]

Consequently, as an immediate—or even short-term—solution to poverty, civil society does not seem to be the answer. One expert says, "A healthy civil society cannot be artificially created or imposed: it needs to grow spontaneously, over a considerable length of time and sometimes in ways not readily comprehensible to outsiders not familiar with the culture in which it has developed."[25] Much of the protest movement(s) mentioned above can be subsumed under civil society, since they represent neither government nor the economy.

One World

Since the existence and continuation of poverty is in great measure caused by the current movements of privatization and globalization, one proposed method of "taming" their excesses is the establishment of supragovernmental entities with the power to enforce policies and activities. The idea of "world governance" is not new, of course. Both the Romans and Greeks, among others, ruled all of what was thought to be the civilized world at one time. However, with the emergence of national states, international agreements have taken the place of world governance. These agreements require consensus, which is not only hard to reach but—as witness numerous UN human rights treaties—usually have no real enforcement powers. As one writer puts it:

> A lack of universally accepted standards covering human and international behaviors is an area that cries out for global governance, able to set such standards for people and member states worldwide, *and enforce* them. [26]

There are and have been such supragovernmental entities, although their powers of enforcement were and are very limited. The League of Nations was one example, although considerably hampered by the refusal of the United States to join. A more current example is the United Nations, which has acted in the interests of world governance in some specific areas, such as whale hunting, and has attempted to do so over a vast array of concerns elaborated in international human rights treaties, which it has had limited success in enforcing. Other examples: the World Court in The Hague, especially in its genocide trials, and the recently created International Criminal Court. However, all such organizations are made up of or governed by the representatives of individual states. They depend upon the willingness of sovereign governments to give up some of their powers. Allowing trials in other countries for crimes committed at home, so to speak, which has begun, is an abdication of part of such powers, and may be a good omen. However, the question is whether governments will be or are willing to give up power in ways that cost them money, or are inimical to their economic systems or bodies. In any case, the rise of supragovernmental bodies is at least possible, if not probable, in the near future.

THE FUTURE OF POVERTY

Predicting the future is a risky business, and yet people have been trying to foretell the future from the earliest days of recorded history. In some places and at some times these were medicine men, shamans, witch doctors, seers and oracles, of which the Greek oracle at Delphi is perhaps the best known, prophesying the future. Personal prophets are exemplified by Cassandra, who always predicted correctly, even though her predictions were invariably ignored. Many of the Hebrew prophets discussed events to come, some at the end of time, but most for shorter periods. The Middle Ages saw Nostradamus reading the stars and making predictions from them—a tradition that continues both in modern astrology and in continuing quotations from that medieval astrologer.

Indeed, we cannot live without predicting the future, as we plan our next moment, hour, day, month or years. In many cases we do this intuitively, while in others we look for trends, signs and predictions to help. In recent years methods of predicting the future have become more scientific and more precise as futurism has become a semi-profession. The methods used are various—one source lists seventeen currently-used methods of consciously predicting the future,[27] including the consensus of experts, mathematical equations, computer simulations, content analysis, analogies, comparisons, and trend analysis, among others. The results of such predictions have proven more useful than pure guesswork.

For example, of the 137 inventions predicted by George Orwell in 1946 as becoming usable by 1984, over a hundred were,[28] and others come into being every day. Similarly, a study of predictions made in *The Futurist* magazine over a thirty-year range found that 68% of the measurable things predicted by futurists had come about.[29] In fact, even items that were thought fantastic in their day have come into being, as witness Jules Verne's submarine, and Dick Tracy's radio wristwatch. Consequently, in attempting to portray the possible future or futures of poverty, I have used a combination of trend projection, content analysis, consensus of experts, analogies and examples.

Recent history indicates that poverty has been constantly growing. A few statistics should suffice: In 1979 only one in ten persons in the United Kingdom was in poverty—in 1998 it was one in four (fourteen million).[30] In the United States 12.6% of the American population was poor in 1970, but in 1997, 13.3% of the American population were poor,[31] and many neighborhoods in large cities now suffer greater concentrations of poverty than they did then.[32] In addition, the number of people with incomes less than 50% of the poverty line has doubled in the last twenty years.[33] From 1970 to 1996 the percentage of children under the age of six who were living in poverty rose from 16.6% to 22.7%, while the percentage of children in "extreme poverty," doubled.[34] In Britain, one in three children was in poverty in 1999 compared to one in ten in 1979. In the United States in 1997, 19.2% of its children were poor, contrasted with 15% in 1970.[35] In Israel there were 14,000 more households living below the poverty line in 1999 than there were in 1997.[36] Danker points out that worldwide, infant mortality has been halved since 1960, malnutrition is down by a third, and more children are going to school. Yet the number of poor people continues to grow.[37]

This is true of countries as well as people. In 1971 the United Nations categorized twenty-one countries as "least developed countries" (LDC). In them average life expectancy is 51 years, as compared to 78 years in the developed world. One child in every ten in the LDCs dies before the first birthday, and half of the population is illiterate. By 2001 the number in the category of LDCs had grown to forty-nine,[38] more than double the original number. At the end of the nineteenth century the ratio between the richest and poorest countries in the world was a factor of eight; at the end of the twentieth century this had increased to a factor of at least forty.[39]

Or, to take another example: The United Nations reports that the growth in the number of the poor far exceeds the non-poor; the amount of water available per person is about a third of what it was fifty years ago, and half the forests are gone.[40] This litany of increasing poverty could be extended with many other examples, but in any case the increase in poverty is tangible.

The extrapolation of present trends is not decisive, of course, but this is supplemented by expert opinion concerning the future, which is not optimistic. Sullivan, for example, says:

> The ratio of private to state provision rose during the 1980s and early 1990s in most countries and this trend is likely to accelerate...the effects of private provision are likely to be disadvantageous to lower socio-economic groups...it is likely that inequality and relative poverty will increase in all countries in the near future...the expansion in low-paid, part-time employment, changes in taxation, the growth of private provision and the retrenchment of state welfare are the main reasons for this trend.[41]

Others agree: "Poverty is deep-seated in many rich and not only poor countries and seems destined to get worse in both groups.[42] The outlook for living standards in Eastern Europe, most Third World countries and the poorest 20% or 30% in the rich EC countries, the United States and Japan is gloomy."[43] "It is likely that inequality and relative poverty will increase in all countries (in Europe) in the near future."[44] The Global Scenario Group see inequity increasing in every region of the world through 2050.[45]

Content analysis, which is another method of prediction, adds weight to the dismal prospects for the poor. Conference proceedings, newspaper and journal articles, radio and television programs and reports of government activities (although not government promises) all point in the same overall direction. Given the continuation of privatization and globalization—which seem assured at least insofar as the short- and medium-ranges are concerned—and their professed goals, which is acquisition of profits at almost any cost, it is all but certain that the poor people will continue to suffer, and/or suffer even more than they do now.

And yet, things do change. Some changes come about like tidal waves, sweeping away everything built up. Other changes are more like the tides themselves, which quietly, slowly, but inexorably change the face of the ocean and the shore. Still other changes are more like aquifers, or underground water, which must be searched for in order to be observed.

During the 1800s there was a growing—tidal—feeling that government intervention in the market was necessary because of the unbridled avarice of the unrestricted, uncontrolled "robber barons." Governmental intervention was needed because, in the words of one contemporary, corporations engaged in "double-shuffling, honey-fugling, hornswoggling and skullduggery."[46] And this was before Enron. The need for government intervention was expressed in the Populist Party platform of 1892, "The powers of government...should be expanded...to the end that oppression, injustice, and poverty shall eventually cease in the land."[47]

World War I brought about an intensification of proposed and actual government activism—nationalization of the railroads, nationalization of the mines, federal operation and ownership of international radio and more. In the immediate post-War period, many of these innovations were seen as worthy of continuation.

However, the pendulum swung back. "War," according to Schlesinger, "had produced a season of moral dedication. With peace, selfishness returned."[48]

It reached the point where President Calvin Coolidge proclaimed, "The chief business of the American people is business." He held that the law that builds up the people is the law that builds up industry. Washington thus began to encourage tendencies toward economic concentration, where it had previously disapproved. The result was, again, almost unbridled competition and lack of regulation.

The tidal wave of change came with the Great Depression of the 1930s—a depression so wide and deep that it was clear to the most unlettered observer that private sources could not deal with the consequences.[49] The shouldering of social welfare by the government through the entire complex of social security and social welfare legislation was a revolutionary movement at the time, and it is not surprising that the move was described as communism, socialism, and the end of democracy by its opponents.

The protest movements of the 1960s improved the lot of women and African-Americans, among others. These were popular—although not majority—uprisings that basically called attention to social evils that demanded redress. Nor should the role of the judicial system be overlooked in this area. It is possible that school, restaurant, housing, and other forms of segregation would still exist in the same virulent form—if not worse—to this very day, had the courts refused to institute change.

In each of these cases, the private market and voluntary organizations would not or simply could not cope with the extent of need, and governments came to the rescue of their citizens. Consequently, the current return to unbridled capitalism can be seen as a move back to the unregulated economy of the nineteenth century, with nefarious modern trimmings. Obviously, history does repeat itself, but—as Marx said—the first time as tragedy and the second time as farce. We are now in the farcical period, when neo-liberal capitalism is being touted as certain to bring about universal prosperity, more equality and equity, and better living conditions for everyone, despite its tragic record the first time around.

Finally, there is also the possibility that none of these factors, or no combination of them, will bring about basic underlying changes in society, or in large segments of it. Castells, for example, speaks of areas in the modern world that seem to be beyond the reach of all positive possibilities—including Africa, Caucasia, slums and remote areas.[50] But changes take place over long periods of time, often for reasons that are only dimly perceived even in hindsight. Thus, it may be that we are in for a very long period of poverty on the part of some and inequality and/or inequity on the part of others, until some sea-change takes place in society, and the wheel turns once again towards a more just, humane society. Ideologies do change, and even current ideologies can be used for constructive purposes. As has been commented, "Anything can be done with ideology, the most plastic of human inventions."[51]

At the moment, however, there is nothing in sight to slow, let alone reverse, the establishment of deeply divided societies, with two-tiered systems arising in health, education, social welfare, housing and other areas that directly impinge upon the poor, and cruel economics determining individuals' fates.

EPILOGUE

No one—writer or reader—likes to end on a pessimistic note. And yet the world seems destined for decades, if not generations, of continuing poverty amidst comparative wealth. Privatization and globalization will continue, although there may be some public relations gestures made toward being less ruthless.

Unless some major—now unimaginable—event takes place to bring about an entirely different economic system, the future of poor people seems bleak.

Nevertheless, there are optimists like Dunham, who says, "We have no longer need of a transcendental paradise, 'a kingdom not of this world.' An ideal society...is...quite attainable. If we do the right things, our descendents will possess it."[52] It is in this spirit that *The Ethics of the Fathers* enjoin, "It may not be given you to complete the task, but neither are you free to desist."[53] Pelagius put this into positive terms. When someone complained, "What can I do? I'm only human," he gave a blunt reply: "Make the effort!"[54]

ENDNOTES

[1] The term is from Jasper, J. M., *The Art of Moral Protest.* Chicago: University of Chicago Press, 1997, p. xiii.

[2] Crossette, B., "Population Estimates Fall as Poor Women Assert Control," *New York Times*, March 10, 2002, internet edition, p. 1.

[3] For example, the unemployed in Argentina. See Petras, J., "The Unemployed Workers Movement in Argentina," *Monthly Review*, 53, 8, January, 2002, internet edition, pp. 1-8.

[4] Pear, R., "Budget Would Cut Medicaid Payments State and Local," *New York Times*, February 2, 2002, internet edition, p. 1.

[5] For further clarification concerning movements, etc., see Caygill, M., *Do the Labels Matter? Contested Categories and the "Movement."* Paper delivered at the 8th Conference on Alternative Futures and Popular Protests. Manchester, UK, April, 2002.

[6] Terms used to identify the movement mentioned include Seattle movement, post-Seattle movement, anti-globalization movement, alter-globalization, globalization from below, de-globalization, movement against corporate capitalism, anti-capitalism, movement against global capitalism, movement for social justice, global democracy movement, global justice movement, network of networks, movement of movements, a new left on a world scale, and more. *Ibid.*

[7] See, for example, Waterman's discussion of the World Social Forum, quoted by Caygill, *op cit.,* see endnote 5.

[8] See, for example, the *Proceedings of the Eighth International Conference on Alternative Futures and Popular Protest.* Manchester: Manchester Metropolitan University, 2002.

[9] Dunham, B., *Heroes and Heretics: A Social History of Dissent.* New York: Knopf, 1964, p. 7.

[10] Jasper, *op cit.*, p. 3, see endnote 1.

[11] Steinberg, J., "Forty-two Schools in Philadelphia to Be Privatized." *New York Times*, April 18, 2002, internet edition, p. 1.

[12] *Ibid,* p. 374.

[13] Tuchman, B. W., *The Proud Tower.* New York: Ballantine, 1962, p. 360.

[14] Dwyer, P., and D. Seddon, *The New Wave? A Global Perspective on Popular Protest.* Paper given at the 8th International Conference on Alternative Futures and Popular Protest, April, 2002, Manchester Metropolitan University, Manchester, UK.

[15] *Ibid.*

[16] *Ibid.*

[17] *Ibid.*

[18] Caygill, *op cit.*, p. 3, see endnote 5; see, also, Alexander, P., "Globalization, Inequality and Labour's Response: A View from Africa, and Some Thoughts for Further Research." In Barker, C., and M. Tyldesley, (Eds.) *Conference Papers, Vol II. 2001. 7th International Conference on Alternative Futures and Popular Protest.* Manchester, UK: Manchester Metropolitan University, 2001.

[19] Whitmore, E., and M. Wilson, "Research and Popular Movements: Igniting 'Seeds of Fire'." *Social Development Issues*, 21, *1*, 1999, pp. 19-28.

[20] For more information on protest movements, see Bircham, E., and J. Charlton, (Eds.), *Anti-Capitalism: A Guide to the Movement.* London: Bookmarks, 2001.

[21] Deakin, N. *In Search of Civil Society.* Houndmills: Palgrave, 2001, p. 5.

[22] See Etzioni, A., *Next: The Road to the Good Society.* New York: Basic Books, 2001.

[23] Radwan, S., "Preface," in Lipton, M., *Success in Anti-Poverty.* Geneva: International Labour Office, 1998, p. vii.

[24] Edwards, M., and D. Hulme, (Eds.), *Non-Governmental Organisations Performing and Accountability: Beyond the Magic Bullet.* London: Earthscan, 1995; quoted by Deakin, *op cit.,* p. 171, see endnote 21.

[25] Deakin, *op cit.,* p, 14, see endnote 21.

[26] Albert, G., "Revising Global Governance." *The Futurist,* 36, *1,* January/February, 2002, p. 4 (emphasis added).

[27] Glenn, J. C. (Ed.), *Future Research Methodology.* Washington: United Nations University, 1999.

[28] Rada, M., "The Impact of Micro-electronics." Geneva: International Labour Office, 1980.

[29] Cornish, E., "Forecasts Thirty Years Later," *The Futurist,* (January/February, 1997), pp. 45-48.

[30] "Poverty," *Poverty Watch,* 106, Summer, 2000, p. 20.

[31] *Social Security Bulletin—Annual Statistical Report—1999.* Washington: Social Security Administration, 1999, p. 151.

[32] Bok, D., *The Trouble with Government.* Cambridge: Harvard University Press, 2001, p. 65.

[33] Anelauskas, V., *Discovering America As It Is.* Atlanta: Clarity, 1999, p. 65.

[34] *Ibid.*

[35] *Social Security Bulletin—Annual Statistical Report—1999, op cit.,* p. 151, see endnote 31.

[36] Fishbain, E., "Numbers Show Increase in Poverty," *HaAretz,* December 21, 1999, internet edition, p. 1.

[37] Danker, S., "Global Cohort of Poverty Increases," *Earth Times,* 8, *15,* August 16-31, 1999, pp. 22-23.

[38] Freeman, J., "New Approach to Aid the Poorest," *Earth Times,* April, 2001, p. 3.

[39] Weber, S., "International Organizations and the Pursuit of Justice in the World Economy," *Ethics and International Affairs,* 14, 2000, pp. 99-117

[40] Sullivan, R. E., "Number of Poor is Increasing Daily." *Earth Times,* April, 2001, p. 4.

[41] *Ibid.*

[42] Townsend, P., *The International Analysis of Poverty.* New York: Harvester Wheatsheaf, 1993, p. 3.

[43] *Ibid.,* p. 234.

[44] Bonoli, G., V. George and P. Taylor-Gooby, *European Welfare Futures: Towards a Theory of Retrenchment.* Cambridge, UK: Polity Press, 2000, p. 155.

[45] *Global Futures Bulletin,* 111, July, 2000, p. 7.

[46] Ripley, W. Z., quoted by Schlesinger, A. M., Jr., *The Crisis of the Old Order—1919-1933.* Boston: Houghton Mifflin, 1957, p. 70.

[47] Schlesinger, A. M., Jr., *The Crisis of the Old Order—1919-1933.* Boston: Houghton Mifflin, 1957, p. 17.

[48] *Ibid.,* pp. 21-22.

[49] For graphic descriptions of the results of the Great Depression, see Bird, C., *The Invisible Scar.* New York: Pocket Books, 1966.

[50] Castells, M., *The Rise of the Network Society.* Oxford: Blackwell, 1996; quoted by Junteunen, E. K., and J. Hamalainen, in *Social Care Service and Social Work Shaped by Globalisation: Example Finland.* Paper delivered at the Symposium 2001: Globalisation and Small Countries. Dubrovnik, June, 2001.

[51] Dunham, *op cit.,* p.77, see endnote 9.

[52] Dunham, *op cit.,* p.144, see endnote 9.

[53] *Ethics of the Fathers,* circa 200 A.D., Raskin, S., New York: Academy Photo Offset, 1940.

[54] Dunham, *op cit.,* p. 144, see endnote 9.

Index

N

Naess, A. 103, 115
NAFTA (see North American Free Trade Agreement)
National Association of Social Workers 158
National Insurance Institute 36, 80
Native Americans 64
near-poor 15, 31
NEC (see Net Earnings Capacity)
Needs
    common 20
    special 20
    societally induced 15, 16, 20
negative income tax 153
neo-liberalism 114, 164
Net Earnings Capacity (NEC) 19
Netherlands 25, 28, 31, 39, 56
New Attack Submarine (NSSN) 149
New York 18, 22, 43, 122, 128, 143
New York City 29, 49, 69, 87, 100, 109, 134, 160
New Zealand 68, 74, 81, 95
NGO (See Non-Governmental Organization)
Non-Governmental Organization (NGO) 108, 168, 169
normative poverty 16, 26, 27, 30, 61
Nortel Networks Corporation 95
North American Free Trade Agreement (NAFTA) 104, 107
Norway 61
Nostradamus 170
nursing homes 80, 83, 99
nutrition 42, 82, 149, 156, 159, 170

O

OECD (see Organization for Economic Cooperation and Development)
Office of Economic Opportunity 88
Ohio 135
older people (see aged)
Oregon 85
Organization for Economic Cooperation and Development (OECD) 22, 31, 33
organized labor (see labor unions)
Orwell, G. 170
Overeaters Anonymous 73
Overseas Development Institute 76

P

Papua-New Guinea 106, 110
part time workers 30, 32, 34, 64, 78, 92, 104, 109, 125, 126, 128, 129, 134, 136, 138, 139, 140, 171
PCP (see Poverty, lines)

Pelagius 173
pension 110, 113, 131, 132, 137, 140, 141, 158
pension funds 94
Peru 89
pet food 149
Philadelphia 56, 88, 97, 100, 167, 173
Philippines 80, 81, 88, 114, 120
Phillips 66
Planned Parenthood 83
Poland 77, 97, 100, 141
poor 11, 12, 13, 42-66 69, 71, 72, 74, 76, 77, 78, 79, 80, 81, 83, 84, 85, 89, 90, 91, 92, 95-97, 102-105, 107-114, 117, 118, 121-129, 132, 133, 135, 136, 137, 138, 140-153, 154, 155, 164-172, 173, 174
Populist Party 171
poverty 11, 12, 34, 42-46, 48-52, 53, 56, 58-65, 68, 72, 76-79, 81, 83, 85, 89, 90, 92, 93, 103, 104, 109, 111-114, 115, 120-129, 132-138, 140-153, 154, 160-165, 167, 169-172, 174
    poverty line 14-19, 21-31, 34, 35, 36, 93
    poverty rate 22, 28, 30, 36, 39, 44, 64
    relative poverty 15-17, 21-25, 61
    subjective poverty 15, 16, 25, 26, 27, 39
prejudice 26, 64
prescription drugs 43, 44, 79, 82, 83, 107, 144
prisons 26, 39, 70, 75, 92, 98, 100, 105, 126, 130
private consumption 19
private health 84, 98
private hospital 68, 79, 82, 95, 98
private schools 69, 73, 86, 87, 88, 89
privatization/privatisation 12, 36, 40, 44, 45, 47, 55, 65, 68-87, 89-93, 95, 96, 100, 101, 104, 108, 109, 112, 114, 121, 133, 164-169, 171, 172
privatization by stealth 71
production 43, 61, 89, 99, 102, 103, 107, 109, 111, 128, 129, 131, 135,148
productivity 79
products 12, 83, 85, 88, 99, 103, 131, 137, 147, 149
projection 41, 132, 142, 154, 170
prostitution 51, 53, 56
protests 11, 51, 77, 97, 112, 166, 167, 168, 173
Providence, R.I. 18
public housing 21, 47, 55, 90, 100
purchase of services 68-69